D0310430

MARY RUSSELL MITFORD

Mary Russell Mitford, 1852, *by John Lucas.*

MARY RUSSELL MITFORD

by

VERA WATSON

LONDON
EVANS BROTHERS LIMITED

MADE AND PRINTED IN GREAT BRITAIN BY
PAGE BROS. (NORWICH) LIMITED

To my great-aunt
EMILY C. WHITE
in whose company I have
spent so many gay and
delightful hours.

PREFACE

The preface of a biography is necessarily a record of other people's kindness, for no biographer, however diligent and conscientious, however perspicacious in his researches, can hope to complete his task without the co-operation and assistance of those in possession of special sources of information. If, therefore, I have been fortunate in obtaining much hitherto unpublished material, it is due, in no small measure, to the help I have received.

My gratitude is due to the Committee of the Reading Public Library and to Mr. S. H. Horrocks, F.L.A., Borough Librarian, for permission to examine and to publish extracts from their collection of Mary Russell Mitford's letters; and to Miss Swaddling, the Reference Librarian, Miss Loam and Mr. Lee (also of the Reference Library) all of whom have given me much valuable assistance.

I also wish to thank Mr. C. K. Adams, of the National Portrait Gallery; Mrs. M. Knowles of Sutton, who permitted me to examine her interesting collection of Mitford relics; Captain the Hon. Bertram Mitford, D.S.O., R.N., who supplied me with much information about the Mitfords of Hexham; Mr. R. L. Watson, who lent me the print reproduced on p. 132, and the authorities of the John Rylands Library, who allowed me to quote from the Mitford letters in the library. I wish to record that I have quoted from Mary Russell Mitford's diary and other MSS. in the British Museum, by kind permission of the Trustees.

My acknowledgments are also due to the following publishers: Messrs. J. M. Dent, Ltd., for permission to quote from *Jane Austen*, by R. Brimley Johnson; Messrs. William Heinemann, Ltd., for permission to quote from

Portraits and Sketches, by the late Sir Edmund Gosse; Messrs. Hutchinson & Co. Ltd., for permission to qoute from *English Wits*, edited by Leonard Russell; Messrs. John Lane The Bodley Head, Ltd., for permission to quote from *Mary Russell Mitford and Her Surroundings*, by the late Constance Hill; Messrs. John Murray, for permission to quote from the *Order of Release*, edited by Admiral Sir William James, and the *Letters from Elizabeth Barrett to B. R. Haydon*, edited by Martha Hale Shackford.

It is impossible adequately to express my gratitude for the help so willingly given by my two friends, Mavis MacKinnon and Maboth Moseley, and my uncle, Hugh S. Watson, who not only assisted me in the researches, but undertook much of the laborious routine work, without which no biography could be compiled.

CONTENTS

CHAP.		PAGE
	Preface	vii
	Foreword	xiii
I	1787-1791	1
II	1791-1795	11
III	1795-1797	25
IV	1798-1806	40
V	September-November, 1806	54
VI	1806-1810	68
VII	1810-1811	84
VIII	1811	98
IX	1812-1819	109
X	1820-1821	127
XI	1821-March, 1823	141
XII	1823-1825	156
XIII	1825-1828	172
XIV	1829-1831	185
XV	1832-1835	200
XVI	1836-1837	215
XVII	1838-1842	233
XVIII	1842-1844	248
XIX	1845-1848	266
XX	1849-1852	282
XXI	1853-1855	294
	Appendix I	308
	Appendix II	310
	Appendix III	312
	Appendix IV	314

ILLUSTRATIONS

Mary Russell Mitford, 1852, by John Lucas *Frontispiece*
Dr. Mitford, by John Lucas . . . *facing page* 48
The garden at Three Mile Cross in 1835, by George Baxter . . . . *facing page* 49
The lake at Oakhampstead, by George Baxter, from the sketch "Hopping Bob," in *Our Village* . . . *facing page* 49
Three Mile Cross, 1835, by George Baxter *facing page* 80
Mary Russell Mitford, 1835, by George Baxter . . . . *facing page* 80
Letter from Dr. Mitford to Mrs. Mitford, on the occasion of the second performance of *Fascari*, 7th November, 1826 . . . . *facing page* 81
Letter from Mary Russell Mitford to William Harness, 28th July, 1825 . *facing page* 81
Bertram House . . . . . . *page* 105
The Cottage at Three Mile Cross, before the alterations, from *The Mirror*, June 28th, 1834 . . . . . . *page* 132
A page of the Diary, by courtesy of the Trustees of the British Museum . *facing page* 176
Mary Russell Mitford, by John Lucas (by courtesy of the National Portrait Gallery). See Appendix IV . . *facing page* 177
Mary Russell Mitford, 1824, by B. R. Haydon (by courtesy of the Reading Museum and Art Gallery) . . *facing page* 177
Mary Russell Mitford, aged three . . *facing page* 177
The Author of *Our Village*, reproduced from the drawing by Maclise in Fraser's Magazine, May, 1831 . . *page* 197

The Cottage at Three Mile Cross, *circa* 1836, from a lithograph from a sketch by E. Havell . . . . . . *facing page* 208
The Cottage at Three Mile Cross, *circa* 1896. This is how it must have appeared after the structural alterations in 1837. . . . . . *facing page* 209
The Cottage at Swallowfield . . . *facing page* 209

FOREWORD

The principal source of information for any biography of Mary Russell Mitford is her letters. She was a prolific correspondent at a period when letter writing was still practised as an art, and when people, separated by the immeasurable distance of bad communications, were in the habit of writing long letters to one another.

Mary Mitford, even as a young woman, had a large circle of friends; and when she became famous, her correspondents increased tenfold. In her old age, she mentions searching through "five boxes, trunks and portmanteaux, two huge hampers—baskets innumerable—and half a dozen great drawers" containing letters and papers; and after her death this great mass of papers passed into the possession of one of her executors, the Rev. William Harness.

In accordance with her wishes,* he decided that an edition of her correspondence would form the best record of her life, and in addition to sorting those papers which had devolved upon him as executor, he appealed to Mary Mitford's friends—among them Mrs. Browning—to supply him with her letters for publication. But the classifying of such a vast quantity of material occupied so much time and proved so onerous that he asked his friend, the Rev. A. G. L'Estrange, to help with the task; and when the book, *The Life of Mary Russell Mitford*, was eventually published after many vicissitudes in 1870, fifteen years after Mary Mitford's death, it appeared with L'Estrange's name on the title page. Although Harness died in 1869, there is no doubt that he was the dominant partner in the association

* She had sent him a letter, post-marked 26th August, 1854 (now in the possession of Mrs. Duncan-Jones of Chichester, his great-great niece) giving directions for the compilation of a biography and the publication of her letters.

for he states that the work was to be carried out "under my superintendence;" * and part of the text of the biographical note still exists† in his handwriting.

What happened to Mary Mitford's papers after Harness's death can only be surmised. They must have remained for some years with L'Estrange, despite the action brought against him by her residuary legatees, for in 1882 he published a further selection, *The Friendships of Mary Russell Mitford*, consisting mostly of letters from her friends; but somewhere about 1890, we think them bulk of the may have passed into the hands of Miss E. Langley, the successor to Lovejoy, the Reading bookseller. At all events, the majority of the letters which constitute the three volumes of *The Life of Mary Russell Mitford* are now in the Reading Public Library, together with a number which Harness did not publish.

When I came to compare the printed text with the original letters, I found that many alterations had been made. Wording and phraseology had frequently been changed; paragraphs had been extracted from one letter and added to another, by a different correspondent. Thus it often happens that events recorded under one date actually occurred on different days, sometimes far apart. Vast excisions had also been made in the text, without any indication having been given to this effect, and many of the letters are wrongly dated. Editing, at the end of the 19th century, was a haphazard affair, and a high standard of accuracy was not considered necessary. Thus the task of sorting and identifying this collection was not an easy one; and it was not lightened by Mary Mitford's execrable handwriting. Well might she write gaily to Sir William Elford "What a fine job the transcriber of my letters will have! I hope the bookseller of those days will be liberal and allow the man a good price for his

* Copy of a letter from Harness to Samuel Sweetman, dated 9th March, 1857.
† Also in the possession of Mrs. Duncan-Jones.

trouble; no one but an unraveller of state cyphers can possibly accomplish it." Far be it from me to disagree with this pious hope; although some of the reward for my pains has undoubtedly been the entertainment I have derived from her wit and worldly wisdom.

In 1872, a further two volumes of her correspondence were published, *The Letters of Mary Russell Mitford* (*Second Series*) edited by her friend, Henry Chorley; and in 1871, her correspondence with Charles Boner appeared in the first volume of *The Memoirs and Letters of Charles Boner*, edited by Rosa Mackenzie Kettle. These last were reprinted, with some letters to Ruskin and his father in *Mary Russell Mitford: Correspondence with Charles Boner and John Ruskin*, edited by Elizabeth Lee (1914). In addition there are many hundreds of unpublished letters in libraries and private collections in this country and America. In fact, I have been faced with an *embarras de richesse* so far as material is concerned; and I found, as was inevitable, that many letters to different correspondents dealt with the same subjects. In the following pages, all quotations from letters are from the published text of the above volumes, unless otherwise stated; but I have made much use of the unpublished material, particularly in the reconstructions of her literary and dramatic experiences. I have also dispensed with annotations when the quotations are from her own works, in order not to hold up the narrative.

V. W.

I

1787-1791

It is an unfortunate fact, and one of the many injustices imposed upon us by an inegalitarian Nature, that we can neither choose our birthplace nor our parents. But there is no reason to believe that Mary Russell Mitford, despite the vicissitudes of fortune, would have wished to change either of these necessary adjuncts to her entry into this world.

So far as her birthplace was concerned, she had little cause for complaint. The small town of Alresford in Hampshire where she was born at a quarter to ten on a winter's evening, on 16th December, 1787, is a perfect setting for one who has been described as a " country lady," and whose writings are redolent of the atmosphere, the scents, the sounds and the sights of the English countryside. Alresford is to-day much what it was at her birth, for it was rebuilt at the end of the seventeenth, or the beginning of the eighteenth, century following a fire which totally destroyed the town in 1689.* It has had a varying history having been prosperous in the fourteenth century and during the Commonwealth (Oliver Cromwell frequently stayed at The Swan, the principal inn), but it has now declined into little more than a beautiful village and a perfect specimen of eighteenth century-architecture.

Whether Mary Russell Mitford was as fortunate in her parentage as in her birthplace is a matter to be resolved in these pages. To her mother, however, no exception could be taken. She was the only surviving child of Dr. Russell, a descendant of the Bedford family, Rector of Ash and Vicar

* *History of Alresford*, by A. J. Robertson, p. 25, 1937.

of Overton; a gentleman with literary tastes and a propensity for marrying, whom his grand-daughter succinctly describes as "faithful to his wives, but not to their memories." His third* venture into matrimony, with Mary Dickers the daughter of a rich Hampshire landowner, was particularly successful; and it is on record that their "large parsonage house was generally overflowing with guests," and that the hospitality dispensed there was both liberal and generous. Dr. Russell died in 1783 in his eighty-eighth year; and after his death his widow and daughter moved to Alresford, where two years later Mrs. Russell followed her husband to the grave.†

Thus their daughter, Mary Russell, in her thirty-fourth year (she was born on 4th June, 1750) found herself alone in the world and mistress of what was, in those days, a considerable fortune. This amounted to £28,000, as well as "houses and property in land," of which only a small sum, her mother's marriage settlement, was in trust. It is therefore scarcely surprising that, despite her plain face, prominent eyes and teeth, and bad complexion which "was scarcely redeemed by the kind and cheerful expression which animated her countenance," Mary Russell was not lacking in suitors.

Among the aspirants to her hand, and it is to be feared her fortune, was George Mitford, a young man some ten years her junior. He was the second son of Francis Mitford, of Hexham, Northumberland, and of his wife Jane Graham, daughter of the curate of Hexham. It has been stated that George Mitford was a "younger son of a younger brother" of Mitford of Mitford, Northumberland,‡ but there is no evidence to support this statement. He came of an ancient north country family, and was descended from Roger

* Harness (*Life of M. R. M.*, p. 4,) only refers to two wives, but M. R. M. (*Our Village*, Vol. I, p. 223) says ". . . my three grandmothers (pshaw! I mean my grandfather's three wives!). . . ."

† M. R. M. states that it was after the death of both parents that her mother moved to Alresford.

‡ *Life of M. R. M.*, Vol. I, p. 5, 1870.

Mitford, Lessee of Heddon Tithes in the reign of Elizabeth;* and if there was any connection between the Mitfords of Hexham and the Saxon family of Mitford of Mitford, it occurred before that time. This non-existent relationship has been referred to, with slight variations, in nearly every biography or biographical note which has appeared of Mary Russell Mitford, for reasons which will be mentioned later.

Francis Mitford died in 1768, when his younger son was eight years old,† and his wife having predeceased him, the child was placed under the guardianship of his uncle and namesake, George Mitford of Morpeth. Little is known of his childhood, except that he was educated at Newcastle School‡; but as in after life he was renowned for his optimistic temperament and buoyant spirits, it is safe to assume that his uncle was a benevolent guardian, and that nothing occurred to mar or embitter his character.

It was decided that the young man should follow his father's profession of medicine; and his daughter states that he studied at Edinburgh University,§ and was for three years a house pupil of John Hunter in London.¶ In those days, the profession of medicine was beginning to emerge from that condition of disrepute in which it had hitherto languished, and there is no doubt that George Mitford's medical education was, for the period in which he lived, an excellent one. It must also have been comparatively costly for Hunter's pupils paid five hundred guineas for a five years' apprenticeship, so that at the lowest computation, three hundred guineas must have been disbursed for this purpose on George Mitford's behalf. Since both he and

* See Appendix I.

† He was born on 15th November, 1860.

‡ In a letter to Mrs. Howitt (*Good Words*, 1895) M.R.M. states that her father was educated at Hexham.

§ *Recollections*, Vol. II, p. 281, 1852. The authorities of the Medical Faculty of the University, however, have been unable to trace his name on any of the old class lists.

¶ Presumably at 42, Jermyn St., where Hunter lived at that period.

his brother William entered professions, it seems probable that sufficient funds had been left by Francis Mitford for his sons' education and maintenance; for it is unlikely that their guardian, who was a surgeon and apothecary in a country town and moreover had four children of his own for whom to provide, would have had sufficient money to spare for this purpose. In addition, as it has been stated by George Mitford's principal detractor that before his marriage "a very brief career of dissipation had reduced his pecuniary resources to the lowest possible ebb," this argues at least that after his education had been paid for, there were still funds left for him to dissipate.

It is not clear how this young man came to be in Alresford about the year 1785. It is variously stated by his daughter that he intended to "settle to his profession" in the town, and that he was staying with Dr. Ogle, Dean of Winchester, who introduced him to the heiress, Miss Russell. As Dr. Ogle was a great friend of her father's, this seems to be the more likely explanation, especially as it is known that the Dean did his utmost to further the match. George Mitford, however, was well acquainted with the neighbourhood, having been on the medical staff of Haslar Naval Hospital for two years, from 1780 to 1782.* At any rate Mary Russell was not long in making up her mind; and as it has happened before, and has happened ever since, a plain, rich woman was captivated by a handsome, impecunious young man. On the 17th October, 1785, their marriage was solemnized by Dr. Buller, Dean of Exeter, the bride being given away by her trustee, Dr. Harness. The entry in the Parish Register at Alresford reads:—

> No. 211. George Midford† of this parish, Batchelor, and Mary Russell of the same, Spinster. Married in this

* He was appointed Asst. Dispenser in Feb., 1780, and rose to the position of Asst. Surgeon at a salary of £5 8s. od. per month in 1782. He left on Sept. 9, 1782. P.R.O. ADM 102/378, 379, 380.

† In his youth Dr. Mitford spelt his name Midford. In the Hexham Parish Register, his baptismal entry runs "George, son of Mr. Francis Midford, surgeon, bap. Jan. 29, 1761."

Church by Licence this seventeenth day of October in the Year One Thousand Seven Hundred and Eighty-five by me, Will Buller, Rector.

This Marriage was Solemnized between us	George Midford Mary Russell
In the presence of	Jno. Harness Elizabeth Anderson

It is obvious what Mary Russell's attractions were for George Mitford. At the start of his career, a wealthy bride, mistress of a well-appointed house and a person of some standing in the neighbourhood, was an inestimable asset. Instead of having to work up a practice while living on the remnants of his capital, he found himself already established. The benefits on her side, too, if less apparent to the onlooker, must have seemed at that time none the less real. She had been able to marry the man of her choice who, possessing "extraordinary personal beauty," must have been much sought after by other women; so that it was something of a triumph that his choice had fallen on her. In addition to his good looks he had, we are told, "excellent natural abilities," "high animal spirits and constitutional good humour;" and "his manners were easy, natural" and cordial. Therefore the prospects for the marriage must have seemed excellent; and if she considered the question of money, it can only have been to express thanks that she had sufficient for them both. She was a gentle, confiding person, addicted to domestic pursuits, and her faith in the future is amply proved by her refusal, on marriage, of any settlement of her own money, thus allowing the control of her fortune to pass to her husband. Nevertheless despite the fact that this union, so far as George Mitford was concerned, could be described as one of convenience, it turned out, in some aspects, surprisingly well. Their personal relations, over a period of forty-five years, seem to have been uniformly harmonious ; and although he was ten years younger than his wife, there is no reason to suppose that he was anything but a devoted and faithful husband. It was only in money matters that he caused her anxiety, for he was a spendthrift, and what was worse from the point of view of domestic comfort, a gambler who habitually played for high stakes.

Neither of these grave flaws in his character can have been discernible when he settled down to married life in his wife's house in Alresford in the autumn of 1785. There is reason to believe, indeed, that they were at first quiescent, for in the early days of his marriage he undoubtedly applied himself to his profession, and acquired patients in the neighbourhood. The town of Alresford consists of two principal streets, the high road from London to Winchester and the west, and Broad Street which lies at right angles to the main thoroughfare, in the centre of the town. Some changes have taken place since the end of the eighteenth century. The church has been restored, the ancient cobblestones have been replaced by smooth pavements and asphalt surfaces* and buildings have sprung up, so that the houses are no longer interspersed by " stables, farm-yards, pigsties and barns :" but in essentials the place remains what it was a hundred and sixty-four years ago. George Mitford and his wife lived in Broad Street, which does not belie its name, for even in these days it would be considered a wide and spacious street. Now all the houses are adjoining, but in 1785, it is possible that some of them were detached, although we know that on one side, at least, of the Mitfords' house there was a barber's shop. It was in this gracious, three storied house, with its large windows and stuccoed front, that a son, Francis, was born thirteen months after the marriage ; and it was here too, a little more than a year after this event, that a girl, Mary

* This work was only executed during the lifetime of one of the older inhabitants

Russell, was born. The son died in infancy,* but the girl survived to become the future authoress and playwright.

Mary Mitford always retained happy memories of her early childhood, possibly because it was one of the few periods of her life not overshadowed by monetary troubles. The household in Broad Street was a pleasant place for a child. There was money in abundance and always something happening to interest the lively little girl. From her nursery window, in the front of the house, she could watch all the events taking place in the street below, the comings and goings of the neighbours, the carriages, the tradesmen's visits, and above all the antics of the lame cobbler, Jacob Giles, across the street, who mended shoes by day and got tipsy by night. It was from this nursery window that she probably acquired those habits of minute observation which are so characteristic of her writings in later life ; and it was from this self-same aperture—a matter of more moment at the time—that her first doll, Sophy, fell into the street below and " had the misfortune to break her neck."

When she was not in the nursery, under the care of her nursemaid, Nancy, she would be downstairs in the company of her mother and father, who, she freely admits, were in the habit of spoiling her. This is not surprising, for apart from the fact that she was the only surviving child, she was something of a prodigy. Before she was three years old, she could read ; and when a guest was present (which often occurred in that hospitable household) her father would place her on the breakfast table, from which eminence she would read aloud the leading articles from the Whig newspapers of the day. The guest, no doubt, was all the more astonished inasmuch as the little girl looked younger than her age. At that time, she tells us, she was a " puny child . . . nicely dressed, as only children usually are, and gifted with

* M. R. M. in a letter to B. R. Haydon (Reading Collection, 11th July, 1825) refers to two brothers, who died young : but we have not been able to trace the baptismal entry of the second son.

an affluence of curls . . ." and this description is corroborated by a miniature of her painted at that time. But apart from this one example of precociousness, her occupations seem to have been those of a normal and healthy girl of her age. Like other children, before and since, she was taken out walking in the afternoon by her nursemaid, Nancy. In these peregrinations, they were accompanied by the lame, and slightly disreputable cobbler (although at this period he had curbed his alcoholic propensities) Jacob Giles ; for it seems that the little girl was not the only person to look out of the window, and Jacob had succumbed to the charms of the pretty nursemaid. Strangely enough, these afternoon walks were always in the same direction, to a wood at the corner of which stood the cottage of the woodman, the handsome William Cotton. When the incongruous trio approached this dwelling Nancy, on some excuse, left the child in charge of the cobbler, and disappeared for some considerable time. These periods of absence became more and more protracted, and their inevitable sequel was that the gay deceiver married the handsome William, and the poor cobbler had to return to his last. He seems, however, to have taken his disappointment in a philosophical fashion, for he got tipsy at the wedding, kissed the bride and staggered home to his shop singing " God Save the King " at the top of his voice.

It is probable that the little girl spent much less time in the nursery than was customary in affluent households ; and that in her childhood she contracted those habits of intimacy with her parents which are so noticeable in later life. She was a far stronger character than either of them, and her intellectual gifts were vastly superior ; and even at this early age, she was able to impose her will. That her parents encouraged this intimate relationship, and enjoyed the society of their precocious little daughter, cannot be doubted. Her father had a special pad made for the saddle of his horse so that she could accompany him when he visited his patients ; and Mrs. Mitford, no doubt, from an early age made her a confidante of all those absorbing details of household chit-chat and gossip which are so delightfully revealed in her letters.

There must have been many occasions when the observant child was present at the entertainments given by her parents. Dr. Mitford was always lavish in his hospitality, and his wife was of a sociable disposition; and there must have been many guests bidden to that hospitable board. The Doctor, with his gaiety and good humour, his frank and easy manners, his interest in politics and his sporting propensities, would soon make acquaintances in the neighbourhood, while his wife, through long residence in that part of Hampshire, had a large circle of friends. Foremost among these were Dr. and Mrs. Harness, old friends of the Russell family. Dr. Harness, who lived in the neighbouring village of Wickham, was trustee for the money Mrs. Mitford inherited from her mother. This sum of about £3,500 was the only money in trust of all her fortune, and consequently could not be touched by her husband ; and frequent reference will be made to it in these pages. After Dr. Harness's death, the trusteeship devolved on his son William, who was born at Wickham in 1790, and was thus a little more than two years younger than Mary Russell Mitford. Of William Harness, too, more will be heard, for he was the first biographer of his childhood's friend and it is owing to the information vouschafed by him that so many erroneous statements about the Mitford family, and in particular Dr. Mitford, have been perpetuated.

An idyllic picture has been painted of the association at this time between the two children.* In the library lined with Dr. Russell's books, or in the old-fashioned garden among the stocks and hollyhocks, it has been stated, William and Mary would " chase away the summer hours " until the time when the carriage came to take Mary's

* *Literary Life of the Rev. William Harness*, by A. G. L'Estrange, p. 2, 1871.

playmate back to Wickham. As, however, the Mitfords left Alresford in 1791, William can only have been a baby of twelve months old, and we venture to state that his *rôle* of " playmate " must have been a purely passive one. That this pleasant figment of the imagination came to be published is due, in the first place, to Mary Mitford's vivid description of her birthplace, and secondly, to Harness's erroneous statement that Dr. Mitford left Alresford eight or nine years after his marriage.

The reason for the family's removal is unknown, but various factors may have contributed to it. The house in Broad Street did not belong to them ;* and if Mrs. Russell took it on a seven years' lease after Dr. Russell's death in 1783, this would have expired, supposing she did not at once move from her comfortable rectory, about 1791.† Then again it is probable that Alresford was too quiet a locality for the gay Dr. Mitford. He, who had already passed three years in London and who all his life craved for excitement, must have found the sleepy little Hampshire town insufferably dull, for there would be few boon companions for gambling and card playing. Also, his daughter says that being " a zealous and uncompromising Whig . . . when Whiggery was sometimes called sedition and sometimes treason he . . . ruined his fair professional prospects . . . by plunging into the fervent hatreds of a hotly contested county election." In other words, he scandalised the staid clerical circle of his wife's friends by his violent Radical opinions. At any rate, whatever the reason, some time in 1791, when Mary Mitford was not quite four years old, the family moved to Reading.

* Information derived from a Schedule of Deeds and Documents relating to a freehold messuage and premises in Broad Street, Alresford, Hants, kindly supplied by the present owner.

† Mr. W. J. Roberts (*Life and Friendships of Mary Russell Mitford*, p. 30, 1913) states that the only two entries in the rate books at Alresford of payments by George Mitford, are in 1787 and 1790.

II

1791-1795

William Harness states that when Dr. Mitford left Alresford, he was obliged to sell his library and furniture, and that his wife's fortune was irretrievably ruined: in other words, that in the short space of six years, the extravagant Doctor had managed to dispose of £28,000. While we do not doubt that Mrs. Mitford's capital was considerably diminished, neither of these statements is true; and another five years were to pass before the optimistic Doctor was reduced to the painful necessity of parting with his goods and chattels. No doubt when he arrived in Reading, he had not even considered such an unpleasant prospect and the town, with its easy access to London, its noisy politics, it opportunities for indulging in his favourite pursuits of card playing and coursing, must have seemed an ideal place in which to settle.

Reading, at the end of the eighteenth century was, in Mary Mitford's own words, "clean, airy and affluent; well paved, well lighted, well watched; abounding in wide and spacious streets, filled with excellent shops and handsome houses." "It is not a manufacturing town," she continues, "and its trade is solely that dependent on its own considerable population, and the demands of a thickly inhabited neighbourhood; so that, except in the very centre of that trade . ., the stir hardly amounts to bustle. Neither is it a professed place of gaiety, like Cheltenham or Brighton; where London people go to find or make a smaller London out of town. It is neither more nor less than an honest English borough, fifty good miles from 'the deep, deep sea,' and happily free from the slightest suspicion of any spa, chalybeate or saline." Nevertheless despite this pleasant description, written forty years later, she never really cared for the place, for it was ever afterwards associated in her mind with the disastrous events which occurred there, and the total ruin of the family's fortunes. For the town was not quite the sleepy backwater which her description implies. There was a good deal of card playing, for high stakes, in private houses, and a card club held its weekly meetings at the King's Arms: and at the end of the eighteenth century, it was an asylum for French *emigrés* fleeing from the rigours of the Revolution. Among them was a Monsieur de St. Quintin, the son of an Alsatian nobleman, who at one time had been secretary to the Comte de Moustiers, one of the last ambassadors of Louis XVI to the Court of St. James's. St. Quintin was a clever, well educated man, but unfortunately addicted to high play, as the result of which he was in such financial straits when he came to Reading that he was thankful to take up the post of French teacher in the Grammar School, presided over by the famous Dr. Valpy.* Apart from this well known scholastic institution there was an establishment for girls situated near by in the Abbey House.† This was run by two women, Mrs. Latournelle, an elderly person, and her young partner, Miss Pitts. As was only to be expected, there were connections between the staffs of the two schools and eventually M. de St. Quintin was recommended to teach French to the Abbey pupils. In due course, such is the influence of proximity on human affairs, the French ex-diplomat married Miss Pitts and became the owner of the establishment for young ladies.

When Dr. Mitford arrived in the town, St. Quintin was already installed in the Abbey House; and since like attracts like, the two men formed a connection which was to last nearly thirty years. They were associated in many enterprises of a speculative nature—apart from card playing—

* *Life and Times of Mrs. Sherwood*, ed. Darton, p. 123, 1910.
† Jane Austen received part of her education there.

in which, to judge from the correspondence, the astute Frenchman invariably outwitted the more simple Englishman. At first, however, Dr. Mitford seems to have made some attempt to earn his livelihood by more prosiac methods, and it has been stated that he settled in a house in Southampton Street, now pulled down, with a view to practising his profession. Southampton Street is in the Parish of St. Giles's, and Miss Constance Hill, in *Mary Russell Mitford and her Surroundings* says " It is in connection with this very church [St. Giles's] that we have a pleasant glimpse of the little Mary from the pen of Mrs. Sherwood,* then a young girl living in Reading. [She was at the Abbey School]. 'I remember,' she writes, 'once going to a church in the town which we did not usually attend, and being taken into Mrs. Mitford's pew, where I saw the young authoress, Miss Mitford, then about four years old. Miss Mitford was standing on the seat, and so full of play that she set me on to laugh in a way which made me thoroughly ashamed.' "† There is no reason to suppose, however, that the church referred to is St. Giles's. The girls of the Abbey School would, presumably, have attended the church of St. Laurence, which is in the vicinity, and " another church in the town which we did not usually attend " might easily have been St. Mary's, in which parish we have incontrovertible proof that the Mitfords were living in 1793. Therefore if Dr. Mitford lived in Southampton Street, it can only have been for a short time, and this residence is not mentioned by his daughter. On the contrary, when writing of this period she refers to Coley Avenue which is at the top of Castle Hill in the parish of St. Mary's. In addition she states : " It is now about forty years ago, since I . . . first became an inhabitant of Belford [Reading]; and really I remember a great deal not worth remembering concerning the place, especially our own

* Author of the *Fairchild Family*.
† *Mary Russell Mitford and her Surroundings*, Constance Hill, pp. 23-25, 1920.

garden, and a certain dell on the Bristol road to which I used to resort for primroses. Then we went away; and my next recollections date some ten years afterwards, when my father *again** resided on the outskirts of the town . . ." Considering that Castle Hill, off which is Coley Avenue, leads to the Bristol road, and that she refers to her two residences as being on the outskirts of the town, the occupation of the house in Southampton Street, which is in the centre of Reading, seems at least open to doubt. It is probable that at this period the family lived in one of the eighteenth-century houses on Castle Hill, near the top.

Whether Dr. Mitford had any previous knowledge of Reading, or whether he selected it purely by chance, will never be known; but after his arrival, it did not take him long to form a circle of acquaintances and to plunge into the affairs of the town. He was a man to whom action was vital; not the planned action of the clever man who follows certain courses with a fixed end in view, but action for action's sake. He had superabundant energy, an optimistic temperament and high spirits; and not for him was that steady attention to affairs, that concentration on detail, which is so necessary to success in every walk of life. Work, it must be admitted, was an anathema to him (although he would have been astounded at such an assertion), and during the course of his long life, he probably did less than the average modern schoolboy. But an outlet had to be found for that abounding energy, with or without a motive. Before long he had become embroiled with that influential body of citizens, the Corporation; and then not content with alienating his Alresford patients by the violence of his Radical opinions, he committed the same offence in Reading, with the result that he affronted a rich cousin to whom his wife was heir, who inconsiderately died a few months later, leaving his fortune elsewhere. To a man of the Doctor's temperament, therefore, it is not surprising that the building

* The italics are ours.

up of a physician's practice seemed intolerably tedious and slow ; and that he attempted to augment his fortunes by the dubious expedient of card playing. At least that is doubtless how he would have justified himself if he had been called to account for his actions. But even if he had been rich, he would still have gambled, for the vice was inherent in his nature, and he was not of a sufficiently reflective character to assess the mathematical possibilities of being constantly successful at games of chance. Besides it must be remembered that gambling was the fashionable vice of the eighteenth century, and he was very much a child of his age.

A glimpse of his activities at this time can be obtained through the observant eyes of the pupil of his boon companion, de St. Quintin. Mrs. Sherwood writes : "Had I been older, or seen more of the world, I might have guessed that things were already going amiss with the establishment at the Abbey, which three years afterwards broke up under very painful circumstances. Mr. St. Quintin would go out and not return till near morning, and we used often to see Mrs. St. Quintin in tears. I, who was a parlour-boarder, sometimes witnessed violent quarrels. The truth was he had begun again to gamble, and it is painful to add that Dr Valpy constantly met him where he played high, and that Dr. Mitford was another of their associates."

Gambling all night was scarcely the best way in which to earn a reputation for reliability and medical skill ; nevertheless the Doctor undoubtedly acquired some patients, for his daughter speaks of a remarkable cure which made his medical talent advantageously known, and it is stated that about this time he obtained his M.D.* There is, however some mystery about this degree—as there is about so much connected with the Doctor—and we have been unable to trace where it was obtained. His daughter says that he was "a graduate of Edinburgh," but his name does not appear in

* *Annual Biography*, 1843. Obituary Notice of Dr. Mitford. His daughter supplied some of the details for this notice.

the published records of the University.* It is possible that he qualified as an apothecary, and then arrogated to himself the title of doctor, for there was a certain laxity in these matters in his day.† The immature, childish strain in his character made him self-important, and he delighted in any title which gave him an official position.

While Dr. Mitford was disposing of his wife's fortune, how was his little daughter occupying her time? One thing is certain, there were no violent quarrels in the Mitford family comparable with those which took place between the St. Quintins at the Abbey; for Mrs. Mitford was an amiable woman who never, at any time, reproached her husband for his extravagances, no matter how desperate the financial situation might be. For the first few years in Reading the little girl must have had an enjoyable life, gathering primroses, as we already know, in the dell in the Bristol road, playing in the garden and taking part in the festivities of the household. There were dinner parties, tea parties, supper parties, concerts in the town, visits to friends in the neighbourhood and above all, coursing meetings, for this was the Doctor's favourite sport, in which he indulged to almost the end of his life, and for which he always kept a number of greyhounds. Then for several months in 1793, the household was enlivened by another occupant, the Doctor's cousin, Alicia Mitford, the daughter of his uncle and guardian George Mitford of Morpeth.‡ She, having inherited a large fortune from her great uncle, Gawen Aynsley, had adopted his surname. It so happened that at this time Lord Charles Murray, brother of the Duke of Atholl and an Oxford undergraduate, was spending the long vacation with his mother in the neighbourhood. The young couple met in Dr. Mitford's house, and Lord Charles

* *List of Graduates in Medicine in the University of Edinburgh from* 1705-1846.

† See Appendix II.

‡ In the *Medical Register* for 1779 (Murray), p. 11, under *Morpeth*, appears the following entry "Surgeons and Apothecaries: Messrs. William Fenwick and John Wilson, Mr. Francis Laidman, Mr. George Mitford."

Murray immediately fell in love. Mary Mitford h
entertaining account of this courtship.

"How the first step in the business, the inevitab
awful ceremonial of a declaration of love and a proposa
marriage, was ever brought about, has always been to m
one of the most unsolvable of mysteries—an enigma without
the word.

"Lord Charles, as fine a young man as one should see in a summer's day, tall, well made, with handsome features, fair capacity, excellent education, and charming temper, had an infirmity which went nigh to render all these good gifts of no avail: a shyness, a bashfulness, a timidity most painful to himself and distressing to all about him . . . . I myself, a child not five years old, one day threw him into an agony of blushing, by running up to his chair in mistake for my papa. Now I was a shy child, a very shy child, and as soon as I arrived in front of his Lordship, and found that I had been misled by a resemblance of dress, by the blue coat and buff waistcoat, I first of all crept under the table, and then flew to hide my face in my mother's lap; my poor fellow-sufferer, too big for one place of refuge, too old for the other, had nothing for it but to run away, which, the door being luckily open, he happily accomplished.

"That a man of such a temperament, who could hardly summon up courage to say 'How d'ye do?' should ever have wrought himself up to the point of putting the great question, was wonderful enough; but that he should have submitted himself to undergo the ordeal of what was called in those days a public wedding, was more wonderful still.

"Perhaps the very different temper of the lady may offer some solution to the last of these riddles; perhaps (I say it in all honour, for there is no shame in offering some encouragement to a bashful suitor) it may assist us in expounding them both.

"Of a certainty, my fair cousin was pre-eminently gifted with those very qualities in which her lover was deficient.

Everything about her was prompt and bright, cheerful and self-possessed. Nearly as tall as himself, and quite as handsome, it was of the beauty that is called showy—a showy face, a showy figure, a showy complexion. We felt at a glance that those radiant, well-opened hazel eyes, had never quailed before mortal glance, and that that clear round cheek, red and white like a daisy, had never been guilty of a blush in the whole of its life . . . she would not have minded a coronation ; on the contrary, she would have been enchanted to have been a queen-regnant ; but as a coronation was out of the question, she had no objection, taking publicity as part of the happiness, to a wedding as grand as the resources of a country town could make it."

The glory of the wedding procession certainly rivalled that of a public pageant. All the chief members of the two families were present ; and the first carriage, a low pony phaeton, contained three children, a nephew and niece of the bridegroom and Dr. Mitford's little girl, whose *rôles* were those of bridesmaids and page. They were dressed in white and the little girls wore white beaver hats trimmed with ostrich plumes. The last carriage contained Dr. Mitford and the bride-to-be, Alicia Aynsley. The procession was so long that it stretched from Coley Avenue (as the bride was married from Dr. Mitford's house, this points to its having been situated at the top of Castle Hill) to St. Mary's Church in the Butts, a distance of nearly half a mile. The entry of the marriage in the Parish Register is as follows :

No. 122. Lord Charles Murray of this Parish and Alicia Aynsley of the same Parish were married in this Church by Licence this eighteenth day of June in the year One thousand seven hundred and ninety three by me

George Martin Clerk.

This marriage was solemnized between us { Charles Murray* / Alicia Aynsley }

* After his marriage, Lord Charles Murray took his wife's surname of Aynsley.

In the presence of {George Midford
Mathias Deane

After the ceremony, the young couple left immediately for their honeymoon in Bath and Bristol, while the rest of the party returned to Dr. Mitford's house to drink their health, which pleasant duty was followed by a dinner party. During the preparations for this feast the servants, even those connected with the nursery, were so busy that the children were left to their own devices. Wearied and bored by their part in the ceremonies they turned to the more congenial occupation of hide and seek. When it was the boy's turn to hide, he chose the innermost recesses of the coal cellar, from which he emerged the colour of a chimney sweep. His mother stormed, but as nothing could restore his white suit to its original spotlessness, he was ignominiously consigned to bed, in which comfortable retreat he was stuffed with sweetmeats by the servants to keep him quiet. The little girls, on the other hand, who had been more careful of their finery, were obliged to come into the drawing room, make their curtsies and remain for two or three hours, while thinking enviously of their companion upstairs. "With so little justice are the rewards and punishments of this world distributed—even in the nursery!" commented Mary Mitford.

Shortly after this celebration, another event took place a month later, in the middle of July, which was much more to her taste—she paid her first visit to London. Dr. Mitford, with his usual lack of premeditation, suddenly announced his intention of driving her there in his gig. She was only five at the time, and it is surprising that no female, either nurse or mother, accompanied them; but doubtless the novelty of the situation greatly added to its charm. There was so much of the child in Dr. Mitford that he must have made an ideal companion for his little daughter, and he probably enjoyed himself as much as she did. It was this quality which, despite all his faults, endeared him to his wife and daughter, and consoled them when faced with the bitter consequences of his actions. It is necessary, however, to distinguish between the strain of youthfulness which is to be found in all charming and lovable characters and the immaturity which amounts to a pathological case. Dr. Mitford's childishness belonged to the second category. His irresponsibility and thoughtlessness, his absurd optimism and desire to impress, his petulance and injured innocence, and his moral cowardice when faced with the consequences of his own follies, are all traits of an adolescent mentality scarcely normal in an adult.

On this excursion to London, when nothing occurred to mar his pleasure, his more endearing qualities, gaiety, high spirits and enthusiasm, were uppermost. The two travellers set off early in the morning, and arrived at Maidenhead bridge in time for the midday meal. There they picked up a spare horse, sent on over night, and drove swiftly to London. The child was starry eyed with excitement, and revelled in the journey. She mistook Brentford for London, and when, after passing the turnpike gate at Hyde Park Corner, they reached their headquarters, Hatchett's Hotel in Piccadilly, she spent some time watching the crowds in the street and wondering innocently when the procession would come to an end. But so little tired was she by the journey, and so buoyed up by the novelty of the situation, that her father took her that night to the theatre, where, sitting on his knee, she clapped and laughed to her heart's content. The other occupants of the box, who at first were rather annoyed at the noisy antics of the excited little girl " finished," she says, " by being amused at my amusement."

These three days in London were an enthralling and never-to-be-forgotten incident in her childhood, and to read her account is to realize that what amused and entertained a child in 1793 still amuses children to-day. She went to St. Paul's, and clasping her father firmly by the hand, clambered up as fast as her short legs would carry her to the whispering gallery and then on to the gallery below the ball, where she gazed at the panorama of the city before her. In those days, London was compact and limited. It stretched along the river from Billingsgate to Westminster; the West End started at the turnpike gate at Hyde Park Corner; Paddington and Chelsea were isolated villages; there were fields in Eaton Square and Belgravia, and it was possible to gather blackberries in a muddy lane on the site of Cromwell Road. From St. Paul's they went to the Tower and inspected the jewels and the armoury, and in the evening, a visit was paid to the circus which she did not enjoy so much as the theatre. Next day, they set off on another sightseeing expedition, for like all children her energy was inexhaustible. Their first call was at the Houses of Parliament where she sat on the Woolsack and on the Speaker's chair; then on to Westminster Abbey, Cox's Museum in Spring Gardens (a fascinating place where, she says "I sate down upon a chair, and the cushion forthwith began to squeak like a cat and kittens, so like a cat and kittens, that I more than half expected to be scratched,") the Leverian Museum in Blackfriars Road, ending this glorious day at the Haymarket, where they saw another comedy. It must have been a tired and cross little girl who eventually arrived back at Coley Avenue: and what an anti-climax the next few days must have seemed, although doubtless she spent the greater part of them retailing her experiences to whoever would listen.

During this first period of residence in Reading, another incident took place over which there has been much controversy. In the town at that period was stationed the 15th or King's Regiment of Light Dragoons. An officer of the regiment was Captain Ogle, an intimate friend of Dr. Mitford and son of that Dr. Ogle, Dean of Winchester, who was instrumental in bringing together the Doctor and his wife; and a trooper of the regiment was Silas Tomkyn Comberbacke, the assumed name of Samuel Taylor Coleridge, who, fleeing from Cambridge on account of his debts, had enlisted in the army on 2nd December, 1793. As may be imagined, Coleridge was scarcely the ideal trooper being unable to keep on a horse; and he proved so incompetent in other ways that he was relegated to the ignominious *rôle* of sick nurse to a comrade suffering from smallpox. This remarkable recruit attracted Captain Ogle's attention by, it is stated, the words " *Eheu, quam infortunii miserrimum est fuisse felicem* " which he had written on the stable wall.* The officer's sympathies were aroused, and he did his best to alleviate Coleridge's lot; and the poet, writing to his brother, says " a Captain Ogle, of our regiment . . . has taken great notice of me. When he visits the stables at night he always enters into conversation with me, and to-day, finding from the corporal's report that I was unwell, he sent me a couple of bottles of wine. These things demand my gratitude."†

It so happened that the Dean of Winchester came to spend a few days with Dr. Mitford, and was visited by his son. During the course of dinner, Captain Ogle mentioned his learned recruit, and discussed the means being taken to obtain his release from the Army. According to Mary Mitford, one of the conditions was the procuring of a substitute, and a servant waiting at the dinner table was induced to undertake this *rôle*. This account has been dismissed by Ernest Hartley Coleridge, who says: " In various and varying reminiscences of his soldier days which ' fell from Coleridge's own mouth,' and were repeated by his delighted and credulous hearers, this officer [Captain Ogle] plays an important part. Whatever foundation there may be for the touching anecdote that the Latin sentence . . . scribbled on the walls of the stable, caught the attention of Captain

* *Life of Coleridge*, by S. J. Gillman, Vol. 1, p. 60, 1838.
† *Letters of Samuel Taylor Coleridge*, ed. E. H. Coleridge, Vol. 1, p. 63, 1859.

Ogle . . . and led to Comberbacke's detection, he was not, as the poet Bowles and Miss Mitford maintained, the sole instrument in procuring the discharge. He may have exerted himself privately, but his name does not occur in the formal correspondence which passed between Coleridge's brothers and the military authorities."

It is true that Bowles, in his account,* attributes Coleridge's release solely to the efforts of Captain Ogle; but Mary Mitford makes no such claim. She merely affirms that the arrangements for his discharge, that is to say the procuring of a substitute, were made at her father's house in Reading. Therefore if this were a condition of release, there is no reason why her statement should not be true.† It is thus probable that while Coleridge's brothers were negotiating with the War Office, Captain Ogle, with the help of Dr. Mitford, procured the substitute. At any rate Coleridge undoubtedly considered himself under an obligation to Dr. Mitford, for many years later he corrected two of Mary Mitford's poems for the press, and her letters of that period abound in references to him, his advice and the help that he gave her.

The veracity of Mary Mitford's account, however, has been doubted on other grounds. Mr. W. J. Roberts writes: "The dates relative to Coleridge's enlistment and discharge are incontrovertible, [he was discharged on 10th April, 1794] therefore in view of the lack of evidence to support the idea of the Mitfords being in Reading in 1794, we are inclined to doubt—as others have doubted—the authenticity of Miss Mitford's narrative."‡ But if they were in Reading in June, 1793, for Lady Charles Aynsley's wedding, there is every likelihood that they were in the town in April, 1794. Mr. Roberts, in fact, doubts the whole of this period of residence in Berkshire, and copying Harness, transports

* *Mr. Coleridge—a Common Soldier. The Times*, 13th Aug., 1834.

† Sir Edmund Chambers (*Coleridge*, p. 24, 1936) states "But the negotiations for his release lingered on, because the Army authorities asked for a substitute recruit."

‡ *Life and Friendships of M. R. M.*, p. 79.

them direct from Alresford to Lyme Regis. His argument therefore cannot be sustained.

Notwithstanding all the gaieties, or perhaps in some measure because of them, the family's financial situation was desperate. Dr. Mitford's practice did not bring in sufficient money to compensate for the losses he incurred at cards even though he was, according to his daughter, one of the finest whist players in England. He did not tell his wife of his pecuniary anxieties, for he had all the secretiveness of the confirmed gambler; nevertheless both she and her daughter were aware that matters were going awry, possibly by the frequency with which strange men, obviously creditors (the only constant feature of Dr. Mitford's career) called at the door and demanded to see the master of the house. At any rate, Mary Mitford says that at this period most of her mother's fortune had disappeared—except the trust funds—and that her father resolved to remove to Lyme Regis " feeling with characteristic sanguineness that in a fresh place success would be certain." There was probably no more thought given to the matter than that; fresh places, fresh experiences, fresh friends were the breath of life to the Doctor. One idea, however, may have flashed across his mind; that it might be wise to put as many miles as possible between himself and his creditors. Therefore when the child was eight and a half years old, about June 1795, the family were once more on the move, this time to the west of England.

III

1795-1797

The Mitfords' residence in Lyme Regis lasted about twelve months, for the Doctor, with the gambler's instinct, never had any idea of retrenchment and imagined that a change of habitation would automatically bring a change of luck. The house he rented was one of the most spacious in the town which, some twenty years previously, had been inhabited by the sons of the great Lord Chatham, the future Earl and William Pitt, the latter of whom was Prime Minister when the Mitfords lived in the town. It was in Broad Street, and still stands to-day, although many alterations have taken place both internally and externally.* Behind the house in those days was a delightful garden which, says Mary Russell Mitford writing many years later to her friend Elizabeth Barrett, " descended by terraces to a small stream, a descent so abrupt that a grotto with its basin and spring formed a natural shelter under the hilly bank, planted with strawberries. Arbutus, passion-flowers, myrtles, and moss-roses abounded in that lovely garden. . ." Then again, in her *Recollections*, she remarks "... I have never seen anything like that garden. It did not seem to be a place to be sad in; neither did the house, with its large, lofty rooms, its noble oaken staircases, its marble hall, and the long galleries and corridors, echoing from morning to night with gay visitors, cousins from the North, friends from Hampshire and Berkshire, and the ever shifting company of the old watering place."

During one of the gay dinner parties, the expenses of

* For an account of the house as it is to-day, see *Lyme Regis, a Retrospect*, by C. Wanklyn, pp. 218-219, 1927.

which must have contributed considerably to the Doctor's pecuniary difficulties, the ornamental ceiling in the dining room fell on to the assembled guests. The eight year old child, who was standing by her father, was instantly clasped protectively in his arms; while the rest of the party had a most providential escape, the only casualties being the glass and china on the table and the scratched, bald head of an elderly clergyman. Apart from these adult festivities, the child spent many enthralling hours with her father on the sea shore when he, hammer in hand, tapped the cliffs in search of the fossils in which the district abounded. On other occasions, they walked towards the beautiful bay of Charmouth which, on a summer's day, sparkles the azure blue of the Mediterranean; or if the tide were high, they paced the stone pier, known as the Cob "to which," says Mary Mitford, "Miss Austen has since given such an interest."

One night, when the little girl was asleep, a violent storm arose. Her father took her from her bed at midnight and carried her up to the top storey of the house so that, she says, "I might see the grandeur and glory of the tempest, the spray rising to the very tops of the cliffs, pale and ghastly in the lightning, and hear the roar of the sea, the moaning of the wind, the roll of the thunder and, amongst them all, the fearful sound of the minute guns, telling of death and danger on that iron bound coast." That night made such an impression on her mind that fifteen years later she made reference to it in one of her poems.

"For I had heard old ocean roar
And chafe 'gainst Dorset's rocky shore;
Had listen'd to the sea-bird's cries,
Had mark'd the gath'ring tempest rise,
And, fearless 'mid the deaf'ning jar,
Had watch'd the elemental war."

The storm, she remarks, was the one exception to the

brightness of the scene, for the little port " had a peculiar air of cheerfulness and comfort," which it still retains to this day. Yet she was sad. With the child's instinct, she detected amidst the gaiety, the undercurrent of anxiety and worry, for the Doctor's financial situation was now desperate. His plans, if he had ever conceived any, had gone astray ; and his money and sources of credit were at an end. Extravagant living, gambling and other speculations had taken their inevitable toll. Also it has been stated that as the great revolutionary wars had broken out and the militia was being raised all over the country to repel the threatened invasion, Dr. Mitford equipped and maintained a troop of yeomanry cavalry in Lyme Regis.* Although such an action would have undoubtedly appealed to him being both spectacular and extravagant, the author of this statement is unreliable and confirmation cannot be found elsewhere. In his plight, Dr. Mitford made one last desperate attempt to retrieve his fortunes. He went to London, staked all his remaining resources on some gamble, probably the turn of a card, and lost. Then he returned to Dorset to break the news to his wife, if indeed it were news, that he was totally ruined. There followed interviews with lawyers, landlords and auctioneers, when the disposal of his property was arranged ; and then he once more departed from the town, possibly to escape arrest, leaving his womenfolk behind. "And I knew . . . ," says his daughter, to whom this was the first experience, but not the last, of poverty, " that everything was to be parted with, and everybody paid."

A few days later, Mrs. Mitford, her daughter, Mrs. Mosse, the old housekeeper who had worked for Dr. Russell (how she must have deplored such a situation) and another maidservant made their way as best they could to London. They had intended to travel post, but when they reached Dorchester, a camp in the vicinity was dispersing, and there were

* *Book of Memories*, by S. C. Hall, p. 34, 1871.

neither horses, nor chaises, nor any rooms in the place. All they succeeded in obtaining was a lift in an old cart without springs. This was the final humiliation for poor Mrs. Mitford, and her daughter never forgot her mother's heart-broken expression as they jogged along in the rickety old cart, nor her tears when they spent the night at a miserable alehouse, where instead of tea, they were offered stale bread and dirty cheese which, as her daughter philosophically remarks, is always the fate of those who arrive in shabby equipages.

The following day they arrived in London and went to dingy lodgings which presumably the Doctor had found. Once again, it has been difficult to trace his movements, and we have to rely on his daughter's account, written fifty years later, and that of William Harness, for there are no letters extant for this period. She says their rooms were in a suburb beyond Westminster Bridge, and although she was not cognizant of her father's plans, she imagined that he intended to gather up all the money which remained after paying his debts, and with this, and his greatly lessened income, (the dividends from the trust funds and from a legacy) to start a practice in some distant town. " At all events," she continues, " London was the best starting place, and he could consult his old fellow-pupil and life-long friend, Dr. Babington,* then one of the physicians to Guy's Hospital, and refresh his medical studies with experiments and lectures, whilst determining in what place to bestow himself."† William Harness, on the other hand, states categorically " His next removal [from Lyme Regis] was to London; and there, we have heard from those who knew him well, that about the year 1795 or 1796 [it was 1796] the doctor was living with his wife and child on the Surrey

* William Babington, M.D., F.R.C.P., F.R.S.

† It has been asserted (*Life and Friendships of M. R. M.*, p. 30) that Dr. Mitford at this period performed " odd jobs " for Dr. Graham of " Celestial Bed " fame. But as Dr. Graham's Temple of Health was only in existence from 1780-1782 (vide *History of Medicine*, F. H. Garrison, 4th ed., p. 387, 1929) when Dr. Mitford was at Haslar, there seems to be no truth in this statement.

side of Blackfriars Bridge, and finding a refuge from his creditors within the rules of the King's Bench." In other words, the Doctor was imprisoned for debt.

It is important that this matter should be fully investigated, for as a rule, the consequences of his actions usually fell on others, generally his wife and daughter, rather than on himself. Also, although he undoubtedly had great faults, there is no reason why he should be considered more base than he actually was. We therefore consulted the records of the King's Bench Prison, and Dr. Mitford's name does not appear among the list of prisoners.* Moreover, it must be rememberd that Harness's statement was made over seventy years after these events, and that he was only a child of six when they occurred. Dr. Harness, his father, who as Mrs. Mitford's trustee might reasonably be expected to know about her affairs, was in 1796 appointed Physician to the Mediterranean Fleet, and he and his family were absent from the country for several years, which accounts for William's having no personal knowledge of what occurred at this time. Furthermore, it must always be borne in mind that Harness disliked Dr. Mitford and while, being a clergyman, we do not think he would deliberately lie, we feel that he would not take much trouble to verify any information derogatory to the Doctor. On the other hand, it cannot be denied that for some cause or other the Doctor remained in London from the middle of 1796 to early 1798; but this might have been due to lack of money to set up an establishment elsewhere. In view of the prison records, therefore, it can only be concluded that he was not an inmate of the King's Bench, for even if he had been living within the Rules, his name presumably would have been on the Commitment Books.

The Doctor's release from his pecuniary difficulties was obtained in a fashion which must have strengthened his

* Alphabetical List of Prisoners for the years 1794 and 1797 (P.R.O. Pris. 10/140 and 10/141), and the Commitment Books for the years 6th Nov., 1793-28th Sept., 1795 (P.R.O. Pris. 4/14) and 28th Sept., 1795-13th Nov., 1797 (P.R.O. Pris. 4/15).

faith in the Goddess of Chance. On the 16th December, 1797, when he was taking his little girl for a walk, he entered what she describes as "a not very tempting-looking place," which was a lottery office. An Irish lottery was about to be drawn, and he asked her to choose one of the pieces of paper which lay on the counter.

"Choose which number you like best," he said, "and that shall be your birthday present."

The child picked up a ticket marked No. 2,224 and placed it in his hand.

The Doctor examined it. "Ah, you must choose again. I want to buy a whole ticket, and this is only a quarter. Choose again, my pet."

But the child was obdurate. "No, dear papa, I like this one best."

"Here is the next number," said the lottery clerk ingratiatingly. "No. 2,223."

"Ay," said the Doctor, "that will do just as well. Will it not, Mary? We'll take that."

"No!" she exclaimed petulantly, "that won't do. This is my birthday, you know, papa, and I am ten years old. Cast up *my* number, and you'll find that makes ten. The other is only nine."

Thus the affair was arranged and the secret kept between father and daughter. Whenever they were alone the Doctor, like all his successors who participate in Irish Sweepstakes, discussed his plans for spending the prize money. Then a few weeks later, on a Sunday morning when the family were about to go to church, a man appeared at the dreary lodgings, whose face was familiar to the child, but whom the father had forgotten. It was the clerk from the lottery office to announce that an express had just been received from Dublin intimating that No. 2,224 had drawn the £20,000 prize. The day of liberation had dawned, and the Doctor could start his hectic career of spending once again. It might be thought that the experiences of the last eighteen months would have had a salutary effect on Dr. Mitford; but such was his temperament that the winning of £20,000 without physical or mental effort seemed the normal course of events, and the dreary privations of London just an unfortunate interlude to be forgotten as soon as possible. To commemorate his good fortune, he had a dinner service made with his arms on one side and the Irish harp on the other, and the mystic number 2,224 interwoven into the design. This fragile souvenir, his daughter remarks, outlasted the money.

Early in 1798, as soon as the necessary arrangements could be made, he moved back to Reading, where he resided in a red brick house, still in existence to-day, in the London Road.* He was superstitious but not sensitive, and the fact that ruin had overtaken him once in that town in no way affected his partiality to the place. Not so his daughter: she retained her aversion to Reading to the end of her life. Dr. Mitford, however, was not the only one in his circle to have been overwhelmed by financial disaster. Somewhere about the year 1794, M. de St. Quintin was obliged to close up the Abbey School for girls. However he, too, was smiled on by fortune; for his young pupil, Mrs. Sherwood, having published her first work *The Traditions*, handed over the profits to her old schoolmaster, which enabled him once more to start his school, this time at 22, Hans Place in Chelsea. To this establishment, therefore, it was decided to send the young Mary Mitford in the mid-summer term, when she was ten years old.

It is not known whether the Doctor attempted once more to practice medicine in Reading; but if he did, his efforts can only have been sporadic. Why, indeed, spend one's days in laborious toil when by mere perspicacity one can select a piece of paper the value of which is equivalent to several years' income? There were, indeed, far more interesting ways of passing the time; and shortly after his

* No. 39, London Road.

arrival, he had re-established his greyhound kennel, was attending coursing meetings, dabbling in the affairs of the town, driving about in his phaeton, filling the house with guests, attending parties and balls and no doubt once more putting in an appearance at the card clubs.

In the meantime, his daughter was receiving her education at 22, Hans Place. In those days, the house had just been built, and was ideally suited for a school. It was situated in the midst of fields and there was a garden where the pupils could take their recreation. No. 22 to-day stands on a corner site with the entrance in Hans Place, while the back looks out over Pont Street. This house, however, is not the one in which Mary Mitford received her education, for it is a comparatively modern building; but there are still some of the original houses in the square so that some idea of its architecture can be obtained. It is probable that the garden was at the back of the house, and that it eventually merged into the surrounding fields. For the first few days, Mary Mitford was thoroughly miserable as is traditional with young ladies who go for the first time to boarding schools. She had always been accustomed to adult society, and the noise and laughter of her youthful companions overwhelmed her. She was so shy that she dreaded being spoken to, and blushed when anyone looked at her: yet although she was sure, inevitably, that she would never laugh again, her pride prevented her from crying or showing her distress. But being a normal and healthy little girl, she soon became accustomed to the conditions, and settled down to enjoy her school life.

Scattered throughout her writings, especially in the five volumes of *Our Village*, are many delightful reminiscences of her schooldays; and in her first slender volume of poems, published in 1810, she pays tribute to the place in verses entitled *On Revisiting the School where I was Educated*.

Her education was certainly excellent. The pupils were made to speak French throughout the day; and if they infringed this rule, were obliged to wear a medallion with the word *English* engraved on it and to pay a fine. The punishment was not so harsh as it seems, for the fines were put into a box and eventually provided a feast for the pupils. From this rule emanated her love and great knowledge of French literature which were to give her such pleasure in later life. Of course she made friends at school, those intimate friendships so dear to the heart of the young, and one of them was with a Polish countess, Sophia, whom she afterwards apostrophized in verse. Then there was Miss Rowden, the English teacher, who in her spare time coached the talented pupil, " so that," says Mary, " instead of passing half hours and whole hours, half days and whole days, at the side of my beautiful countess, in the full enjoyment of my dearly beloved idleness, I found myself, to my unspeakable discomposure, getting by rote (an operation which I always detested) sundry tedious abridgements of heraldry, botany, biography, mineralogy, mythology and at least half a dozen other ' ologies ' more. . . ." There was, however, a lighter side to this coaching, for Miss Rowden introduced her to English literature, and together they read Shakespeare, Pope's Homer, Dryden's Virgil, *Paradise Lost* and doubtless other works from that vast and wonderful store which is our national heritage. In addition, Miss Rowden took her to the theatre, to which they were both passionately attached. The mistress's interest in the drama was so great that she could never look at the large school room at Hans Place without wishing to transform it into a theatre, and had visions of her pupils acting *Comus* or Shakespeare. One day she imparted these visions to Mrs. St. Quintin, and that excellent lady, no doubt with a view to possible parental reactions, refused to sanction the presentation of Milton or Shakespeare, but gave her consent to the more prosaic production of Hannah More's pastoral drama *Search after Happiness*. Great was the consternation and contempt of her pupils, and when the play was eventually cast, two of the youthful actresses, in the true tradition of the stage, threw up their parts in a pet. The production nevertheless took place. Mary Mitford was cast for the role of Cleora, the blue stocking, and she also recited the prologue. At first she grieved over the choice of play, and longed " to come out in Milton and Shakespeare ; " but she soon discovered that she had mistaken " the love of an art for the power of excelling in it ; " and to the great improvement of her humility that " *The Search after Happiness* was only too good for me, in short, that I was about as bad an actress as ever trod the stage." On the night of the production, after the audience had assembled, one of the youthful actresses laced her stays so tightly that she could hardly breathe, and between that and fright, fainted away. Water was immediately called for, and the gardener who was helping behind the scenes, at once produced an enormous watering-can full to the brim. In the *mêlée* which followed, someone knocked against the swooning one's harp, which fell on to a house-maid, who in turn crashed on to the watering-can in the middle of the stage, with the result that there was " water, water everywhere." Mops, cloths, warming pans and more housemaids were sent for to clean up the deluge ; but the disaster had at least one salutary effect—the noise brought the fainting heroine to her senses, whereupon she burst into tears which unfortunately removed her rouge. Altogether it might be said that this schoolgirl effort was a great success, and that it conformed, by its catastrophes, to the true schoolgirl tradition.

As at the Abbey School in Reading, many French *emigrés* came to dine with the hospitable St. Quintin ; and Mary Mitford says : " Something wonderful and admirable it was to see how these Dukes and Duchesses, Marshals and Marquises, Chevaliers and Bishops, bore up under their unparalleled reverses ! How they laughed, and talked, and squabbled and flirted." But in addition to the *habitués* of Hans Place, she had other opportunities for observing the habits of the *emigrés*. Often at the week-end she spent from Saturday afternoon to Monday morning in the house of a female relative in Brunswick Square. The husband of this lady was a French marquis who had dropped his title, become completely anglicised and made a fortune on 'Change. On Saturdays, however, there was always a *petit souper* for his French friends, and the child, wide eyed and silent (she regarded it as an imposition to be forced to talk French on her half holiday) participated in the parties, at any rate to the extent of enjoying the good fare. Eventually she became accustomed and even attached to the guests. There was a certain Chevalier, who fancied himself as a verse maker, and was married to a pretty but foolish, wife who never opened her mouth without making a *faux pas*. One evening, two distinguished guests, the Abbé de Lisle and M. de Calonne*, the financier, joined the circle. The Chevalier, wishing to display his poetic talents, went into a profound study, walked two or three times up and down the room, slapped his head, called for a pen and paper, and then proceeded to write down the product of his sudden inspiration. The act of composition finished, he handed the paper to his host who read out the verses to the applauding company. But the effect of the impromptu was entirely spoilt by the Chevalier's wife who, delighted at the approbation received by her husband, exclaimed : " How glad I am they like the impromptu ! My poor dear chevalier ! No tongue can tell what pains it has cost him ! There he was all yesterday evening, writing, writing—all the night long—never went to bed,—all to-day—only finished just before we came,—My poor chevalier ! I should have been so sorry if they had not liked his impromptu ! Now he'll be satisfied." " Be it recorded to the honour of French politeness," says Mary Mitford, " that, finding it impossible to stop or to out-talk her . . . the whole party pretended not to hear, and never once alluded to the impromptu *fait à loisir*, till

* Controller-General of Finance to Louis XVI, 1781-1787.

the discomfited chevalier sneaked off with his pretty simpleton, smiling and lovely as ever, and wholly unconscious of offence. Then, to be sure, they did laugh." There are many more of these delightful stories, told in her own beautiful, limpid prose, which prove that the silent little girl was not only keenly observant, but had a retentive memory.

The combination of personal beauty and great intelligence is a rare one, and it must be admitted that this ideal did not obtain in the youthful Mary Mitford. She was, at this period of her life, small and far too plump for her age; and although her features, when taken separately, were good and a replica of her father's—she had fine grey eyes* a slightly acquiline nose and silken light brown hair—her countenance as a whole was not handsome. She had, however, even as a child, a sweet smile, great self-possession and that peerless asset in a woman, an incomparable voice. In later life, this self-possession turned into the imperturbability and the gracious manners of a woman of the world; and the beauty of her voice rather increased, than decreased, with age. Altogether it might be said that her charm, good-breeding and wit made the observer almost unaware of any lack of physical attributes.

Throughout her schooldays, she was in constant touch with her parents, for apart from the usual holidays which she spent in Reading, Dr. and Mrs. Mitford paid frequent visits to London, her mother often staying at Hans Place. During the periods of separation, many letters passed between them, and a note to her father, written when she was not yet eleven, shows that at an early age she had great facility of expression.

* In her portrait, painted by John Lucas, in the National Portrait Gallery, her eyes are shown as blue.

"Hans Place, Sept. 15, 1799

My dear Papa,

I sit down in order to return you thanks for the parcels I received. My uncle called on me twice while he stayed in London, but he went away in five minutes both times. He said that he only went to fetch my aunt, and would certainly take me out when he returned. I hope that I may be wrong in my opinion of my aunt; but I again repeat, I think she has the most hypocritical drawl that I have ever heard. Pray, my dearest papa, come soon to see me. I am quite miserable without you, and have a thousand things to say to you. I suppose that you will pass almost all your time at Odiam* this season, as it is a very good country for sporting; and that family is so agreeable, that it would be very pleasant for mamma to stay there with you.

Remember me to all the family, particularly to grandpapa† and William."‡

And then on February 23rd, 1801, she writes: "I really think that my dearly-beloved mother had better have the jackasses than the cart-horses. The former will at least have the recommendation of singularity, which the other has not; as I am convinced that more than half the smart carriages in the neighbourhood of Reading are drawn by horses which work in the team."

Mrs. Mitford, in her turn, kept her daughter informed of all those incidents which delight a child separated from beloved parents—the domestic affairs of the household and the gossip of the neighbourhood. Her letters are a delight to read and give a vivid picture of life as it was lived at the end of the eighteenth century. In 1798, she writes: "Your dear papa and I dined with Mr. Annesley yesterday. After dinner papa attended Mrs. Bouchier to the play that she might see young Banister§ act the part of Sheva in *The*

* Mr. and Mrs. Raggett, relatives of the Mitfords, lived there.

† A pet name for Dr. Harness.

‡ Presumably William, son of Dr. Harness.

§ Possibly John Banister, the actor (1760-1836) son of Charles Banister.

Jew. I remained to play cribbage with the Mrs. Davidsons, the two Mrs. Annesleys and their sister." And then again, " The concert went off extremely well, the house quite full. We had no vacancy in either of our boxes, as Mrs. Terry (her sister not coming as she expected) applied to me on Thursday morning, and I was happy in giving her the only vacant place." Then she displays her tact as hostess : " For fear of consequences, I durst not put Monck* and her in the same box, therefore we marshalled our company in the following order :—In the first row of the Stage-box Mrs. Dolly, your aunt, and Mrs. Terry ; on the back seat Mr. Annesley, Mr. Robinson senior and your father. The other box in front Mrs. Nicholl, Miss Valpy and myself ; and behind us Mr. Monck, Mr. Southgate and Mr. Mathew Robinson." After the concert, the Mitfords spoke to Mr. Shaw Lefevre† and his wife, who were among the audience, and as a result were invited back to his house, Heckfield Grange. " The night was dry, though cold, and, being moonlight, our drive was a very pleasant one ; and we reached their truly hospitable mansion before twelve. Sandwiches, negus etc., was immediately brought in, and after half an hour's pleasant chat, we separated for the night. I cannot attempt to detail what an agreeable day we had on Friday. The gentlemen dedicated the morning to field sports ; the ladies accompanied me round the grounds, and afterwards we took a ride round Lord Rivers' park‡ before we dressed for dinner, when there was an addition to our numbers of a Mr. Milton, his wife, and two daughters ; the youngest of whom, Miss Fanny Milton§ is a very lively, pleasant young woman. I do not mean to infer that Miss Milton may not be equally agreeable, but the other took a far greater share in the conversation . . . ."

* Bligh Monck, M.P. for Reading, later of Coley Park, Reading.
† M.P. for Reading, 1802-1820.
‡ Strathfieldsaye, afterwards the home of the Duke of Wellington.
§ Fanny Milton was the daughter of the Vicar of Heckfield, and afterwards became the celebrated writer, Mrs. Trollope, mother of Anthony Trollope. She and Mary Mitford were lifelong friends.

It is easy to imagine how the child enjoyed these letters, giving, as they did, a minute picture of her parents' actions, and how eagerly she longed to be at home to share in them. In one of her old notebooks, under the date 30th November, 1800, she scribbled, " Where shall I be this day month ? At home. How happy I shall be. I may do what I like then, and shall be ready to jump for joy." School, no doubt, was all very well ; but home was better. How many schoolgirls have since echoed her sentiments ?

IV

1798-1806

Enthusiasm for his profession was not, as we have seen, one of Dr. Mitford's principal qualities, and his ambitions lay in other directions. He wanted to be an English country gentleman, with an estate, and the dignities accruing to the position. This was not an ignoble aim, provided he remembered that property carried its duties as well as its rights. Up to this period, although the houses he had lived in were spacious, well furnished and comfortable, they were, by their situations, habitations suitable to professional men, rich burghers, business men or their widows. In the eighteenth century, there was a wide gap between the social status of such people and the landed gentry, and Mary Mitford, writing of Reading at that period, says: "To live in that respectable borough was in general a recognised exclusion from the society of the neighbourhood." This state of affairs was not congenial to Dr. Mitford, and he determined to change it.

At the end of 1801 or early in 1802, he bought Grazeley Court, an old farmhouse, situated about three miles from Reading as the crow flies, and a little more than a mile from the Basingstoke road. The house, which had fallen into disrepair, had stood for about two hundred and fifty years, and with skill, could easily have been made into a suitable residence. But Dr. Mitford, with his passion for novelty and delight in change, decided to raze it to the ground (a costly business, as it turned out, for the walls were thick and demolition difficult) and build a new house in the then prevailing style. The first stone of this new residence which was to metamorphose the Doctor into a country gentleman was laid on 29th April, 1802. Mrs. Mitford, writing to her schoolgirl daughter, says, " We got to our rural retreat about half past nine, both the men-servants attending us on horseback. At ten o'clock your old Mumpsa [a pet name for herself] laid the first brick, and placed under it a medal struck in commemoration of the centenary of the Revolution in 1688. Your darling father then placed another for himself, and a third for his beloved treasure, which he made Toney [a dog] put her foot upon ; and after the little rogue had done so, you would have laughed to have seen how she wagged her tail, and nodded her head upon it, as much as to say she was very proud of being admitted to have, not a finger, but a foot, in the business. The men worked merrily on till two o'clock, and then repaired to the public house, where two legs of mutton, and bread, beer, and potatoes were provided for them. There they enjoyed themselves for the rest of the day, and this morning cheerily resumed their labours."

While this new residence was being built, the Mitfords continued to live in Reading. Dr. Mitford, in spite of his previous dispute with the Corporation, still took part in the town's affairs. We learn that in 1802, at a meeting of the inhabitants under the auspices of the High Steward of the Borough, Mr. Addington,* he seconded an address to His Majesty King George III on the occasion of the peace treaty with France.† At the end of the same year, his daughter left the school in Hans Place, and rejoined her parents in the house on the London road. How did this accomplished young lady of fifteen spend her time ? Although there is no correspondence available for this period, we can gain some idea of her activities from the pages of her novel, *Belford Regis*. Writing of the society of the town at that period, she says : " The gentlemen had frequent dinner-parties, and the young people occasional dances at such houses where

* Afterwards Viscount Sidmouth.

† *The History and Antiquities, Ancient and Modern, of the Borough of* Reading, by John Man, pp. 96-7, 1816.

the rooms were large enough; but the pleasant meetings were social suppers, preceded by a quiet rubber and a noisy round game, succeeded by one or two national airs, very sweetly sung . . . enlivened by comic songs . . . and interspersed with more of fun and jest, and jollity, of jokes that nobody could explain, and of laughter no one knew why, than I ever happened to witness amongst any assemblage of well-behaved and well-educated people." The public diversions of the town were "limited to an annual visit from a respectable company of actors, the theatre being, as is usual in country places, very well conducted and exceedingly ill attended; to biennial concerts, equally good of their kind, and rather better patronised; and to almost weekly incursions from itinerant lecturers on all the arts and sciences, and from prodigies of every kind, whether three-year-old fiddlers or learned dogs.

"There were also balls in their spacious and commodious town-hall, which seemed as much built for the purposes of dancing as for that of trying criminals."* Her own introduction to society took place at one of these balls, at the time of the Reading Races in August, 1803. It was apparently the custom of the Steward of the Races to dance with the girls who were to come out, and Mary Mitford, writing to her mother in anticipation of this alarming experience, says: "I think myself very fortunate that Mr. Shaw Lefevre will be steward next year, for by that time I shall hope to know him well enough to render the undertaking of dancing with him much less disagreeable."

She was not, even as a young girl, fond of dancing, nor did she care much for riding, which she referred to as a "detestable exercise." Her figure was not, it must be confessed, one that would lend itself to athletic pursuits; and the only form of exercise she practised was walking. When she was well past middle age, she was capable of

* The proceedings of the local Bench and the Assizes were held in the Town Hall.

covering fifteen miles without excess fatigue: but it must be admitted that she walked more for the pleasure of observing the countryside than for the love of exercise. As a girl, she was gay and high-spirited, but there was a reflective side to her nature, which combined with an intellect which matured early, made her more at ease in the society of her elders than that of her contemporaries. This is particularly noticeable in her relations with her parents, to whom she was more of a sister than a daughter. Writing to a friend, she says: "I have lived so little with girls of my own age, and have been so much accustomed to think papa my pleasantest companion, and mama my best friend that . . . I have escaped unscathed from all the charming folly and delectable romance of female intimacy and female confidence." The truth is that being intellectually superior to her parents, she was, even at the age of fifteen when lacking all wordly experience, at least their equal. As time passed, the difference between their respective mentalities became even more apparent, which accounts for the fact that towards the end of her father's life, her attitude towards him was maternal. Not that she ever expressed such an opinion—she would never have deigned to discuss the matter—but she was undoubtedly aware of it. And she practised the same reticence in regard to the weaknesses of her father's character which others have stated that she ignored. That she was cognizant of them, and that despite all the suffering and anxiety she endured, she preferred to keep silent, is what we hope will be proved in these pages.

Besides taking part in the social activities of her parents, she spent a great deal of her time in reading. The excellent education she had received at Hans Place had stimulated her natural abilities and her love of literature. William Harness describes her as lying for hours at a time on a sofa, with a dog by her side, reading any book she could procure. The number of books she read was phenomenal, and from a list kept by her mother as a check on the local circulating library, we learn that in January, 1806, she obtained from this source alone, fifty-five volumes in thirty-one days. This habit of reading continued all her life, so that it was no idle boast when writing to a friend later in life, she says she doubts whether any woman alive has read more than herself. Indeed her knowledge of recondite subjects was such that, in 1854, Ruskin wrote "You know everything that was ever written, I believe—" and another friend commented "Miss Mitford lived and breathed and moved in an atmosphere of books; and when she was not writing books, she was writing about them."* On another occasion, she refused to remove to a residence which was otherwise suitable, owing to the lack of facilities for obtaining books, without which, she said, she could not exist. All this time she was fitting herself for her *rôle* later in life, when by the products of her pen, she was enabled to support both her parents. She was learning and observing. Although Dr. Mitford's financial star was still in the ascendant, and although she was only a young girl, she must have realized that there might be a time when he would be unable to provide his family with the necessities of life, and that what had happened before might happen again. Mary Mitford was not a woman who deliberately chose a literary career; she had it, so to speak, thrust upon her. She often expressed the opinion that she would never have published a line had she not been forced to do so; and although this can be doubted, she certainly would have preferred the rôle of one who, in her spare time, indulged in literary activities for her own amusement, a dilettante in the art, rather than that of being forced to write in order not only to keep herself but her parents.

How long the mansion at Grazeley took to build is not known, but in June 1804, eighteen months after Mary Mitford left school and a little more than two years after the laying of the first stone, the family was established

* *Some Literary Recollections*, by James Payn, p. 81, 1884.

there. The ancient name of Grazeley Court was dispensed with, and the Doctor named his new residence Bertram House, after Sir Robert de Bertram, one of the Conqueror's knights, who married Sibella, daughter and heiress of the Saxon Sir John de Mitford, owner of the castle and barony of Mitford.* A description of the house is in the files of the Public Record Office.† It was "an elegant, uniform and substantially built mansion, occupying a front of fifty-three feet, stuccoed all over," with Venetian windows and a flight of stone steps. It contained four "large bed chambers or servants apartments, presenting views of great extent and beauty," three smaller bedrooms, a further four large ones and with adjoining dressing rooms, a drawing room twenty-two by eighteen feet, a library, dining room, butler's pantry and "a noble entrance hall with principal and secondary staircase." In addition to the usual offices of kitchen, wash-house, pantry, dairy, larder and brew-house, there were "capital arched wine cellars with catacomb bins, ale cellars, coal and beer ditto." The detached offices, we are informed, "are removed at a proper distance from the mansion and completely secluded by a thriving plantation." They consisted of a double coach-house, stabling, bailiff's cottage, piggery, cow-house and barn and a gardener's cottage. "The mansion is most delightfully situated in the rural village of Shinfield, in the centre of near five acres of rich land laid out with singular taste in lawns and pleasure grounds and plantations, ornamented with a profusion of the most rare and curious shrubs, with serpentine walks and a carriage approach to the villa through a romantic plantation. A small sheet of water ornaments the front . . . the park meadow and orchard are immediately contiguous and abundantly stocked with full grown timber." The entire property consisted of about 60 acres and we are told that it entitled the owner to a pew in Shinfield church.

* Until 1310, the lords of Mitford bore the surname of Bertram, but in that year the property passed to a cadet branch who resumed the ancient name of Mitford.

† P.R.O. C.13 1643/40.

Allowing for the fact that this description is taken from an auctioneer's catalogue, it will be seen that Dr. Mitford had acquired a property which was of much more lavish proportions than anything he had yet inhabited. At long last he had achieved his ambition, and had become a member of the landed gentry. All that was lacking was the income necessary to keep up the establishment; but so long as some of the £20,000 lottery capital remained, such an unimportant detail was not likely to disturb him. The interior of the house was furnished in a style commensurate with the exterior. William Harness, who had visited the place, remarks: "The domestic appointments of Bertram House were on a par with those of their wealthier neighbours. The servants were numerous. The furniture—bright, new, abundant, and of the latest pattern—was from a fashionable London upholsterer. The walls were ornamented by a fair collection of pictures, which, though many were by nameless or inferior artists, did no discredit to their companions—a charming Gainsborough, two sweet female heads by Greuze, and a portrait of the Doctor by Opie."

All that remains of this edifice to-day are a few of the outbuildings, the kitchen garden with its old wall, the orchard, the drive and some of the "rare and curious shrubs" and trees planted by the Doctor, a segoia, cedar of Lebanon, white beam, sweet chestnut, evergreen oak and acacias. Bertram House was demolished a few years ago, and a new residence erected in its stead but not on the same site. It is still possible to discover where the old house stood, for although the site has been ploughed and sown with grass, this does not grow so luxuriantly as that which once constituted the lawns surrounding the old house. Indeed as we walked round the grounds and gazed at the high hedge which marked the boundary of the Doctor's sixty acres, and the thriving market garden which now occupies the site of the park meadow and some of the pleasure grounds and plantations, we could not help reflecting that the almost total obliteration of this monument to the Doctor's ambitions was not unmerited. Never at any time had he the income necessary to uphold the position of a country gentleman, nor the stability of character to enable him to discharge the duties of a member of that now almost non-existent class of the community. All he cared for was the outward show, which even in his lifetime passed from him and now, a little more than a hundred years after his death, does not exist at all.

The next few years were some of the happiest of Mary Mitford's life, for they were free from acute monetary worries. Dr. Mitford's capital was certainly diminishing, but enough remained to keep up his household and to indulge in those pursuits to which he was most attached—card playing, coursing and politics. Grazeley, unlike Alresford, was conveniently near to London, so that he was able to make frequent visits to the metropolis, where he mixed with the Whig aristocracy of the day. It may be asked how this comparatively obscure man, who although he bore an ancient name and passed as a member of an ancient family had no position in the world, was able to obtain the *entrée* into that exclusive oligarchy. The answer is that it was due to a number of factors. Dr. Mitford, where his pleasures were concerned, was a determined man: if he had made up his mind to play a part in politics, however subsidiary, his object would be achieved, for unlike a more sensitive character, he would be unable to recognize any of the obstacles which stood in his way. Then again, his love of coursing and card playing would lead him to places where the political leaders of the day congregated. It is known, for instance, that he met Cobbett at a coursing meeting at Alton in Hampshire, presented him with a greyhound and invited him to another meeting near Reading. After that the two men became friendly, visited each other's homes, and it was doubtless through Cobbett that he became acquainted with the extreme Radical leaders of the day. In addition, he was intimate with Sheridan, whose second wife was the youngest daughter of Dr. Ogle, Dean of Winchester, and in whose company he must have met many of the great Whig leaders. It is therefore not difficult to understand how the Doctor numbered among his acquaintances such men as Lord Holland, Sir Francis Burdett, Lord Cochrane, Lord Folkestone, Charles James Fox and Brougham. But the political world was not his only interest, and he seems also to have mixed in literary circles. He was not an erudite man, but he had a facility of expression and a superficial knowledge of literature which enabled him to converse freely with men of letters. These connections proved useful when his daughter embarked on her literary career.

After the removal to Bertram House, the family settled down to what was to be their normal routine for the years they resided at Grazeley. Mrs. Mitford and her daughter paid and received visits ; they went shopping in Reading in their green carriage, had friends to stay with them and took part in the local festivities. Mrs. Mitford, in addition to attending to the domestic affairs of the household, also supervised the management of the estate, in the Doctor's absence. Her daughter, when she was not engaged in social activities, read widely or spent many hours wandering in the country lanes, observing all those changes in nature which she was afterwards to describe so graphically. Sometimes in the evening, she composed verses in honour of her father's political friends. Often the two women went away for a few days to visit friends. Mrs. Mitford went to Winchester while her daughter visited London or Richmond. These visits were nearly always paid singly, for it is a curious fact that the Mitfords, although so devoted, rarely went away together. While his wife and daughter were spending their time in this innocent fashion the restless Doctor, during the coursing season, went all over the country with his greyhounds ; or if sport did not

Dr. Mitford by John Lucas.

The garden at Three Mile Cross in 1835 by George Baxter.

The lake at Oakhampstead, by George Baxter, from the sketch 'Hopping Bob,' in "Our Village."

occupy his attention, he paid protracted visits to London where his time was spent in the gaming clubs. Probably in this connection, he became involved with a Lt. General Baron Hompesch who owed him £2,025 and who, in November 1803, wrote him the following curious letter: "Nine Elms, Battersea Fields, Friday Evening. Lt. General Hompesch's compliments to Dr. Mitford. Has found his note of this morning at his return home, and to assuage the prudent anxiety expressed in it, he acknowledges hereby his debt to the Doctor of £2,025, which together with Mr. St. Quintin's witness, will be more than sufficient proof in case of any accident the Doctor foresees may happen to General Hompesch in the short interval to get a legal instrument drawn which Baron Hompesch having promised, Mr. Mitford may fully depend the General shall get completed according to the verbal agreement between the Doctor and him. And which instrument he shall then put in Mr. St. Quintin's hands for the Doctor in case of his absence from town."* It is not, of course, possible to state with any certainty that this was a gambling debt, but in view of the Doctor's propensities and that M. de St. Quintin was also involved, it seems likely that this was the result of a night's play. Whatever the cause, Dr. Mitford did not receive his money, for two years later he lodged a Bill of Complaint in Chancery. On this occasion, at any rate, his "prudent anxiety" seems to have been justified. Nevertheless it was to his disastrous habits of gambling that we owe an almost daily record of his daughter's life at this time, for she wrote to her father frequently when he was in town, and kept him informed of everything which happened during his absence.

Mary Russell Mitford's letters are some of the best in the English language. They sparkle with wit and vitality, and abound in shrewd observations on men and affairs. Furthermore, although she nearly always wrote in haste (perhaps because of it) she had the perfect style for letter writing,

* P.R.O. C.13. 1981/17.

incisive, scintillating yet intimate, giving expression to the mood of the moment. Her letters are a mirror of her own personality, and whether she is grave or gay, she is never dull, which in this bleak and turgid age of ideologies, is something for which to be thankful. James Agate says: "Mary is to me one of the great letter-writers, far closer to my heart than your wan Dorothy Osbornes or wordy Wortley Montagus."* Writing to her father, she remarks gaily: "Mamma says the great art of letter-writing is to construct an epistle without one possible subject. And truly, if such be the fact, no two people have a better opportunity of improving in this way than those who have the honour of sending you a sheet full of nothings. Indeed, my dearest love, upon a careful revision of our letters, I do not suppose that upon an average they would be found to contain one piece of intelligence a week." Many years later, when commenting upon the possibility of her correspondence being published, she differentiates clearly between two kinds of letters; those written formally to impart information and those composed in complete abandonment to intimate friends "where the pen plays any pranks it chooses." Fortunately for posterity, the greater part of her correspondence comes into the second category.

Those letters which provide such an intimate record of her life really begin in 1806, and from that year onwards, both the Doctor and his wife seem to have kept most of the notes she wrote to them. We can only speculate on the reason why this particular year was selected for the collection of her letters, but it may have been that even at the age of eighteen, her talents were beginning to manifest themselves, and both parents realized that their daughter might, at no distant date, achieve fame. That year she wrote some of the verses which were afterwards published in her slender volume *Miscellaneous Poems;* and she also

* *English Wits*, ed. Leonard Russell, *Mary Russell Mitford*, by James Agate, p.347, 1940.

occupied herself in arranging some of her grandfather's verses for the press. These were forwarded to the Doctor who spent the early months of 1806 in London, with instructions " to take the precious MS. to Mr. Phillips,* or any other publisher he liked better, and get as much money as he could for it." Apparently Mr. Phillips did not view the collection with favour, for it was never published, although later some of Dr. Russell's verses appeared in the *Poetical Register*.

In May, Mary Mitford paid a few days' visit to the St. Quintins at Hans Place, during which she engaged in a round of sightseeing and gaieties which would have exhausted anyone not imbued with the boundless energies of extreme youth. Her father, who was still in London, procured her a ticket for Westminster Hall, where Lord Melville's trial was taking place.† She listened spellbound to the oratory of the prosecuting counsel, Samuel Whitbread,‡ and in her enthusiasm for his eloquence, promised her father to make verses in his honour. Dr. Mitford also took her to the Exhibition of Water Colours, and in the evenings to the theatre, where she saw representations of *Henry the Eighth*, *The Provoked Husband* and *The Forty Thieves*.§ The latter was not at all to the taste of one whose intellect was capable of appreciating political trials, and with the pedantry of eighteen she remarks scornfully to her mother, " *The Forty Thieves* is a very magnificent spectacle, but nothing more ; for the language and music are equally vulgar and commonplace." Notwithstanding her preoccupation with weightier matters, she was not able to

* Richard Phillips (1767-1840) bookseller and publisher, founder of the *Monthly Magazine*. In 1807, he became a Sheriff of London and was knighted the following year. His name appears in the correspondence of most of the eminent literary figures of the day, including Hazlitt's and Coleridge's.

† Henry Dundas, Viscount Melville, a member of Pitt's administration who, in 1805, was impeached in the Commons for malversations of public funds. He was acquitted on this charge and only found guilty of neglect of duty where his agents were concerned.

‡ Samuel Whitbread, brewer and M.P. for Bedford.

§ The scenario was by R. B. Sheridan.

resist the lure of that Mecca of all women, Oxford Street, where, accompanied by her former schoolmistress, Fanny Rowden, she bought a dress skirt for half a guinea, which she wore at one of her appearances at the trial.

On her return to Bertram House, she redeemed her promise to her father and sent him the following verses. These lines are the earliest known to have been written by her, although they are doubtless not the first she composed.

Impromptu on hearing Mr. Whitbread declare in Westminster Hall, on Friday, May 16, 1806, *that he "fondly trusted his name would descend with honour to posterity."*

" The hope of Fame thy noble bosom fires,
Nor vain the hope thy ardent mind inspires,
In British breasts, whilst purity remains,
Whilst Liberty her blest abode retains,
Still shall the Muse of History proclaim
To future ages thy immortal name.
And while fair Scotia weeps her favoured son.*
By place corrupted, and by pow'r undone,
England, with pride, her upright Patriot sees,
And Fame's unfading wreath to thee decrees."

The youthful versifier seems to have experienced some trepidation and doubts about her powers, for in the letter to the Doctor accompanying this production, she remarks : " Do not impute the faults and deficiencies in these lines to my laziness ; for I assure you they cost me an infinite deal of trouble ; but they are not good enough to show, and I had rather you would return them to me immediately." When, however, Dr. Mitford was prevented from delivering them personally, she exclaims, with female inconsistency : " I will not deny, my dearest beloved darling, that I am a little disappointed at your not having seen Mr. Whitbread, after you had taken so much pains to obtain an interview." Evidently, the object of her admiration had

* Lord Melville.

communicated his gratification in a letter, for she adds, "His eulogium is far higher than I either merited or expected."

Shortly after her return from town, the correspondence ceases for a few months. Dr. Mitford must have been in residence at Bertram House, or the letters have been lost. Whatever the reason, nothing is known of her movements until September when her father took her on a round of visits to relatives in Northumberland.

V

September-November, 1806

This visit to Northumberland had a special significance in Mary Mitford's life. The memory of it lingered in her mind, and throughout her works and her inimitable letters there are many referenccs to it and the people she met there.

It has already been stated that George Mitford was not related to the Mitfords of Mitford; or if there was any relationship between the two families, it occurred so far back as to constitute scarcely a connection. He was the third child of Francis Mitford, surgeon, of Hexham. His elder brother William went into the Church and lived in the Isle of Man, while his sister Elizabeth*, the eldest of the family, died in infancy. Of his other sister, Dorothy Mary, who was baptised in 1763, nothing is known, so presumably she, too, must have died in her youth.

Nevertheless, although there was no blood relationship between Dr. Mitford and the Mitfords of Mitford, he always claimed to be a member of that ancient family. He was, as we have seen, a man with certain ambitions. He was not content to be a country practitioner at a time when the profession of medicine only carried a lowly social status. He wanted to be a country gentleman with an established position in his neighbourhood. With these pretensions, he might well have claimed a relationship with an influential family which had no real basis in fact. But in spite of all his failings, we do not believe this to be the case: it is our opinion that he implicitly believed in his kinship with the Mitfords. It must be remembered that they were a Border family, and the prevailing sentiment on these matters would

* Bap. 10th June, 1757.

be analogous to that of a Scottish clan—that all who bore the same name were of the same clan. Kinship, under such circumstances, spreads its net rather widely. And if George Mitford considered himself a member of the Mitford family, they certainly reciprocated the sentiments and recognized the relationship, for both he and his daughter were on friendly terms with the Squire of Mitford, Bertram Mitford, whom they not only met frequently in Northumberland, but afterwards in London. Even as late as 1842, Mary Mitford was invited to stay with the then head of the family, Admiral Osbaldistone Mitford. Therefore if Dr. Mitford, in arranging the Northumberland tour, was actuated by the wish to introduce his clever daughter to his relations, he also probably wished her to see the important position they held in the county. All his life, he was proud of his family connections which was, perhaps, just as well, for this family pride probably prevented him from behaving a good deal worse than he actually did. There is, after all, a very thin dividing line between the selfish, foolish extravagant man and the rogue.

The Doctor and his young daughter left Bertram House on 20th September, 1806. Mrs. Mitford accompanied them as far as Reading, and after she had bidden them what were, no doubt, tender and tearful farewells (for a journey of three hundred miles was somewhat of an undertaking in those days) there was a long wait before the London coach departed, during which time they were joined by the Doctor's schoolmaster friend, Dr. Valpy. When the coach finally rumbled out of Reading, Dr. Mitford travelled on the box, while his daughter, who was somewhat depressed at leaving her mother, had a seat inside. In London, the travellers stayed at the Bath Hotel,* where M. de St. Quintin and his daughter Victoire paid them a visit.

The journey up north was to be made in the carriage of

* This was erected on the site of Hatchett's Hotel (see p. 20). It was subsequently pulled down and a block of flats erected in its place, to be followed by the Ritz Hotel.

Mr. Nathaniel Ogle, the eldest son of Dr. Newton Ogle, the Dean of Winchester, and squire of Kirkley Hall, Northumberland. Under the impression that an early start was to be made the next morning, Mary Mitford retired to bed as soon as the St. Quintins had left; but as Mr. Ogle did not rise until half-past ten, the party did not leave London until midday. Dr. Mitford and his daughter whiled away the time by visiting a bookseller's, where they bought one of Cobbett's works, a Cary's Itinerary, an edition of "Peter Pindar"* and some plays to take on the journey. Their route lay by Enfield, where they dined with a friend, Waltham Cross and Wade's Mill, at both of which places they changed horses, eventually arriving at Royston, where they spent the night. The next day, the journey was continued, and the party proceeded at a leisurely pace until, eight days after leaving London, they arrived at Little Harle Tower, Northumberland, the seat of Lord Charles Aynsley, whose wife was first cousin to Dr. Mitford, and whose wedding celebrations had taken place in 1793 at the Doctor's house in Reading. The journey was about three hundred miles, so they had travelled at a rate of thirty-eight miles a day. At Little Harle Tower, they were within easy reach of most members of the family. George Mitford, father of Lady Charles and uncle and guardian to Dr. Mitford, lived at Morpeth, thirteen miles away. Bertram Mitford, the head of the family, resided at Mitford, two miles from Morpeth, and Nathaniel Ogle, with whom Dr. Mitford spent a great deal of his time, lived at Kirkley, seven and a half miles south west of Morpeth. Mary Mitford was therefore in a position to become intimate with her relations. That she did so, and that with one exception she enjoyed herself greatly during this visit, is proved by the letters she wrote to her mother.

Most of her time was spent in visiting places of historic interest in the vicinity and attending dinner parties and

* Dr. Wolcot.

other festivities given by the neighbouring gentry or her hostess; and although her headquarters were at Little Harle Tower, she also stayed at Kirkley and Morpeth. In spite of these entertainments, she did not disdain the more humble occupation of a walk, and in her *Recollections* she records her fright when forced to cross by means of stepping stones, one of the narrow foaming, swirling Northumbrian rivers, for as we have stated, she walked for the enjoyment of the scenery rather than for exercise. Physical discomfort was not at all to her taste and in an account to her mother of a walk she had taken with Lady Charles in the rain, she remarks ruefully, ". . . the scenery, although extremely beautiful, by no means compensated me for all the mud I was forced to wade through. Lady Charles minds it no more than a duck; but I have begged to be excused from such excursions for the future." The same letter contains an amusing and shrewd commentary on a dinner party she attended that evening at the house of Sir William Lorraine, a neighbouring landowner. Mary Mitford, as a writer, was defective in imagination, and that, perhaps, is why she never reached the highest rank. But when the facts are before her, when she is describing what she has seen and experienced, she has never been surpassed. Her mellifluous prose, allied to her acute powers of perception and her wit, bring to life the people she is describing.

"We had a very pleasant party—" she writes, "not at all formal—Sir W. and Lady Lorraine, Mr. and Mrs. Lorraine (his eldest son and his wife, who live with Sir W.), Mrs. John Lorraine, the Beaumonts* and ourselves. Mrs. B. told Lady Charles that they received last year a hundred thousand pounds from their lead mines in Yorkshire; and they never make less than eighty thousand, independently of immense incomes from their other estates. Mrs. B. was dressed in a lavender-coloured satin, with Mechlin lace, long sleeves, and

* Colonel Beaumont, who lived at Hexham Abbey, was immensely wealthy, and one of the principal landowners in that part of the country.

a most beautiful Mechlin veil. The necklace she wore was purchased by her eldest son, a boy of eleven, who sent it from the jeweller's without asking the price. It is of most beautiful amethysts; the three middle stones are an inch and a half long and an inch wide; the price was nine hundred guineas. Mrs. B. wished to return it; but the Colonel not only confirmed the purchase, but gave his son some thousands to complete the set of amethysts by a bandeau and tiara, a cestus for the waist, armlets, bracelets, brooches, sleeve-clasps and shoe-knots. All these she wore, and I must confess, for a small dinner party appeared rather too gaily decorated, particularly as Lady Lorraine's dress was quite in the contrary extreme. I never saw so strong a contrast. Her ladyship is a small, delicate woman, and Mrs. B. large and strong; and she wore a plain cambric gown and a small chip hat, without any sort of ornament either on her head or neck. Colonel Beaumont is generally supposed to be extremely weak . . .; but I sat next to him at dinner, and he conducted himself with infinite propriety and great attention and politeness; yet, when away from Mrs. Beaumont, he is (they say) quite foolish, and owes everything to her influence with him. They live in immense style at the Abbey; thirty or forty persons frequently dine there; no servants but their own admitted; and there is constantly a footman behind every chair. I hope I have not tired you with this long account . . ."

What, we wonder, would the buxom Mrs. Beaumont have said had she known she was being described as "rather too gaily decorated," and that her ostentatious remarks about her husband's wealth had been preserved for posterity by the eighteen-year-old girl at the dinner table? She would, we feel sure, have said a good deal, and what is more, have said it loudly and stridently. Nor do we think the gallant Colonel would have been much flattered by his youthful neighbour's opinion that he was dominated by his robust wife; and despite his perfect propriety towards her, we rather fear for the virtue of the female section of that huge retinue of servants.

The morning following this diverting party, Lady Charles ordered her landaulet, and drove Dr. Mitford and his daughter to Wallington, the seat of Sir John Trevelyan. There, escorted by the owner's son, they were shown over the house which was decorated in the Egyptian style—a rather bizarre adornment for an English country house. Then, their appetite for sightseeing by no means assuaged, they went on to the house of Sir John Swinburne* at Capheaton ; but, as the family were out, they had to content themselves with admiring the park and driving along the borders of the large lake which was its principal feature. That afternoon, Bertram Mitford, the Squire of Mitford, came to stay at Little Harle Tower, in order to shoot with Lord Charles. Mary Mitford's opinion of the head of the family was by no means one of unalloyed admiration. " I told you I was not enamoured of Mr. M."† she writes to her mother " and I will now describe him to you. In person he something resembles Mr. P.; but he is an oddity from affectation ; and, I often think, no young man affects singularity when he can distinguish himself by anything better. He affects to despise women, yet treats them with great respect ; and he makes the most extraordinary assertions to provoke an argument, from which he generally escapes by some whimsical phrase." As it was rumoured, in later years, that Bertram Mitford's feelings for her had been of a tender order, it is interesting to note that his sentiments, if they existed, were by no means reciprocated.

So passed the days. A week after their arrival at Little Harle Tower, the Doctor and his daughter moved on to Morpeth for the week-end, and then spent two nights with Nathaniel Ogle at Kirkley, after which they returned to

* Sir John Swinburne, 6th Baronet, and grandfather of the poet A. C. Swinburne.

† In a letter dated 28th Sept., 1806, to her mother (Reading Collection) she says " The squire of the Castle dined at Morpeth to-day, but I am not enamoured. His manners are too easy and free for me."

Little Harle to prepare for the most important event of their tour—a visit to the Duke of Northumberland at Alnwick Castle. As part of her preparations, Mary Mitford had her hair cut by Lord Charles's *friseur*, a joiner by trade, who attended her in an apron covered with glue and carrying a rule in his hand instead of scissors. Apparently he performed the important operation successfully, for she told him to call the next morning to put the final touches to her hair before the journey.

The next day, Thursday, 9th October, the party rose early. Mary Mitford put on her ball gown and Lady Charles kindly lent her a necklace of Scotch pebbles with brooches and ornaments to match. The versatile joiner evidently kept his appointment for she records that her front hair remained in curl papers until Alnwick Castle came into view; and although she travelled all day in her evening clothes, her dress was "never the least discomposed," although they had travelled thirty miles over bad roads.

A detailed account of this visit was sent to Mrs. Mitford, whose vicarious enjoyment, no doubt, equalled her daughter's. "I would not attempt a description of Alnwick Castle, my dear mamma," says this observant young scribe, "for you may meet with it in almost any northern tour; but I tell you that it is by no means so very princely a residence as I had imagined. The entrance is extremely striking. After passing through three massy gateways, you alight and enter a most magnificent hall, lined with servants, who repeat your name to those stationed on the stairs; these again re-echo the sound from one to the other, till you find yourself in a most sumptuous drawing-room of great size, and, as I should imagine, forty feet in height. This is at least rather formidable; but the sweetness of the Duchess soon did away every impression but that of admiration. We arrived first, and Lady Charles introduced me with particular distinction to the whole family; and during the whole day I was never, for one instant, unaccompanied by one of the charming Lady Percys, and principally by Lady Emily, the youngest and most beautiful.

"We sat down sixty-five to dinner, and I was within three of the Duchess. The dinner, of course, was served entirely on plate, and the middle of the table was decorated with a sumptuous *plateau*. I was seated next a young man of large fortune, a Mr. Selby, who was particularly polite and attentive to me; and I met Sir Charles Monck, my cousin Mitford, and several people I had known at Little Harle. After dinner, when the Duchess found Lady Charles absolutely refused to stay all night, she resolved at least that I should see the castle, and sent Lady Emily to show me the library, chapel, state bed-rooms etc.; and she likewise—thinking I was fond of dancing—persuaded Lady C. to go for an hour with herself and family to the Sessions Ball, which was held that night. This dear, charming Duchess is generally thought very proud; and Lord Charles says he never knew her so attentive to any young person before. She is still a most lovely woman and dresses with particular elegance. She wore a red shawl gown, ornamented round the bosom with vandykes of point lace, and a head-dress of the same, with a helmet of diamonds which Lady C. valued at about eleven thousand pounds. She had likewise splendid diamond bracelets, necklace, armlets, brooches, etc. The young ladies were elegantly dressed in white and gold. The news of Lord Percy's election * arrived after dinner, and Lady Julia read me his account of it. He writes a most elegant letter, however ineffectively he may speak.

"At nine we went to the ball; and the room was so bad and the heat so excessive, that I determined, considering the long journey we had to take, not to dance, and refused my cousin Mitford of Mitford, Mr. Selby, Mr. Alder, and half a dozen whose names I have forgotten. At half-past ten we took leave of the Duchess and her amiable daughters, and

* He was elected M.P. for Westminster, following the death of Charles James Fox; but before he could take his seat, parliament was dissolved.

about thirty other people, to whom I had been introduced at the ball, and commenced our journey homeward, after a most delightful visit. We went on very quietly for some time, when we suddenly discovered that we had come about six miles out of our way; and, as the four horses were waiting at Framlington, Lord Charles and the footman were obliged to walk before the carriage with candles to find out a cross-country road. This so much delayed us, that it was near seven o'clock in the morning before we reached home. Seventy miles, a splendid dinner, and a ball all in one day! Was not this a spirited expedition, my darling? But I am now quite recovered from the fatigue, and Lord and Lady C. never felt it."

The day after this astonishing display of stamina, she left Little Harle Tower for Morpeth, while Mr. and Mrs. George Mitford went to spend a week with their daughter, Lady Charles. She was not, however, alone, for her second cousin, Mary Mitford, Lady Charles's sister, was there to keep her company. Dr. Mitford, too, took his departure and joined his friend, Nathaniel Ogle, at Kirkley Hall. In recording their movements from place to place, we cannot help reflecting on their almost boundless vitality, for there is nothing so exhausting as a change of residence every few days. Perpetual motion, however, was a stimulant to the Doctor, and as we shall see, only spurred him to further efforts; but his daughter was beginning to feel the strain. Although the entertainments at Morpeth were on a less lavish scale than at Little Harle, she says "The good people . . . would consider it the very height of ill manners to leave me a moment at peace; and between morning calls and evening visits I am harassed to death, and extremely happy to go to Little Harle for a day's rest." But Lady Charles was also imbued with the Mitford vitality, and twenty-four hours after her young relative had returned to her hospitable roof, they set off on another long distance tour. The first day they drove to Roddam on the Cheviot

Hills, where they spent the night. The following day they visited Chillingham Castle, the seat of Lord Tankerville, who took them on a conducted tour of his estate; and on Friday, 24th, they drove to Alnwick, where they dressed and then went on to dine at Lord Grey's at Falloden. It was here that Mary Mitford found a letter awaiting her from her father which contained very disagreeable intelligence.

A hint of its contents can be obtained in her own letters and one from Mrs. Mitford, dated 21st October, in which she says: "Your letter of the 16th, my beloved, I have just received and, encompassed as I am with all the horrors of an election before my eyes, it is the greatest cordial that can be. Nothing can exceed the madness of the people of Reading for your father's return. I own I hope his squire* will keep him where he is till he bring you both back." This hope was not to be fulfilled, for an election to Dr. Mitford was an irresistible magnet; all the more so on this occasion as his friend, Shaw Lefevre, who was seeking re-election, had been ill and there was the excuse that he needed the Doctor's help. Therefore while his host, Nathaniel Ogle, was away making one of the dinner party at Falloden, he left Kirkley and returned to Berkshire.

This ill-considered action was typical of the Doctor. He liked elections; therefore he must go. The issue was perfectly clear. That he was behaving discourteously to his host and leaving his young daughter stranded, probably never entered his head. Premeditation was not in his character. If it had been, with his total unconsciousness of any point of view but his own he might have been—until his ruthlessness aroused opposition—more successful in material matters. But his departure was not viewed in so simple a light by those whom he had left behind. His host, Nathaniel Ogle, was deeply affronted, although he magnanimously promised to remain in Northumberland till the 12th November, in case the Doctor should return and

* Nathaniel Ogle, who was proposing to bring back the Mitfords in his carriage.

they could all travel south together. Lady Charles, too, was much distressed. She and her family were due to leave for Bocking* in Cambridgeshire on 4th November, but as they had a large travelling party, there was no possibility of their guest's accompanying them. The only place where Mary Mitford could find refuge was in her great-uncle's house at Morpeth. He, however, appears to have had a slight stroke at this time, so that it would scarcely have been convenient to receive her. In her dilemma, she wrote to her father expressing her views in no uncertain terms.

"Morpeth, Oct. 22† 1806
Saturday morning.

It is with great reluctance, my dearest darling, that I am compelled to say that I never have experienced so disagreeable surprise as in receiving your letter yesterday at Lord Grey's. What could possibly influence you to prefer Mr. Lefevre's paltry vanity of being head of the poll (for of his election he was certain) to Nat Ogle's friendship and your daughter's comfort? Lady Charles leaves Little Harle on the 4th. On the 1st she is obliged to bring me to Morpeth; and *she* says that she shall be miserable in the idea of leaving me there, for your uncle, you well know, is in a state which must be dreadful to any one, and to a visitor most particularly so. . . .

"Is this a time for me to stay, or for my aunt to receive me with comfort? If you need any other motive to return, I must tell you that Mr. Ogle is extremely offended at your leaving him in this manner; and nothing but your *immediately* coming back can ever excuse you to him.

"I now implore you to return, and I call upon mamma's sense of propriety to send you here directly. Little did I suspect that my father, my dear, beloved father, would desert me in this manner, at this distance from home. Every one is surprised. They had thought that your parental

* Lord Charles Aynsley was Dean of Bocking.
† The date was 25th October. This mistake must have been due to her agitation.

affection was the strongest sentiment of your heart, and little suspected that it would yield so entirely to your *friendship* for any one. I expect no answer but a personal one, for it is utterly impossible that you should have any motive to detain you so strong as those I have given you for your return. . . ." And to her mother, a few days later she said: "You have no notion how very much I am offended with Papa for leaving me without even waiting a few hours to inform me of his intentions in person. I shall never again go to such a distance from my Mamma . . . for I perceive that on him I can place no reliance. . . ."*

I perceive that on him I can place no reliance. This was the first time that she had personally experienced her father's lack of consideration, (for previous disasters must have seemed to her, child that she was, as acts of fate over which there was no control) and she was deeply mortified and hurt. Furthermore she was in a most unenviable position. From all sides she heard criticisms of her father's conduct which she knew to be just, but which must have greatly distressed her. Apart from her natural affection, she had been taught by that simple and kindly soul, her mother, to respect and admire him; and only a few days previous to this unfortunate occurrence, Mrs. Mitford had written; "You smile at local attachments, but I think the enthusiasm of your character will kindle into affection when you behold the spot that gave birth to a parent you have so much reason to love and revere." The shattering of illusions is peculiarly painful to the young, and when Mary Mitford underwent this experience, there was no one in whom she could confide. With her strong sense of loyalty, it is inconceivable that she agreed with the censures passed on her father's conduct; but whether she attempted to defend him, or whether she merely kept silent, will never be known. Although this was the first occasion on which Dr. Mitford through his selfishness, had placed her in an intolerable position,

* Reading Collection, 29th October, 1806.

it was unfortunately not the last, nor the most serious. All her life, she was forced to conceal the defects of his character and to make excuses for him ; and she did it so skilfully and so urbanely that she has been accused of ignoring those very traits which caused her such suffering and anxiety. The idea is preposterous. She, whose perceptions were so keen that, in a few phrases, she could sum up the salient characteristics of a person whom she had met for the first time, was scarcely likely to ignore what was daily before her. But why, it may be asked, did she always defend and excuse him ? To that we can only postulate : what else could she have done ? Even in these days, when the ties of family are loosened, he who abuses a parent is thought to be lacking in taste, if nothing more. But in the early nineteenth century, when an unmarried daughter always lived at home and when her circle of friends was confined to those in the immediate neighbourhood, the family bond was much stronger, there was a far greater respect for the conventions (and what are conventions but a code of behaviour evolved by experience ?) and all peccadilloes were, as far as possible, carefully concealed. This concealment nowadays is considered as mere hypocrisy but it was at least a recognition that the moral code necessary to conduct the affairs of mankind had been broken. Therefore Mary Mitford, in our opinion, in defending her father took the only course open to her. In addition, there was her mother to be considered. She, poor woman, never wavered in her loyalty and affection, despite the financial disasters her husband had brought upon her ; and her daughter, who was devoted to her, would never have done anything to cause her suffering. Besides Dr. Mitford, despite his faults, had some endearing qualities. He was generous, too generous perhaps ; he had great sympathy with the under dog and he was devoted to children and animals, all of which must have compensated, in some degree, for his egotism. His very irresponsibility and immaturity must have aroused the protective instinct in his daughter; and while the cold analysis of his character conducted at a distance of more than a hundred years places more emphasis on his vices than his virtues, we can understand that in his lifetime, there must have been something attractive in his personality.

On this occasion, however, Mary Mitford was rescued from her dilemma by her father's sudden reappearance in Northumberland. Whether he came in answer to her anguished appeals or whether the Reading election was over, is not known: but on her return from a drive with Lady Charles to view his birthplace at Hexham—"a shocking gloomy place"—she found a letter, forwarded from Morpeth, announcing his return for that day. This was Saturday 1st November, so that Dr. Mitford had travelled six hundred miles and fought an election in about eleven days, which testifies to his powers of endurance if not to his common sense. No wonder his daughter wrote impatiently to her mother, "I cannot think, my darling, why you did not send him off on Wednesday, for the eating and drinking, and bawling at the election will do him more harm than twenty journeys." Then she adds, "I hope the Doctor will make his peace with Nat but I should not wonder if we had to return at our own expense . . . The letter he writes to me consists of a few lines but he can write long epistles to his uncle and other people."*

Fortunately the situation she envisaged did not materialize. Nathaniel Ogle was apparently placated, for the party travelled south at the end of November, but not before the Doctor had taken part in the Morpeth and Newcastle elections.

* Reading Collection, Nov. 2nd, 1806.

VI

1806-1810

The year 1806 marked the zenith of the Doctor's prosperity. Not only had he established his position as a landowner, but as a reward for his services the Whigs, in power that year in the ministry of All the Talents with Lord Grenville as First Lord of the Treasury and Charles Fox, until his death, as Foreign Secretary, appointed him a magistrate. Thus his ambitions were achieved. But in spite of these outward signs of prosperity, the Doctor's position was thoroughly unsound. His income, based on what remained of the lottery capital and Mrs. Mitford's small sum in the funds, was wholly inadequate to meet his expenses, and he trusted to gambling and speculation to enlarge it. No doubt like all gamblers, he had periods of good luck which, with his sanguine temperament, would only encourage him—although he scarcely needed any encouragement—to further follies. In the long run his fate was that of all those who rely on such expedients ; he was completely ruined, and for the last twenty years of his life was wholly dependent on his daughter's earnings. This unfortunate climax, however, was not reached immediately : the process was rather that of gradual decay. But as early as 1807, there were indications that all was not well. The first signs were the Doctor's long absences from Bertram House, which were indicative not only of gambling activities in London but of reluctance to meet creditors at home. An examination of the correspondence, which is by no means complete for there are few letters for the years 1807, 1808 and 1809, reveals that in 1807, he was in London in February, April and May ; in 1808, in February and June ; in 1809, February, April,

May and June; in 1810, January, March, May, July and December, and in 1811, when his financial situation was well nigh desperate, he remained there practically the entire year.

Besides these lengthy sojourns in London, there are actual references in the letters—few at first but increasing as the situation became more serious—to monetary affairs; and on February 11th, 1807, Dr. Mitford received these words of advice from his twenty-year-old daughter; "As lottery tickets continue at so high a price, had not you better dispose of yours, for I am not sanguine with respect to its turning out a prize, neither is Mamma; but consult your better judgment. I think you have to deal with a slippery gentleman. You would do well to introduce a rule, that whoever introduces a gentleman should be responsible for him; that is, supposing that you mean to continue to play there; though my advice has always been, that you should stick to Graham's, where, if you have not an equal advantage, you have at least no trouble, and know your society. You have always gained more there, on an average, than with chance players like the Baron,* or at inferior clubs, like the one you now frequent."

This is, for several reasons, a remarkable letter. If we had not known the writer, we might easily have supposed from its tone—that of absolute equality with the recipient—that it had been penned by one of the Doctor's friends, the advice of man to man. Then it proves that not only was Mary Mitford fully cognizant of his habits of high play, but that she apparently accepted them as the natural course of events. Considering that gambling was customary in the circles which the Doctor frequented, she should not, perhaps, be blamed for her acquiescence. Nevertheless this raises the wider issue of how far she condoned her father's conduct in financial matters; and we are bound to admit that while she frequently warned him that certain debts,

* Probably Baron von Hompesch.

through fear of the consequences, must be paid, or informed him of the steps which had been taken to meet some stringent financial situation, she never once exclaimed at the moral issues involved. Again we say she was scarcely to be blamed, for she had been brought up in an atmosphere of debts and uncertain speculations, and she was imbued with the eighteenth-century spirit of indifference towards monetary affairs. She was, by nature, broad minded and tolerant, and while in her own personal financial transactions she was scrupulously honest, for she had a horror of debt, "merely," she wrote ruefully to Harness later, "as a question of personal comfort," she was undoubtedly too tolerant towards her father's activities. And she was to pay heavily for this tolerance for the greater part of her life.

In addition to the evidence already adduced of the decline of the Doctor's position, other signs were not wanting. In 1808, William Harness, then a schoolboy at Harrow, wrote:

"Harrow, 31st July, 1808

My dear Dr. Mitford,

I was impudent enough to invite myself to your house, and you were kind enough to say that I should be welcome; it was afterwards settled I should come to the Races. I am too selfish to let such an opportunity slip, and fully intend to bore you for some time at Grasely. I hope Mrs. Mitford will not turn me out. Will you then, my dear Sir, let me know when the Races are, and when I shall be least troublesome to you; for as soon as you appoint I shall come down and harass Miss Mitford to death! My father and grandmother send their love and compliments to Mrs. and Miss Mitford and yourself. I shall keep all my civil things till we meet.

Believe me,
yours sincerely,
W. Harness."*

* *Literary Life of Rev. William Harness*, by A. G. L'Estrange, p. 9, 1871.

It was doubtless due to his observations on this visit that we are indebted for the information that " within six years of the completion of Bertram House—so early as 1808—great reductions had been required in the establishment. The servant out of livery had been dispensed with. There had ceased to be any lady's maid. The footman had degenerated into an awkward lad, who was not only expected to wait at table and go out with the carriage, but to make himself useful in the stable or the garden. The carriage horses were employed on the work of the farm, and it was not every day in the week on which Mrs. and Miss Mitford could command the use of them." It is also on record that the young gentleman from Harrow was thoroughly ashamed of the shabby carriage in which the party appeared on the race-course.

Notwithstanding the decline in the family's fortunes during the years 1807-1810, Mrs. Mitford and her daughter did not, apart from reductions in the household staff and other minor economies, experience any great inconvenience, and appear to have continued the even tenor of their ways. They entertained and were entertained, and Mary Mitford observed to her father, " Mama will tell you how good I am grown with respect to going into Reading. I have lost much of my aversion to morning calls and I shall perhaps twenty years hence be as accomplished a votary of cards and scandal as any of the amiable Sisterhood to which I shall most probably belong."* In September, 1808, the family paid a visit to William Cobbett at Botley, one of the few recorded occasions when they went away together, and Mary Mitford has left a lively description of her host. "The coarseness and violence of his political writings and conversations almost entirely disappeared in his family circle, and were replaced by a kindness, a good humour, and an enjoyment in seeing and promoting the happiness of others which was infinitely attractive in itself, and appeared

* Reading Collection, March 24th, 1808.

perhaps to even greater advantage from the contrast it exhibited with his sterner mood. He had, too, occasionally uncommon powers of unintentional description. Living constantly in the country, and a very beautiful part of the country, and going out daily into the fields and woods, he could not always divest himself of those picturesque associations to which the distinctiveness of his conceptions, and his clear and direct language were so well calculated to do justice ; and in pointing out where a spaniel sprung a pheasant, or a greyhound killed a hare, he would sometimes strike a landscape so distinct, so glowing, so vivid that the dullest imagination could see the very spot."

It was probably on this visit that Dr. Mitford was confronted with a Mrs. Blamire,* with whom he had carried on a flirtation before his marriage. This encounter is humourously depicted by his daughter. "I was a little curious to see how my own dear mother, my mamma that was, and the stranger lady, my mamma that might have been," she says, "would bear themselves on the occasion. At first, my dear mother, an exceedingly lady-like, quiet person, had considerably the advantage, being prepared for the *rencontre* and perfectly calm and composed; whilst Mrs. Blamire, taken, I suspect, by surprise, was a good deal startled and flustered. This state of things, however, did not last. Mrs. Blamire having got over the first shock, comported herself like what she evidently was, a practised woman of the world—would talk to no one but ourselves—and seemed resolved not only to make friends with her successful rival, but to strike up an intimacy. This by no means entered into my mother's calculations. As the one advanced the other receded, and, keeping within the limits of civility, I never heard so much easy chat put aside with so many cool and stately monosyllables in my life.

"The most diverting part of this scene, very amusing to

* Her husband, Dr. Blamire, was on the medical staff of Haslar when Dr. Mitford was there.

a stander-by, was, that my father, the only real culprit, was the only person who throughout maintained the appearance and demeanour of the most unconscious innocence." This we have no difficulty in believing, for if anyone was totally deficient in a sense of guilt, that person was Dr. Mitford. Not because he was a conscious rogue, but simply because his powers of reasoning were insufficient to deduce the effect of his actions. This visit to Botley was returned at the end of January, 1809; and on the 22nd of that month, Cobbett wrote this characteristic letter to Dr. Mitford:

" My dear Friend,

I have waited to be able to give you certain intelligence of our movements.

26th. We go to Oxford.

27th. Remain there.

28th. Call at your house, and perhaps sleep.

29th. Return to Botley.

Depend upon nothing as to time of day. A dish of tea will always do for my wife, and a hunch of bread and cheese for me.

I *feed* my wild pheasants in the woods. Shall I get the pied ones? Our kindest respects to Mrs. and Miss Mitford. God bless you and damn the minister.

Wm. Cobbett."

In May, 1809, Mary Mitford visited her old school mistress, Fanny Rowden who, as M. de St. Quintin had retired, was now in charge of the school in Hans Place. She spent about a fortnight in London, and as usual seems to have crowded in as many engagements as possible. She visited Miss Linwood's exhibition of needle-work, the Royal Academy—"It is the worst I ever saw, consisting almost wholly of portraits; and I could scarce name a dozen pictures worth house room—" and the Exhibition of Water Colours in Spring Gardens. These last two visits were paid on the same day, and as there is nothing more exhausting than trapesing round an exhibition, the unathletic Mary Mitford was quite overcome by the exertion. "After this fag," she complains to her mother, "we were obliged to walk into Piccadilly before we met with a coach; and I was so knocked up that, instead of dining with papa and a party at the St. Quintins', I went to bed." Of course she and Miss Rowden went to the theatre; to the Haymarket to see *A Cure for Heartache* and *The Critic*, and with a party to Covent Garden where a tragedy was performed, followed by a concert of Italian singers and the French ballet. This tragedy was apparently effective, for she recounts, "A curious circumstance happened—not one of the party was provided with that article, so essential to a tragedy, yclept a handkerchief; and had not papa (who met us there) supplied the weeping beauties with this necessary appendage, they would have borne some resemblance to a collection of blurred schoolboys. To me, you know, this was of no consequence, for I never cry at a play." Although the tragedy left no outward and visible signs upon her, she was in rhapsodies over the ballet. "The dancing of Vestris is indeed perfection. The 'poetry of motion' is exemplified in every movement, and his Apollo-like form excels any idea I had ever formed of manly grace. Angiolini is a very fine dancer, but her figure by no means equals Vestris's, and I had no eyes for her while he remained upon the stage. The ballet was in itself magnificent, but the last scene excelled in splendour any I had ever seen."

In between her visits to theatres and exhibitions, the time was taken up with social activities. She had "a most delightful walk in Kensington Gardens," during which she met Lord Folkestone, "who was all affability" due, no doubt, to her effusive reference to him in one of her poems, and the two Misses Ximenes*, whose dresses were unfortunately similar to her own: and at a dinner party she met

* Daughters of Sir Morris Ximenes, High Sheriff of Berkshire in 1805.

Lord Suffolk, another friend of her father's—"a most charming old man." During this time, the Squire of Mitford was also in London, and she tells her mother "Bertram Mitford was invited, [to a dinner party] but he had an engagement he could not dispense with, even to meet 'the clever Mary Mitford,' the name by which I find he distinguishes me from three other Mary Mitfords, his sister, his cousin, and our own Mary of Morpeth." He seems also to have been present at a dance given by a Mr. Brett of Brompton, a "most magnificent entertainment," which was the most brilliant event of her sojourn in London. Three hundred persons attended, there was an "elegant" supper, and she danced till five in the morning. "But," she adds, "though my partners were all uncommonly pleasant I do assure you, dear mamma, I am still heart-whole, and I do not think I am much in danger from the attractions of Bertram Mitford!" But dissipations take their toll, and in this case the cost was "a total destruction of gloves and shoes, and no great good to my lilac gown." It must, indeed, have been a very fatigued young lady who returned to the peace and quiet of Berkshire the following Tuesday, June 7th, some time in the evening.

Nevertheless despite these social gaieties, she continued to occupy her leisure hours with literary work which culminated in 1810 in the publication of a slender volume of verses entitled *Miscellaneous Poems*.* This modest work was printed by A. J. Valpy, son of Dr. Valpy, who had recently started in business in Took's Court, Chancery Lane; and it did not make its appearance without those trials and tribulations usually associated with a first production. In the negotiations which preceded publication, Dr. Mitford acted as his daughter's agent, a *rôle* which he

* A copy was exhibited in the National Book League's Poetry Exhibition, 1947. The entry in the catalogue is: "Poems, by Mary Russell Mitford, printed by A. J. Valpy, Took's Court, Chancery Lane, 1810, sold by Longman, Hurst, Rees & Orne, Pater-noster Row, 1810. 8vo First Edition, Original pink paper boards, green paper label on spine. Wholly uncut."

fulfilled till the end of his life. In this capacity, he was remarkably successful, for not only was he astute in the actual business arrangements, but he had a flare for publicity which enabled him to make her works known in the right quarters. This latter quality arose, no doubt, from his paternal pride, for he was naturally delighted to show off the accomplishments of his clever child. In 1810, however, both he and his daughter were novices in these matters, and instead of selling the copyright, as was customary in those days, they arranged to pay for the printing of the poems. As a result they were faced with a bill for £59 for five hundred copies. She was appalled at the cost, and no doubt her father was equally dismayed at this demand for ready money, a commodity in which he was, as a general rule, remarkably deficient. "I was quite shocked, my darling, at the bill, which is really exorbitant," she wrote. "Do you know that if the whole edition is sold in a twelvemonth (a thing I do not expect),* we shall not gain fifty pounds? If ever I write again I will sell the copyright. The charge of four pounds odd for labels and alterations is scandalous. *Alterations*, indeed, I made none; and they certainly ought to pay for their own blunders." The young authoress also seems to have experienced some difficulty in composing a suitable advertisement for her poems, a task with which most modern authors, obliged to this day to write copy to appear on the book jacket, will sympathize. "I am in the horrors respecting the advertisement to be prefixed to the poems, which will soon, I suppose, be wanted. It is usual for people to give some reasons for publishing; but I *cannot*, you know, my darling, for the best of all possible reasons—because I have none to give. Apologies are sufficiently needed, but I had rather write such another volume than undertake to compose any; and I have a mind to turn it out naked into the great sea, the world (as the Indians are reported to do by their children),

* There was a second edition in 1811.

and let it sink or swim as it may." Trouble also arose over the contents, and she seems to have written a poem in order to lengthen the volume. Evidently this addition did not please her father or his friends, for she wrote indignantly, "I was not surprised to find you did not like the tale, for I knew it would not suit your taste. The catastrophe might be easily altered; but I am not disposed to take any more trouble about it; and, if you had known your own mind respecting the quantity of poetry necessary for the volume, I should never have thought of writing this *immoral* production. As, however, I am by no means desirous of having it hawked about among your canting friends, I shall be much obliged to you to put your copy into the fire. You need not fear my destroying my own, for I think too well of it.... I am not angry with you, though extremely provoked at those canting Scotchmen. If any of my things are worth reading, I am sure that poor tale is; and who reads a volume of poems to glean moral axioms? What moral, indeed, have our most celebrated tales?... So that there is nothing offensive to delicacy or good taste, it is sufficient; and I never should think of writing a poem with a sermon tacked to its tale." Like all quick-witted persons, she could express herself forcibly on occasions; and there is more than a little of wounded vanity in this brusque note. But she was only twenty-three, and she had not yet learned to bear criticism with equanimity.

The little book duly appeared about the end of February, 1810. It contained 144 pages, as well as ten pages of notes, and the alterations costing four pounds, over which she was so indignant (not without reason for they numbered only five) are on the last leaf. On reading the poems, twenty-nine in all, the impression is that of a faded, lingering charm, as though we had unexpectedly come across flowers pressed between the leaves of an old book, or a bowl of dried rose leaves culled by some remote ancestress. Poems, however, they are not; rather the pleasant outpourings of a youthful mind, elegantly versified. And the authoress, some twenty years later, was of the same opinion, for when writing to Elizabeth Barrett Browning about these early poetic efforts, she says: "All sold well, and might have been reprinted; but I had (of this proof of tolerable taste I am rather proud) the sense to see they were good for nothing; so I left off writing for ten or fifteen years. . . ." This perhaps is too harsh. Judged by any standards her verses are remarkable productions for a young woman, and they certainly display a fluency of language which she afterwards turned to good account in her own polished prose. But lacking imagination, she had not the poetic fire; and furthermore, she was too witty and too worldly ever to lose herself in those depths of emotion which are the basis of true poetic genius.

It is not possible to state with any certainty when all the poems which constitute this little volume were written; but apart from the *Impromptu* to Samuel Whitbread, already quoted, and some lines to S. J. Pratt,* a popular poet of the period, they seem in the main to have been composed in the years 1808-9. It is possible, however, that *Sybille* was written earlier, perhaps on her return from Northumberland, for the introduction states: "The following poem was written at the request of a near relation, who wished me to compose a Tale adapted to the picturesque and enchanting scenery of the ancient domains of our family, now in the possession of Bertram Mitford, Esq." We can only speculate on the identity of this "near relation"; it may have been Lady Charles Aynsley, or Mary Mitford, but most probably her father. Apart from those verses which are a eulogy on her father's political friends, *The Pen and the Sword*, dedicated to Sheridan, *On a Bust of Fox*, *To G. L. Wardle, Esq.*,† the *Impromptu* on Whitbread and the

* S. J. Pratt (1749-1814) poet and dramatist.

† G. L. Wardle, M.P. In 1809, he brought forward a motion in the House against the Duke of York in connection with the scandals arising out of the Duke's association with Mary Anne Clark.

coursing poem inscribed to Cobbett, these early verses reveal her love of nature ; and although one reviewer jibes unmercifully at her similes, there is no doubt that she already possessed the knowledge, if not the skill, which enabled her to depict so enchantingly the country scenes in *Our Village*. We can imagine her strolling about the spacious grounds of Bertram House observing those signs which portend the changing seasons ; or with a pen in her hand, relaxing in some favourite garden seat, to write these lines :

> " Farewel ! my own romantic bow'r,
> Sweet shelter in the noon-tide hour !
> Scarce yet thy willow buds unfold
> Their silver leaves on stems of gold ;
> Scarce yet the woodbine's clasping arms
> Twine round the elm her modest charms ;
> Scarce yet, in richest robe array'd,
> The oaks display their summer shade ;
> But thy fair bank, in beauty gay,
> Can boast the blooming tints of May ;
> Pure, limpid, sparkling, is the flood
> That murmurs through thy tangl'd wood ;
> And fragrant is the balmy gale,
> That gently whispers through the vale."

It is only right to add that this tender farewell was written before she left for London on that gay visit just described ; and not, as might be supposed, on the occasion of a long absence from home in distant lands.

As was only natural, she had slight misgivings about the treatment her volume would receive from the critics. " I am sadly afraid of not being noticed in the *Edinburgh*," she wrote, " the volume is so trifling." And again, " Shall I be reviewed next number in the *Monthly* ? Will the *Edinburgh* condescend to notice me ? " The *Edinburgh Review*, indeed, remained obstinately silent ; but the verdict of the critics was, on the whole, favourable. The *Eclectic Review* states: "It is possible we may be understood to speak in higher terms of this volume than it deserves, when we say, that the tale with which it commences would lose little in comparison with Mrs. Opie's *Warrior's Return*, and that some other parts of it are nearly as well entitled to be printed in quarto as the introductory epistles in *Marmion*. In fact, we have seldom seen a volume, which, without aspiring to the loftier heights of passion and fancy, was distinguished by such harmony of verse, such elegance of thought, such correct taste, and such a poetical turn of expression." * And most of the other critics dealt with her in an equally gentle fashion. But because her father's political views were well known, and because she had addressed some of the leading Whigs and Radicals, she laid herself open to attack; and the *Quarterly Review*† was not slow to seize the opportunity offered.

"Many of the ladies who have been candidates for celebrity have, we fear, been influenced more by necessity than choice," wrote the reviewer, "and that timidity, which shrinks at the idea of subjecting its productions to the eye of the world, has been goaded forward by motives which admitted no retreat. In such cases, criticism became but a secondary duty; for his feelings would not be much envied, who could pause to examine the construction of a sentence, when not the pursuit of fame, but the fear of distress, evidently dictated the production. Such, however, we believe not to be the case with the writer before us. Indeed, the poems themselves signify that they were composed with the applause of many friends; and that the author's chief motive in their publication was to show how skilfully the lyre might be swept by a lady's hand. The subjects on which her talents are exercised are of a very miscellaneous nature, and such as we should not have

* *Eclectic Review*, April, 1810.
† *Quarterly Review*, Nov., 1810.

Three Mile Cross, 1835, *by George Baxter.*

Mary Russell Mitford, 1835, *by George Baxter.*

45 Frith Street Soho Square
Novr 7th 1826

Our beloved Creature my dearest
Mary attended Covent Garden Theatre
last night & you will rejoice to hear
that altho the night was unfavorable
the Pit was a bumper before
the rising of the Curtain, and Mr
Kemble Mr Fawcett &c admitted
[illegible] was the best House they

Letter from Dr. Mitford to Mrs. Mitford, *on the occasion of the second performance of* Foscari, *7th November*, 1826.

[illegible] — If you happen to know any
thing of the Author of a very clever letter
on the Stage in Blackwood's Magazine
you may tell him with my compliments
that he put the Authoress of Rienzi into
a sound fright. I expected nothing less than
a long pompous answer from Mr Macready
in the next number, holding forth the un-
-lucky Authoress by name — so I wrote to
Mr Talfourd to find out if he could whether
Mr Macready did mean to write to the Editor
Mr Talfourd sounded him accordingly &
discovered that he had formed the wise

Letter from Mary Russell Mitford to William Harness, 28th July, 1825.

supposed peculiarly attractive to a female mind. They are chiefly of an epainetic or commendatory nature, and praise Doctors Mitford and Valpy, Mr. Wardle a "Patriot," Maria a prize greyhound, Lord Folkestone, also a patriot, Zōsia a Pole, Mr. Pratt the Gleaner, Maria again and Jehuda Charizi.

"The first and longest poem in the collection is called *Sybelle*, a Northumbrian tale, the catastrophe of which is taken from Southey's beautiful episode of Laila in *Thalaba*. The next poem is employed in celebrating the young ladies who were educated at Mrs. Rowden's academy, Hans Place. One of those ladies is said to be delightful—

'Whether she join in converse gay
With arch and playful naïveté,'

and the whole of them seem to have spent their time very pleasantly indeed, but not with sufficient attention to the true use of the preterperfect tense.

'While some, reclin'd in verdant bow'rs,
With tales amus'd the passing hours,
And some their fav'rite flow'rs attend,
I roam'd with my selected friend.'

"Some verses soon after occur, discoursing largely in praise of 'dandelions,' by the side of which powerful herb, the poetess, not without danger to her muse, moralizes at leisure, and revolves its various properties. . . . We have then a poem on a glow worm, which we should feel more disposed to commend, if we could overlook the *false fire* in the first two lines of the following stanza—

'Though forked light'ning round thee play,
Though brilliant meteors wildly glare,
Still may thy pale and modest ray
Shed em'rald lustre through the air.'"

The critic concludes his strictures with some words of advice, scarcely designed, however, to bring much consolation to the youthful author. "In our cursory examination of this little volume," he adds, "we have noticed several unpoetical and ungraceful, and not a few ungrammatical lines. It must be apparent, we think, to every one, that Miss Mitford's taste and judgment are not yet matured; that her poems ought to have been kept back much longer, and revised much oftener before they were submitted to the public; and, above all, that she wanted some friend who, without wounding her feelings, or damping the fire of her genius, would have led her to correcter models of taste, and taught her more cautious habits of composition. That such instruction would not have been thrown away, we may judge from many pleasing passages scattered through her little volume, which do no discredit to the amiableness of her mind, and the cultivation of her talents. . . ."

This was harsh measure to deal out to a girl of twenty-three, but Mary Mitford was of too buoyant a temperament to succumb to the blow. She reeled a little, and then rallied. But she never forgot, and only eighteen months before her death, she referred to the article in the preface to her *Dramatic Works*. She always believed it to have been written by William Gifford, the editor of the *Quarterly*,* but Harness states that the author was the Rev. John Mitford, rector of Benhall, Saxmundham.† If this was the case, the reverend gentleman was singularly hypocritical, for he wrote to Dr. Mitford, after the review had appeared, "I have been very much pleased with Miss Mitford's poems generally, and many passages I think excellent. In particular I was delighted to see her muse busy in Northumberland, the scenery of which in many parts is well worthy of a poet. . . . Miss Mitford seems peculiarly fitted to excel in descriptive poetry, which, after all, is the poetry that pleases most and clings closest to the

* The *Encyclopaedia Britannica* attributes the authorship to Scott, but this is unlikely. He was far too kind a man to be so harsh a critic to a young girl.

† J. R. Mitford was a friend of Charles Lamb's.

mind." As for the authoress, she wrote, "Did I not guess well respecting Gifford? It was his quoting an old play that made me think it was he. I have little reason to complain. If he attacked Joanna Baillie,* even to be abused with her is an honour." These comments, considering the flaying she had just received, are commendably moderate.

* Joanna Baillie, poet and dramatist, 1762-1851. Byron (*Life*, Moore, p. 282, 1847) wrote "Women (saving Joanna Baillie) cannot write tragedy. They have not seen enough nor felt enough of life for it." She was an intimate friend of Scott's.

VII

1810-1811

If Mary Mitford suffered from the strictures of the *Quarterly*, she also received consolation from the encouragement of private individuals. In this connection Dr. Mitford, with his large circle of influential friends and acquaintances, was invaluable; and we gain fascinating glimpses of his manifold activities through the medium of the correspondence. "Ten thousand thanks," wrote his daughter, "for the management of the Reviews. . . . Did I . . . make you comprehend that I had not copies enough for Mr. Sheridan and our friends in Hans Place? You will be so good as to convey one to each." And again "It is very kind of Mr. Perry* to invite you to meet Mr. Brougham, and I am sure it will be greatly in my favour. You advertise my poems *viva voce* you know, my dearest, and your manners and conversation are the greatest recommendations." A copy was, of course, presented to Cobbett who wrote to the young author: "Your good and kind father has just given Nancy† a copy of a little volume of poems, in which I find the verses on Maria's winning the cup at Ilsley inscribed to me, and for which honour I beg you to accept my best thanks."

We can well imagine that the task of interviewing—and possibly entertaining—editors, critics and friends, anyone indeed who could be of service, was a congenial one to Dr. Mitford. Any excuse for excitement and change was acceptable to his volatile temperament, and this must have been one of the few occasions in his life when duty and

* James Perry, editor of the *Morning Chronicle*, and an intimate friend of Dr. Mitford's.

† His daughter.

inclination coincided. That his efforts were successful is proved by the second edition of the poems which appeared in the following year. Harness mentions contemptuously his "rough manner and loud talk," and comments many times on what he calls the "filial blindness" of Mary Mitford towards her father's faults; but the fact remains that the Doctor was intimate with many of the great men of his age, and neither his manner nor his vices was such as to alienate them. There is no doubt that Dr. Mitford had an engaging personality, with the bluff and jovial manners of the sportsman; and while his frankness may have offended the susceptibilities of the bachelor Victorian parson, he had sufficient charm to make himself popular with most of the people with whom he came into contact. Both he and his daughter, with their eighteenth-century outlook, were mercifully free from the cant which characterized the middle class of a later era. As we have stated before, we do not believe that Mary Mitford ignored her father's faults; we believe she loved him in spite of them, because of his many engaging and redeeming qualities. And in his fashion, he was devoted to her. It gave him great pleasure to send her expensive presents, to execute commissions for her—"When you return, my dear love, will you bring me the pens and new tooth brush (you know how I like them—neither hard nor soft and very thin of hair)"*—to introduce her to his friends and to take her about with him in London, to pay her, in fact, all those attentions so much appreciated by a woman. The only thing he would not do, perhaps because he could not, was to exercise some sense of responsibility in financial matters; and she, realizing his inability, forgave him and, so far as she was able, exercised it for him. Whether she was right in condoning his actions, and whether, by so doing, she encouraged him to be even more irresponsible, can only be matters for conjecture; but at all events there can be no doubt that

* Reading Collection, 22nd March, 1810.

she paid a very heavy price for her acceptance of his faults.

Dr. Mitford was not the only one to act as a publicist for his daughter's productions. It seems that his wife, in her maternal pride, also played her part and that, on her own initiative, she sent a copy of the poems to Lord Holland, her husband's friend. She evidently anticipated that this gift would be acknowledged to the Doctor, but Lord Holland, to her infinite delight, replied direct. Her excitement at the receipt of his letter is evident in the hasty note she sent to her husband.

"Nov. 21, 1810

Flatter not yourself, my dearly beloved husband, that Lord Holland will favor you with a letter, for believe me, you will find such an idea a mere illusion ; you will stare at my assertion, but patience a moment till I detail the occasion of it, by telling you that it is to your poor wife his Lordship had done the honour of addressing his thanks for our darling's volume of poems. And from the tenor of it I am led to believe he considers himself indebted to me for so valuable a present. As I never feel pleasure, from whatever cause arising, without wishing you to share it with me, I will give you here a copy verbatim of the letter which came with one from your dear self by this morning's post, not even omitting the superscription. . . .

London Novbr. twenty 1810
To Mrs. Mitford,
Bertram House, Reading.

Madam,

Your obliging and flattering present required no apology—I had not only heard of but read with great pleasure some specimens of Miss Mitford's poetry, but that only supplies me with an additional motive for receiving with many thanks the very interesting volume you have done me the honor of sending me. I well remember the verses on Mr. Fox's bust and the pleasure he received from that specimen of so young and so promising a muse.

I am, Madam,

Your obliged humble servant,

Vll. Holland."*†

The publication of her full name, Mary Russell Mitford, on the title page of her poems seems to have caused confusion to the critics and annoyance to the author, for on 2nd March, 1810, she wrote to her father: "My unknown panegyrist has combined with Fanny Rowden and everyone almost that I know, to deprive me of the rights of an only daughter. Miss M. R. Mitford says one, Miss Mary Russell Mitford says another. Would not anyone believe that you had a dozen brats, and another Mary among them, from whom it was necessary to distinguish me by my second appellation? I have no sort of objection to the name of Russell, but it can surely add no lustre to the infinitely more ancient name to which it is affixed, and I am absolutely jealous of the honour of our house in finding this patrician appellation so needlessly and studiously prefixed to that which I inherit from you. I have given a tolerable swing to this excess of family pride in *Sybille*, and I am not without my fears of being attacked on that score."‡

But the background to the natural jubilation and excitement she experienced on the appearance of her poems was a sombre one. The decline of Dr. Mitford's fortunes began in 1807, but the pace was greatly accelerated in 1810 and the climax came in the succeeding year. Interspersed with congratulatory letters, visits to London and friends, balls and dinner parties, were incidents which must have kept her father's desperate financial plight always in her mind. As early as March 17th, 1810, when the poems had only been published a few weeks, she was reminding him that if the

* His christian name was Vassall.
† Reading Collection.
‡ Reading Collection.

tax money was not paid early that week, he would be reported as a defaulter. Then Mrs. Mitford, on 22nd March, forwarded a letter to him from his brother, the Rev. William Mitford, who lived in the Isle of Man and who, there is reason to believe, lent the Doctor over two thousand pounds somewhere about this time. In May of the same year, his daughter again wrote: "And now let me give you a little serious advice, my dear son and heir.* If those Raybould people do not give you secure *indemnity*, stir not a finger in this business. Let them 'go to the devil and shake themselves' for I would not trust one of them with a basket of biscuits to feed my dogs. They have no more honour between them all than you 'might put upon the point of a knife, and not choke a daw withal,' so comfort yourself accordingly; treat them as you would lawyers or the king's ministers, or any other fraternity of known rogues and robbers." We have not been able to discover any further details of this transaction, but from the tone of this letter it is obvious that Mary Mitford, even at the age of twenty-three, mistrusted her father's powers of judgment, and that she thought it necessary to warn him against plausible rogues of whom he was the too easy prey.

It is therefore possible that such incidents and not just the encouragement she had received over her poems, spurred her to further literary efforts. At any rate, whatever the cause, in July of the same year, she started another poem entitled *Christina, the Maid of the South Seas*, based on the mutiny on the Bounty, details of which had only been discovered in 1808. This news is given in a letter to Sir William Elford, one of her father's friends, to whom she had been introduced during a short visit to London in the spring of that year. Sir William was a man of some distinction. He came of an old Devon family, and was Recorder of Plymouth and Member of Parliament for that

* It is curious to note how, even at this youthful age, her attitude towards him was that of an indulgent mother to her child.

Borough. He was also a Fellow of the Royal Society and an amateur painter of merit. At the time of their introduction, he was about sixty-four and it was something of an honour that he should wish to correspond with her. That she felt it to be so is evident from the tone of her letters. Instead of the usual spontaneous wit, her style becomes formal and even, at times, precious. Some of the earlier letters must, we feel, have been copied from a rough draft. They are the letters of a young woman who has the reputation for being clever, and must therefore justify it. Even the handwriting changes. Instead of the usual illegible scrawl, the words are neatly formed and the punctuation impeccable. Fortunately, when the acquaintance ripened into friendship, when she no longer had any need to make an impression, she relapsed into her own inimitable style and the correspondence becomes an interesting record—for Sir William lived to be ninety—of her life and thoughts.

The friendship began propitiously by his promising to send her one of his paintings, which she reciprocated by despatching a copy of the *Poems*, accompanied by the following flattering verses.

"To Sir William Elford Bart.*

The sister-arts at Nature's shrine
In generous rivalry combine ;
Her charms the Painter's soul inspire,
And wake the Bard's immortal fire.†
O doubly blest ! to you are given
These varied powers by favouring Heaven !
The Poet's blissful fairy land,
The charms that wit and sense impart
And, rarer still, a feeling heart.

* *The Poetical Register*, Vol. 7, p. 211, 1812.
† Sir William, too, could turn a pretty verse.

Elford! you first with generous praise
Cherished these simple rustic lays;
With kindness heard the artless strain
And fed the Poet's pleasing pain
With bashful fears and love of song,
The timid maiden struggled long
Till Hope her radiant wings unfurled
And bore the wild flowers to the world;
Bolder, and bolder still, she grew
And sent th' imperfect wreath to you."

Sir William was greatly interested in his youthful friend's work and often enquired about it. In answer to one of his enquiries she wrote, in September 1810, "My dear papa, I am afraid, led you to expect that I had made a greater progress in *Christina* than I have really done. It is true that in a fortnight I wrote a thousand lines (such as they are), which, considering that we keep early hours, and that either from habit or caprice I can never write until candle-light, is really very tolerable work. But I am sorry to say, my dear sir, that I have scarcely written a hundred lines since, having been engaged in our annual dissipation of balls and concerts, races and oratorios." She was anxious to dedicate *Christina* to him, and evidently composed a high-flown address to which he, however, demurred. He wished he said, to be considered a friend of the author, for to him that seemed a higher honour than any he could derive from the superiority of station implied by her dedication. She was naturally delighted at this compliment, and composed another dedication which ended

"So, shrinking from the critic frown, I flew
On trembling wing to Genius and to you;
Proud with your wreath my Indian flower to blend,
Elford, far prouder thus to hail you Friend!"

While *Christina* was being written, Dr. Mitford was

busily negotiating its sale. His daughter suggested that if he had not already taken it to Longman's, he should try John Murray. "He is reckoned a very liberal man, and a more respectable publisher we cannot have." It was eventually printed by John Valpy and published by the booksellers, F. C. and J. Rivington. It was also the Doctor who sought out Coleridge, then living with the Morgans; and it is probable that the poet, in return for the Doctor's services in obtaining his release from the army, offered to read *Christina*. As the proofs came from the press, he corrected them; and in February 1811, Mary Mitford asked her father anxiously: "I want to know what Mr. Coleridge thinks of the third canto, which he has not yet seen, I suppose. This sounds like a bull." The proofs were eventually returned early in March, when she commented: "Mr. Coleridge has only taken out what could well be spared from my poem. I wish he had taken more for what remains is really detestable, always excepting his own beautiful lines." From this it would seem that somewhere in the third canto are lines composed by Coleridge, which presents the students of the poet with a fascinating problem. It is astonishing, in view of the circumstances of Coleridge's life at that period, that he managed to concentrate on the laborious work of correcting and amending the proofs. The final separation from his wife had taken place a few months previously; he had quarrelled with Wordsworth, and in addition, he was totally demoralized by excessive indulgence in opium. Nevertheless, he seems to have applied himself to the task and although Mary Mitford expresses the opinion that he will keep one of her manuscripts for six weeks without looking at it, he does not appear on this occasion to have held up matters for more than the time required to complete the task.

When the final proofs of *Christina* were received, it was found that Coleridge had omitted the Invocation to Scott, because the stanzas contained "bad lines." Mrs. Mitford, usually so gentle and accommodating, took up the cudgels on her daughter's behalf and wrote a most indignant letter to her spouse. She attributed the expunction to bad feeling between Scott and Coleridge, and to a " mean, pitiful spirit of resentment. . . . It is certainly a most extraordinary liberty Mr. C. has taken and will, I hope, be the last he will attempt," she exclaims. When we read this indignant letter, we could not help reflecting on the small part reason plays in human affairs. *Christina* was a narrative poem of five cantos, and as far as we can ascertain, the disputed Invocation had been included in the text, thereby holding up the action. At that time, Coleridge's reputation was established, so that his criticisms might have been expected to bear fruit. Yet so strong was the maternal instinct that this emendation of her daughter's poem aroused Mrs. Mitford's ire to heights of which we would not have believed her capable. In her daughter's words " I did not think it had been in her." Nor did we; and it is easy now to understand that with these strong possessive instincts and fierce loyalties, she so easily overlooked her husband's faults. But her daughter took the excision more philosophically, " . . . it does not at all signify," she remarked. " I would not for the world you had affronted a man to whose kindness we are so highly indebted." Coleridge was not the only person, however, who helped her with the poem. In her preface, she expresses thanks to Captain Burney,* brother of Fanny Burney, who aided her with the notes which contain a large number of quotations from nautical references. On 31st March, she wrote " I do not know if I am right in the inscription for Captain Burney and Mr. Coleridge. I believe I ought to have written to thank them, but really could not summon up resolution. I am terribly afraid of Mr. Coleridge—it is only the eagle, you know, who can approach the sun without trembling."†

* Captain Burney accompanied Captain Cook on his last two voyages and was therefore well acquainted with the South Seas.

† Reading Collection.

Christina appeared either at the end of March or the beginning of April, 1811, and had a good sale, particularly in America. It is a long poem, divided into five cantos and with considerable annotations. She had obviously taken immense trouble to obtain the necessary data for her descriptions, and no doubt the nautical details were checked by Captain Burney. It is a remarkable production for a young woman, both for its execution, the skilful handling of so many characters and the versifying. But it still falls short of the highest standards of poetry. Nevertheless, it seems that Coleridge had a high opinion of her talents, for on June 7th she wrote to her father, "I need not tell you, my dear love, how delighted I am with Mr. Coleridge's approbation. To be, some time or other, the best English poetess . . . is the height of my ambition."* He may, of course, merely have been making a polite remark, but we think it unlikely. He would have scarcely taken so much trouble with her work if he had not thought her worth helping; for not only did he supervise *Christina*, but he performed the same task with her next poem *Blanch of Castille*, which she began immediately after the publication of *Christina*.

Blanch, however, was not the only work she undertook at this time. As early as 1806, she had prepared a collection of her grandfather's poems for the press which had been despatched, with a preface by Mrs. Mitford, to the Doctor in London. At that time, when money was not so urgently required in the household, the Doctor, either through inability or lack of enthusiasm, was unable to find a publisher.† In 1811, however, when Mary Mitford was becoming known, she despatched some of Dr. Russell's poems with a selection of her own, to the *Poetical Register*. The editor, R. A. Davenport, accepted them immediately, and they appeared in the seventh volume. We give below

* It must be admitted that at this period the standard of poetic ability in women was not high.

† See page 51

one of Dr. Russell's poems, as it shows from which side of the family his grand-daughter inherited her humour and wit.

"BURLESQUE EPITAPH
on a very beautiful but High spirited Lady.*
by the late Rev. Dr. Russell

Here underneath, inclos'd in wood,
Lies Mary, wife of Doctor Clark.
Her face was fair, her spirit good,
But death has laid them in the dark.

Oh! Sexton, should it be thy fate
When time has moulder'd this her stone,
To light upon that uncouth pate
Which all in pride and beauty shone.

Shed, prithee Sexton, shed a tear
In memory of her sex's merit;
But gently use her bones for fear
You chance to rouse her sleeping Spirit."

In addition, she brought out a second edition of her *Poems* about the middle of the year, for she sent a copy to Sir William Elford on 30th June. In her *Advertisement* to this new edition, she shows that she is not unwilling to learn from criticism. She states: "In submitting to the Publisher the first edition of the ensuing Poems, the author conceived any preface totally unnecessary. That they were the performance of a very young and unpractised writer was indeed but too obvious. . . . She has now the pleasant task of thanking the professional critics, for praise from which she has derived equal pleasure and encouragement, and for strictures from which she has sedulously endeavoured to improve. All that was pointed out as objectionable either in sentiment or composition has been carefully expunged. . . . The additional Poems in this

* *The Poetical Register*, 1806-1809, p. 156, 1812.

edition exceed in quantity those which have already been printed. In her selections of subjects, the author has directed her attention to objects of more general interest than the addresses to private friends, which occupied perhaps too large a space in the original Volume: in their execution she dares only venture to hope that if there is little to admire, there is nothing to offend." But although she says the additional poems "exceed in quantity" those already published, she is referring to the length rather than the number. There were twenty-nine poems in the first edition, and the second contained twenty-three new ones, including several odes. The price of the volume was raised from seven shillings to half a guinea. To Sir William Elford she remarks: ". . . I hope, my dear sir, you will tell me frankly if you think there is a falling-off or improvement in the new poems—in the lyrical ones, I mean, for the tales are merely to fill pages.* I never attempted odes before, and it is certainly a bold attempt. The few who have succeeded are more terrible than the many who have failed."

In spite of these diversions, however, the greater part of the year 1811 was spent in composing her second narrative poem, *Blanch of Castille*. It was begun about April, but from various causes, some of which will be dealt with in the next chapter, she did not at first make much progress; and by the beginning of August she had only written seven hundred of the five thousand lines which were to constitute the poem. After that, however, she seems to have concentrated on her task, for by the 18th of the month, the number of lines had risen to eleven hundred, and on the 29th to three thousand. She told Sir William: "As soon as I have finished *Blanch* to please myself, I have undertaken to write a tragedy to please Mr. Coleridge, whilst my poem

* It is interesting to note that her friend, Elizabeth Barrett, was also obliged to "fill pages." The first volume of the 1844 edition of her poems was too short, so she finished a ballad, *Lady Geraldine's Courtship* in a few hours to equalize the length of the volumes.

goes to Southey and to Campbell. . . . This will probably not be for some months, as I have yet two thousand lines to write. . . ." By the middle of October, however, the poem was finished and had been sent to Coleridge. She was at first much handicapped by lack of information on Spain, and implored her father to obtain Southey's *Chronicle of the Cid*, " some books about Spain, and an account of the Alhambra, the great Moorish palace at Granada." She believed that this poem would be greatly superior to *Christina*. " It will have the advantage of a very interesting story, and a much greater variety of incident and character." Although an author is often not a good judge of his own work, we consider that her opinion was correct. All her life, Spain exercised a fascination for her, and this seems to have inspired her writing which, in *Blanch*, displays more vitality than in any of her previous productions. The poem did not, however, meet with Dr. Mitford's approval. She told Sir William Elford, " Papa, though he would not suffer anyone to say so but himself, declares the very name gives him the vapours. Is not this shocking ? Mamma, if I but mention tears, professes herself sick of my affectation—Me ! the ' poetess of Nature,' as the newspapers have it—affected ! This is still worse. And a certain *gentille demoiselle*, from whom—upon the score of my having been a most patient listener to divers little feminine distresses, such as ' lovers lost who never dreampt of love,' and suitors gained who little suited my fair heroine—I thought myself entitled to a little commiseration for my literary miseries, suddenly inquired, in the very middle of my first pathetic harangue, where I got the pattern of that sweet morning cap ? This was the worst of all . . . I never will talk to young ladies about poetry again as long as I live." And to R. A. Davenport, who criticized her for killing her heroine, she retorted : " I must, however, ask you what if I had not sent her to heaven, I could possibly have done with her on earth ? "

Although the poem was finished in November, 1811, it was not immediately published, because Lord Holland, to whom it was dedicated, and who had undertaken to correct the proofs, was first of all ill and then too occupied with parliamentary business to carry out the task. Its authoress, however, had no intention of resting on her laurels. At the end of 1811, Lucien Buonaparte,* then living in England, offered £2,000 to Thomas Campbell, the poet, for a translation of his poem *Charlemagne*.† Campbell did not undertake the work, and it seems that Miss Rowden, herself the author of a popular poem ‡ was either approached in the matter or offered her services. She, in turn, applied to Mary Mitford for assistance. There seems, however, to have been some difficulty in reaching agreement between them, and while they were arguing over terms, the translation was given to two clergymen, the Rev. S. Butler and the Rev. Francis Hodgson.

Nevertheless, the year 1811 was, from a literary point of view, a prolific and successful one for Mary Mitford. She had published one narrative poem and finished another, besides issuing a second edition of her poems; and as a result, her name was becoming known to the public.

* Lucien Buonaparte, having been forced to leave Italy through the enmity of his brother, Napoleon, was captured by the English while on his way to the U.S.A. in 1810. He resided in this country until 1814.

† *Charlemagne*, Longman & Co., 1814.

‡ *The Pleasures of Friendship*, 1810. 2nd edition, 1811. 3rd edition, 1818.

VIII

1811

It is astonishing, in view of the circumstances, that Mary Mitford was able to produce any work at this period. The year 1811, from a financial point of view, was a disastrous one, and she was constantly harassed by money troubles, and the disturbances which resulted from them. To add to her difficulties, Dr. Mitford, who was a moral coward, remained in London for the greater part of the year, leaving his wife and daughter to cope with his creditors.

In January, there was a visit to Bertram House from two gentlemen, Mr. Clissold and Mr. Thompson Martin. It seems that the Doctor had commissioned Thompson Martin to paint his daughter's picture and then been unable to pay him.* In lieu of a fee, he gave the artist the choice of his own pictures. Fortunately for him, Thompson Martin chose one of no monetary value. A few days after this visit, Mrs. Mitford was without money for the household expenses, and wrote to her husband "for a little supply of cash" in order to pay the wages of two servants she was dismissing "as the few shillings I have left will not more than suffice for letters and such trifles." Then she adds pathetically: "As to the cause of our present difficulties, it avails not how they originated. The only question is how they can be most speedily and effectually put an end to. I ask for no details, which you do not

* Mrs. Mitford, in a letter dated 23rd March (Reading Collection) says "I am very glad, my dear Mitford, you mean to accede to Mr. Martin's wishes to let him have the painting he selected, as I have long wished the remuneration he expected for our darling's picture should be finally arranged, and now all parties will be satisfied." This might, of course, refer not to a portrait of her, but a painting for her.

voluntarily choose to make. A forced confidence my whole soul would revolt at; and the pain it would give you to offer it would be far short of what I should suffer in receiving it."

Poor, trusting, confiding woman: such nobility and loyalty were wasted upon the Doctor who, having the gambler's instinct of secrecy, would never have revealed his true position and the extent of his liabilities. The cause of his difficulties was, of course, plain to anyone less simple than his wife—gambling and speculation. Apart from his card-playing proclivities, he was always willing to invest money in any scheme which seemed as though it would procure a quick return on his outlay; and being of an optimistic and unreflective temperament, any scheme which was propounded to him appeared to come within this category. A few years previously he had become acquainted, through de St. Quintin, with a French *emigré*, the Marquis de Chabannes, an ingenious gentleman who invented a patent lamp in which the Doctor invested a considerable sum of money. The Marquis, it appears, had other money-making plans, for in all, Dr. Mitford seems to have advanced him about £2,800,* only half of which, by 1820, had been returned to him. How many other ventures of this nature the Doctor was involved in, is not known; but by 1811, he had not only lost his entire capital, but was, in addition, heavily in debt.

His affairs were in such disorder that at the end of February, he was imprisoned for debt, probably in a sponging house. His release was effected by de St. Quintin, who raised a loan on his pictures (it was fortunate that Thompson Martin had been so restrained in his choice), which were afterwards put up for auction by Messrs. Robins, of the Piazza, Covent Garden. The particular debt which placed him in this predicament has not been traced, but his daughter, in a letter dated 3rd March, which

* Harness states £5,000.

bore no address, but which was probably forwarded to St. Quintin for delivery to the Doctor in prison, said "I am happy that the speedy disposal of the pictures will enable you, as I hope it will, to settle this unpleasant affair. Once out of debt and settled in some quiet cottage, we shall all be well and happy again. But it must not be long delayed; for my dear mother must be spared a repetition of such shocks. I have answered Mr. Ogle, and I think you had better call upon him. He is more hurt at your silence than at your nonpayment. . . ." The long-suffering Mrs. Mitford was made really ill by her husband's incarceration, and her daughter reported to Sir William Elford that her mother's health was "in a very delicate state," but that she hoped the spring would bring some amelioration for, in her opinion, "warm weather and sunshine are a cure for all ills, mental or bodily."

Although Dr. Mitford obtained a speedy release on this occasion, he was still on the run from his other creditors; and a letter to him from R. A. Davenport, the editor of the *Poetical Register*, reveals how carefully he was obliged to hide his movements. "I may say to you as Falstaff says to mine hostess Quickly," wrote Davenport, "'One knows not where to take you.' Twice within these five weeks I have been in town, but without being able to find you. Yesterday was the second time of my visiting London. At Russell Street they told me that you had not been in London for the last fortnight; at the Mount* the waiter first told me precisely the same story, and then retracted, and said that you were in town, and that he expected to see you in the evening." Evidently the perspicacious waiter had decided that Davenport had not a writ in his pocket, and that it was safe to give news of his customer.

From these incidents, it can be seen that the Doctor's affairs were in such a state of chaos that a move from Bertram House was imperative and inevitable; and his

* The Mount Coffee House.

daughter's letter of 3rd March is the first indication that such a decision had been taken. After that, implementation followed quickly. The matter was placed in the hands of Messrs. Robins (who had disposed of the pictures), and as early as 28th March, they sent down a Mr. Goldie to look over the house. In May, the auction was advertised in the Reading paper to take place on 22nd June, but for some reason, possibly because the reserve was not reached, the sale was not effected until later in the year. In the meantime, while the culprit was skulking in London, his wife and daughter were grappling with all the manifold complications which arise out of financial ruin, and their situation was far from enviable. News, true and untrue, travels fast in the country, and everyone in the neighbourhood must have known that Bertram House was besieged by creditors, and that the family was ruined. Something of the irritation which Mary Mitford experienced at this unwelcome publicity is expressed in a letter to Sir William Elford. "There is no news in the neighbourhood," she wrote, "excepting what we make ourselves by our intended removal; and truly I think our good friends and acquaintances ought to be infinitely obliged to us for affording them a topic of such inexhaustible fertility. Deaths and marriages are nothing to it. There is, where they go? and why they go? and when they go? and how they go? and who will come? and when? and how? and what are they like? and how many in family? and more questions and answers, and conjectures, than could be uttered in an hour by three female tongues, or than I (though a very quick scribbler) could write in a week."

While she was enduring these humiliations, her father, in the intervals of dodging his creditors, seems to have continued his life exactly as before. It is one of the most extraordinary traits of this extraordinary man that he was totally unable to recognize changed circumstances or to adapt himself to them in any way. He never learned from experience, and this lack of adaptability arose partly from colossal egotism and partly from sheer stupidity. Although his wife was without money to pay the current household expenses, he sent his daughter expensive personal presents, and having himself attended the fête given at Carlton House by the Regent to celebrate the birthday of the King, came down specially from London to fetch his daughter, so that she might see it. She refused to go, and probably wished that she had the price of the coach fare in her pocket.

Nevertheless, he could not entirely escape from the consequences of his own actions, nor was he wholly impervious to their results, for they interfered too much with his personal comfort. When he could no longer ignore their effects, he indulged in orgies of self-pity, considering himself relentlessly persecuted by Fate—that convenient scapegoat of the foolish. But of practical actions to remedy the situation he was totally incapable. His method of dealing with any financial difficulty was to raise money on something, his pictures, his house, a bill or a loan from a friend. When these resources came to an end, for property and good natured friends are not inexhaustible, he had not an idea in his head. Not so his daughter: she, in spite of her environment, was intensely practical, and had she been dealing with a normal individual, would have undoubtedly been able to bring stability to the household. The following letter shows that even the present crisis could have been surmounted had her suggestions been followed.

"Bertram House, Thursday,
July 5th.

The distressing intelligence conveyed in your letter, my best-beloved darling, was not totally unexpected. From the unpleasant reports respecting your affairs I was prepared to fear it.* When did a ruined man (and the belief is as

* This would seem to confirm that the reserve was not reached.

bad as the reality) ever get half the value of the property which he is obliged to sell? Would that Monck* had bought this place last autumn! At present the best we can do seems to me to be, to relinquish the purchase of Lord Shrewsbury's land,† and (if it will be sufficient to clear us, mortgage‡ and all) to sell all we have out of the funds, and with that, and Lord Bolton's legacy, and the money in Lord Shrewsbury's hands, and the sale of the books and furniture, clear off our debts and endeavour to let this house. If this can be done, and we can get from three to four hundred a year for it, we may live very comfortably; not in a public place, indeed, but in a Welsh or Cumberland cottage, or in small London lodgings. Where is the place in which, whilst we are all spared to each other, we should not be happy? For the sale of the money in the funds, or rather for Dr. Harness's consent to it, I think I can be answerable. It will not, four years hence, be worth a guinea, and it would now nearly clear the mortgage, and we should retain our only *real* property. If the thousand pounds of Lord Bolton, the six hundred of Lord Shrewsbury, the three hundred at Overton, and the sale of stock, books, crops and furniture will clear all the other debts, this may still be done. If not, we must take what we can get and confine ourselves to still humbler hopes and expectations. This scheme is the result of my deliberations. Tell me if you approve of it, and tell me, I implore you, my most beloved father, the full extent of your embarrassments. This is no time for false delicacy on either side. I dread no evil but suspense. I hope you know me well enough to be assured that, if I cannot relieve your sufferings, both pecuniary and mental, I will at least never add to them. Whatever those embarrassments may

* Bligh Monck, M.P., who bought Coley Park in 1810.

† Dr. Mitford had paid a deposit on some land he had bought from Lord Shrewsbury, but the deal had never been completed.

‡ From the ensuing remarks, it would seem that the house was mortgaged for about £4,000.

be, of one thing I am certain, that the world does not contain so proud, so happy, or so fond a daughter. I would not exchange my father, even though we toiled together for our daily bread, for any man on earth, though he could pour all the gold of Peru into my lap. Whilst we are together, we can never be wretched; and when all our debts are paid, we shall be happy.

God bless you, my dearest and most beloved father! Pray take care of yourself, and do not give way to depression. I wish I had you here to comfort you. Adieu, my darling!

Ever and ever most fondly your own,
Mary Russell Mitford."

The crux of this letter was the phrase "tell me, I implore you, my most beloved father, the full extent of your embarrassments." This was, perhaps, the first time she had attempted to grapple with the financial situation, and to make plans which, if carried out, would place the family finances on a sound basis. But it was obvious to her that any plan would be inoperative unless it took into account all the relevant factors. Frankness in money matters, however, was impossible to Dr. Mitford. In the first place, any inquest on his transactions would have revealed his incredible foolishness, and that, with his childish vanity, he could not have borne: secondly, had matters been placed upon a rational basis, his future liberty of action would have been curtailed, which he would never have tolerated: thirdly, the only debt which troubled him was the debt of the moment, from the consequences of which he could not escape. All those other bills, interest on mortgages and loans to be paid in a few weeks' time did not in the least upset his composure. To one of his buoyant and optimistic temperament they did not exist, for by the time they were likely to become troublesome, he might have had a run of luck at cards or won another lottery, so it was scarcely worth dwelling upon them. Therefore with such a man to deal with, any plans Mary Mitford might make were bound to prove abortive. She did not know that at the time; but she was to learn from bitter experience.

Bertram House.

Throughout the spring and summer of that year, prospective buyers and angry creditors called constantly at Bertram House. On 7th April, Mrs. Mitford wrote to her husband "Farmer Cover was here on Friday evening to say he must give in his return about the property tax, and by the printed paper he brought last night when he came back from Reading, I see you are returned a defaulter only in the half of it, there being a little longer grace allowed on the second half-year."* And later in the same month, after

* Reading Collection.

thanking her husband for a five pound note which enabled her to pay the wages of a servant she was dismissing, she added " A person rode up to the kitchen door between two and three and enquired for you ; on John saying you were not at home, he laughed in his face, and asked if he was [word illegible] sure of it. John said yes, enquired his name which he said was [word illegible] Simonds* . . . I hope it was no unpleasant thing about cash, any disagreeable occurrence of that nature would be doubly distressing at this time. . . ."† On July 2nd, Mary Mitford reported that a Mr. Rawlings, of Lower Brook Street, had come to look over the house at eight o'clock at night ; and although he had no order to view, she allowed him to do so, mainly because of his physical resemblance to Bertram Mitford. " He had just the same rakish air, but was perfectly well-bred and respectful." And so it continued until the sale of Bertram House put an end to the importunings of one class of caller. During these months, she was never free from worry, for she never knew when some unwelcome visitor would create a disturbance which, witnessed by the servants, would, in two or three hours, be reported round the neighbourhood. And these humiliations must have been doubly distressing inasmuch as they reflected on the honour of a parent, rather than on herself ; for while one can bear the consequences of one's own follies, it is not easy to endure the vilifying of those one loves.

But with the sale of Bertram House on the 14th September, it must have seemed as though her troubles were at an end. The auction took place at the premises of Messrs. Robins, in Covent Garden, and the house fetched the sum of £5,985.‡ The purchaser was Charles Elliott, a Bond Street upholsterer, who in accordance with the terms, paid a deposit of £1,811 and agreed to settle the balance within one month from the date of the sale. As soon as he had

* Messrs. Simonds were bankers in Reading.
† Reading Collection, 20th June, 1811.
‡ P.R.O. C.13. 1643/40.

paid the deposit, however, the upholsterer seems to have repented of his bargain, for his solicitors, Messrs. Dawson and Wratislaw, sent for the title deeds and subjected them to an exhaustive examination. As a result, we find Dr. Mitford writing anxiously on 12th November, a month after the deal should have been completed:

"Bertram House,
12th November, 1811.

Messrs. Dawson & Wratislaw,
Gentlemen,

I am not a little surprised at this strange delay in returning the Abstract* to my solicitor, Mr. Ayrton. You have, of course made your observations upon it, and with them it ought to be immediately sent to him. The estate was conveyed to me by Mr. J. Blandy, of Reading, whom I suppose you know, and he assured me with a most unexceptionable marketable title.

Expecting your immediate attention to this business,
I remain, Gentlemen,
Your humble servant,
G. Mitford."

Messrs. Dawson and Wratislaw, however, were not of the same opinion; and as a result their client refused to complete the sale. Furthermore, he started an action in the Court of King's Bench against Messrs. Robins for the return of the deposit. The point at issue was the land bought by Dr. Mitford from Lord Shrewsbury which, the upholsterer claimed, could not, by Act of Parliament, be alienated from his lordship's estate. Therefore the Title Deeds were not in order, and the sale was null and void.

Thus the anticipated amelioration in the Doctor's finances did not take place. Faced with such a situation, there were two courses open to him: he could agree to

* Of the Title Deeds.

the abandonment of the sale and return the deposit ; or he could take an action against Elliott to compel him to complete the deal. Had he been wise, he would have chosen the former course, for by relinquishing Lord Shrewsbury's land (he had, after all, only paid a deposit on it), he could have put the estate up for auction again, or alternatively, let it, as his daughter had suggested. But with his adolescent mentality, and his total inability to see any point of view but his own, he chose to take action in the Chancery Court against the upholsterer. This decision set the seal on his ruin, for the case dragged on for seven years and cost, so his daughter stated, £11,000. It was eventually settled out of court in 1819, but he must have lost very considerably since the purchase money was only £6,000. In the meantime, during these seven weary years, his position gravely deteriorated. He had all the expenses of upkeep—the interest on the mortgage, taxes and other charges—without the assurance that he would eventually obtain the purchase money. No doubt, however, his sanguine temperament sustained him, but in the meantime, the position of his wife and daughter was far from pleasant.

IX

1812-1819

After the sale in September, the Mitfords had packed their possessions, dismissed most of their servants (they were reduced to two in 1818) and were ready to leave Bertram House at a moment's notice. But by the spring of 1812, it became obvious that Charles Elliott would not complete the deal, so Dr. Mitford, on 14th April, filed a Bill of Complaint in the Chancery Court against him. Having made up their minds to move, however, they could not resume—pecuniary considerations apart—their old way of life, for they were thoroughly unsettled; and the Doctor, at any rate, lost all interest in his home. With the petulance of a spoilt child whose wishes are thwarted, he refused to do anything to the place: as a result the house fell into disrepair, and the garden became overgrown with weeds and almost totally neglected.

The next seven years were, from Mary Mitford's point of view, static, a period of hibernation, during which no progress was made in her literary career. It is true that during 1812, she published *Watlington Hill* a poem on coursing, the *Ode to Genius*,* *Weston Grove* in praise of the estate of William Chamberlayne, M.P., and in the following year, *Narrative Poems on the Female Character*; but with the exception of the Ode, these had all been written previously. The *Narrative Poems* consisted of *Blanch* and the *Rival Sisters*,† and the advertisement states " should the success of these specimens encourage the author to complete the

* Published in the *Poetical Register*, 8th Vol., 1814. It was also issued separately as a pamphlet with the words " Spoken by Mr. Quinn to the Surrey Institution."

† Both R. A. Davenport and Sir W. Elford read this poem in April, 1812. As we have not been able to trace its publication in any periodical, they presumably read it in MS.

series, it will be comprised in three volumes"; but as the British Museum's catalogue states succinctly "no more published," it is to be presumed that the encouragement was somewhat lukewarm. Apart from a play, *The King of Poland*, finished in 1813, but altered so many times to please the manager of Drury Lane that she lost interest in it, and her address for the re-opening of that theatre in 1812,* she appears to have been affected by the general apathy which pervaded the household; and beyond one or two criticisms, she did not take up her pen again until the family moved to Three Mile Cross.

But if she did not write, she read. On a previous occasion we have noted the large number of books obtained on her behalf from the Reading circulating library; and now the pace of her reading was accelerated. In her diary, which begins in the year 1819, she noted the titles of the books she had read, and scarcely a day passes without a new title being added to the list. When she was free from social activities, she often read two books in a day; and she told Sir William Elford "Reading is my favourite form of idleness." If we take at random a few of the books referred to during this period, it will be seen that her reading was heterogenous rather than directed to any particular studies. In contrast to her later life, when she was in the habit of reading as many as fifty books consecutively on one subject, she now devoured anything which came to hand. Here are a few of the volumes she mentions: White's *History of Selborne*—"I really think that I have read it half a dozen times"; *English Bards and Scotch Reviewers*; Maria Edgeworth's *Tales of Fashionable Life*; Anna Seward's *Letters*; *Rejected Addresses*; *Clarrisa Harlowe*; Marmontel's *Memoires*; Rousseau's *Julie*—"I stuck fast in the first volume . . . and have never been tempted to take it up again"; the poems of Burns—"Burns, the sweetest, the

* This address is in the British Museum, but she was not the successful candidate. Lord Holland asked Byron to compose it.

sublimest, the most tricksey poet who has blest this nether world since the days of Shakespeare"; Fanny Burney's *Traits of Nature*; Southey's *Life of Nelson*—"one of the most beautiful pieces of biography I ever met with"; *Pride and Prejudice*—"extremely good"; *Waverley*—"I am still firmly of the opinion that Walter Scott had some share in *Waverley*"; *Sense and Sensibility*—"very good"; *Emma*—"the best, I think, of all her charming books." It says much for her taste that she was one of the first to appreciate the genius of Jane Austen and that she was able to credit Scott with the authorship of *Waverley* when the secret was still closely guarded. This list could be continued almost *ad infinitum*, for leading a retired life, she had plenty of leisure, most of which was spent in this fashion. These were her formative years, when she increased her already wide knowledge of literature. That masculine feminist, Harriet Martineau, has stated that Mary Mitford obtained her literary knowledge while reading to her father;* but as this practice did not start till towards the end of the Doctor's life, such an assertion is absurd. The truth is that, from an early age, she had been an avid reader, and this long period of retirement was one of study and assimilation which prepared her for the tasks which were to come.

During the spring of 1812, she visited Alresford, her birthplace, and in September she stayed at Southampton, "a charming town, which is not a watering place because it is something better," but she does not seem to have gone to London that year. Her last visit to the capital was at the end of 1811, when she attended several of Coleridge's second series of lectures.† Early in 1813, however, she received an invitation to spend a month with Mr. and Mrs. Perry at Tavistock House, Tavistock Square. James Perry was editor and proprietor of the *Morning Chronicle*, then

* *Biographical Sketches*, H. Martineau, p. 357. 1885.
† Given at the Scotch Corporation Hall, Crane Court, Fetter Lane.

at its zenith as the organ of the Whig party.* Little information of her visit survives, but she met Tom Moore, the poet, who many years later was to visit her at Three Mile Cross. "I am quite enchanted with him," she wrote. "He has got a little wife (whom I did not see) and two little children, and they are just gone into Wales, where he intends to finish a great poem on which he is occupied."† She also renewed her acquaintance with Amelia Opie, the novelist and widow of John Opie, R.A.,‡ who, she comments, looked "very ill—thinner, paler and much older." Mrs. Opie's looks, however, belied her, for she lived for another forty years.

On her return to Bertram House, she learned of the death of Lady Charles Anysley, her father's cousin and her erstwhile hostess in Northumberland. Lady Charles, a widow since 1808, had been suffering for some months from an incurable disease; and when she died, her affairs were found to be in the utmost confusion. Dr. Mitford visited Bocking in an attempt to straighten them out and also, it appears, to ascertain if he could recover money lent to his cousin, for his daughter asked: "Pray have *you* any chance of being paid? I must confess the prospect seems to me more remote than ever!" In July, she was again in London, this time staying with a Mrs. Wilson in Fulham. During this visit she attended a *fête* given to celebrate the battle of Vittoria. It was presided over by the Duke of York, and among the eminent personages who attended was Madame de Staël who, Mary Mitford records, was followed about in the gardens almost as much as the royalties. This visit to London was, however, of short duration, and by the beginning of August she was once more back at Bertram House.

* Hazlitt, who wrote for the *Morning Chronicle*, said: "He [Perry] was a man of strong natural sense, some acquired knowledge, a quick tact; prudent, plausible, with great heartiness and warmth of feeling. . . . He was a little of a coxcomb, and we do not think he was a bit the worse for it."

† *Lalla Roohk.*

‡ He painted Dr. Mitford's portrait.

The year 1814, which was to prove a momentous one inasmuch as she was, for the first time, acclaimed in public, started quietly. On January 4th, she wrote to Sir William Elford: "Did you ever see such beautiful weather as we have had for the last week? . . . Here the scene has been lovely beyond any winter piece I ever beheld; a world formed of something much whiter than ivory—as white, indeed, as snow—but carved with a delicacy, a lightness, a precision to which the massy, ungraceful tottering snow could never pretend. Rime was the architect; every tree, every shrub, every blade of grass was clothed with its pure incrustations; but so thinly, so delicately clothed, that every twig, every fibre, every ramification remained perfect; alike indeed in colour, but displaying in form to the fullest extent the endless, infinite variety of Nature. This diversity of form never appeared so striking as when all the difference of colour was at an end—never so lovely as when breaking with its soft yet well-defined outline on a sky rather gray than blue. It was a scene which really defies description. The shrubberies were slightly different; there some little modification of colour obtruded itself. The saffron-tinted leaves of the cut-leaved oak, fringed round with their snowy border—the rich seed-vessels or the sweet briar, blushing through their light veil—and the flexible branches of the broom, weighed down, yet half unloaded of their fine burden, and peeping out in their bright verdure like spring in the lap of winter; all this was yesterday enchanting. To-day it is levelled and annihilated by the heavy uniformity of snow. . . ."

This exquisite description of a winter scene is one of many passages in her letters which express her love and appreciation of the countryside. Her keen powers of observation and her command of language enabled her to paint pictures, delicate miniatures of polished phrase, for her confidant, Sir William Elford, himself a great nature lover. It is her attention to detail—the opening of a bud, the rustle of a leaf, the dew glistening on a spider's web—which makes her a supreme artist in the delineation of Nature in all her varying moods; and it was as natural to her to observe the reflection of the sun on a formation of clouds as it is to most women to note the change of fashion. A concomitant to her delight in rural scenery was her love of animals, particularly dogs, of which there was always a number attached to the Mitford household. Besides the coursing greyhounds, her father bred cocker spaniels, one of which she later presented to her friend Elizabeth Barrett Browning, and which became immortalized as the celebrated Flush. A dog to Mary Mitford was more than an animal; it was a personality and a companion. For she was, despite her numerous friends, fundamentally a lonely woman. Living as she did, with her parents, who were both her intellectual inferiors, she lacked an intimate companion with whom she could discuss her perplexities and problems; and no amount of devotion to her father and mother could compensate for this fundamental need. This state of affairs is usually rectified by a lover; but there is no evidence that she ever contemplated such a solution to her problem. On the contrary, she seems to have made up her mind, at a very early age, to remain in a state of single blessedness. "I intend to die an old maid," she announced to Sir William Elford, on 22nd April, 1812, and again to the same correspondent, a year or two later, "If I ever should happen to be going to be married (elegant construction this!) I will not fail to let you into the secret; but alas! alas! alas! 'In such a *then* I write never.'" And to a female friend she wrote ". . . neither shall I ever marry anybody. I know myself well enough to be sure that if any man were silly enough to wish such a thing, and I silly enough to say 'yes', yet a timely fit of wisdom (caprice some might call it) would come upon me, and I should run away from the church door."

What was the cause of her decision, taken early in life,

to eschew matrimony? In the absence of all direct evidence (for she never gave her reasons, at any rate in writing; and if she confided in her friends, these confidences have not come down to us), we can only draw conclusions from the available facts. It may well be, with the example of her mother and father before her, she decided that marriage was not necessarily the passport to that perfect happiness which young people suppose it to be, for it is a failing of youth to draw general conclusions from particular cases. Also, observing the married couples she knew (and there is little which would have escaped that acute eye) she may well have concluded that their tiffs, quarrels, incompatibilities, infidelities and even the disasters which overtake the most devoted, were not an inducement to her to follow their example. She was too young to realize that such matters are the result of character and not matrimony, and that a quarrelsome person will be equally tiresome whether single or married. By the time she was old enough to understand these truths, it was too late for her to marry, for she was by then the sole support of her parents, and was therefore "condemned to celibacy."* Another factor which militated against matrimony was her inherent conservatism. Although nominally a Whig, she did not like change of any sort. She clung to the people and things she knew and loved; and to detach her from her milieu, the inducement would have had to be strong indeed. No doubt a modern psychologist would find some deep and subtle reason for her antipathy to matrimony; but the fact remains that although she was sceptical about love, as distinct from physical attraction (and it was this slight vein of cynicism which prevented her from ever lapsing into sentimentality, and gave impetus to her wit) she was no hater of men, and many witnesses have testified to her essential femininity. Nor was she a woman soured by lack of masculine attention, for although she was not good-

* William Chambers, Chambers Journal, p. 55, Jan. 28th, 1882.

looking, she had great charm; and there is no reason to suppose that she could not have married had she wished to do so. Therefore in our opinion, the only conclusion which can be safely drawn is that several factors, known and unknown, combined to give her a preference for celibacy.

Towards the end of January, 1814, she was taken ill, probably with some bronchial affection to which she was frequently subject, and she did not recover until the end of March. In April, she learned that her *Narrative Poems on the Female Character** had reached a second edition in America, and in June she went to London to stay with the St. Quintins, now living in retirement at 33, Hans Place. This visit was a memorable one. London was *en fête* celebrating the successful conclusion of hostilities against Napoleon, and the presence of the heads of the allied nations—the Russian Emperor, Alexander, his sister the Grand-Duchess Catherine and the King of Prussia. Through the kindness of Mr. Perry, she was able to watch the royal procession to the Merchant Taylor's Hall from the offices of the *Morning Chronicle*. She was so well placed that, despite her short sight, she had an excellent view of the procession; and she reported that the Emperor and his sister were much alike "with fair complexions and round *Tartar* features"; that the King of Prussia was intelligent looking and that the Regent was hissed. But, she adds, in the true Whig tradition, she was more impressed by the beauty of the Regent's horses and the military spectacle than by the royal personages. The real reason for her visit (although no doubt she enjoyed the public celebrations) was to attend two functions at which her poem *The March of Mind*, written for the Anniversary of the British and Foreign School Society, was to be recited. The first was the Prize-giving at her old school, 22, Hans Place, now presided over by Miss Rowden. As is customary on such occasions, the pupils gave a performance before an admiring audience

* Published in England in 1813.

of parents and friends, during which her own poem was recited by the head girl, a Miss Willes. It was received with great applause " as verses commonly are in the presence of the author " and she was subject to much attention and flattery, by which she would have been overwhelmed had not William Harness, who sat behind her, given her his moral support. It had been arranged that she should present the prizes, but the sudden appearance of Lady Caroline Lamb (also a former pupil) saved her from the ordeal, for she wrote " I insisted on giving her my post."

This minor triumph was far eclipsed a week later when she attended the dinner given by the friends of the British and Foreign School Society, at the Freemasons' Tavern. The Marquis of Lansdowne* was in the chair, and the royal Dukes of Kent and Sussex and many other notable men attended. There were about five hundred persons present, and Mary Mitford, accompanied by two friends, sat in the gallery and watched the proceedings. The *Morning Chronicle* states " The health of the Chairman and Vice Presidents was drunk, and then that of the female members of the Society. After this a poetical tribute of Miss Mitford's was sung, and ' Thanks to Miss Mitford ' was drunk with applause." From a letter to her mother, written two days later, it is possible to amplify this bald statement. After the Chairman had given her health, the Duke of Kent, " observing that Lord Lansdowne's voice was not always strong enough to penetrate the depths of that immense assembly, reiterated it with stentorian lungs." The toast was then drunk three times to the accompaniment of a flourish of drums and trumpets from the Duke's band. The young woman in the gallery could scarcely believe the evidence of her own ears, and thought that the applause was meant for Samuel Whitbread. That gentleman, however, soon dispelled her doubts. "The glowing praises which he bestowed on me still ring in my ears," she told

* John Henry Petty, 2nd Marquis of Lansdowne.

her mother, " and if you find me vainer than any peacock, I beg you to attribute it to the overset which my brains experienced . . ."

Apart from these personal triumphs, her visit proved interesting in other ways. James Perry introduced her to Thomas Campbell, the poet, after she had been to one of his lectures on poetry at the Royal Institution ; she attended the trial of Lord Cochrane, her father's friend,* and had the good fortune to see the Duke of Wellington driving to his house in an open carriage and six. But she was not so occupied by social gaieties that current fashions escaped her. " I see nothing but cottage bonnets trimmed with a double plaiting and sometimes two double plaitings," she informed her mother, " and broad satin ribbon round the edge. Gowns with half a dozen breadths in them, up to the knees before and scarcely decent behind, with triple flounces, and sleeves like a carter's frock, sometimes drawn at about two inches distant, and sometimes not, which makes the arms look as big as Miss Taylor's body. I like none of this but the flouncing, which is very pretty, and I shall bring three or four yards of striped muslin to flounce my gowns and yours. Tell Mrs. Haw, with my love, to prepare for plenty of hemming and whipping, and not to steal my needles."

Although she paid two visits to London the following year, neither of them was as profitable nor as enthralling as the one just described. For the next few years, she seems to have been content to sink into a comfortable obscurity in the country although in reality her life was a dual existence. When she was in London she was the woman of letters, but during her long sojourns at Bertram House, her habits were those of a country gentlewoman. And of her two *rôles*, she undoubtedly preferred the latter. These two clearly defined divisions called for two distinct sets of

* This gallant sailor was accused of fraudulent speculations on the Stock Exchange. He was found guilty and spent the rest of his life trying to get the sentence rescinded.

friends, who rarely intermingled; and although we shall hear more of her literary friends, there is no doubt that she was just as fondly attached to, and perhaps more interested in, the others. One of her intimate friends in the neighbourhood was Catherine Dickinson, wife of Charles Dickinson of Farley Hill Court. Mrs. Dickinson was the ideal companion* gay, sociable and good-looking, and the two friends spent much time together. Then there was Miss James of Richmond, who frequently stayed at Bertram House and who, on one occasion, was driven by Mary Mitford, no great whip, into Wokingham. "Miss James says she was not at all afraid, being so assured of my being reserved to be hanged, that she would not mind going with me even in a balloon. This is very saucy, is it not?" Another great friend was Lady Madelina Palmer, wife of Fyshe Palmer, M.P. for Reading. They do not appear to have met till 1819 when, after a call from the Doctor and his wife, the Mitford family waited for the return visit to Bertram House. Lady Madelina, however, seems to have been an unreliable visitor, for in Mary Mitford's diary are the following entries: *15th April . . . sate waiting for Lady M. Palmer dressed quite fine. Tiresome woman did not come. 17th April: waited again for that tiresome woman who did not come. 22nd April: waited again for that shocking plague Lady M.P. who never came. 23rd April: waited again for my lady—deuce take her.* Despite this inauspicious beginning, their friendship lasted for many years.

In April, 1815, she wrote to Sir William Elford: "*Apropos* to novels, I have discovered that our great favourite, Miss Austen, is my countrywoman;† that mamma knew all her family very intimately; and that she herself is an old maid (I beg her pardon—I mean a young lady) with whom mamma before her marriage was acquainted. Mamma says that she was then the prettiest,

* She was an intimate friend of the Duchess of Wellington.

† Jane Austen lived at Steventon in Hampshire which is near to Overton, Mrs. Mitford's home.

silliest, most affected, husband-hunting butterfly she ever remembers; and a friend of mine, who visits her now, says that she has stiffened into the most perpendicular, precise, taciturn piece of 'single blessedness' that ever existed, and that, till *Pride and Prejudice* showed what a precious gem was hidden in that unbending case, she was no more regarded in society than a poker or a fire-screen, or any other thin upright piece of wood or iron that fills its corner in peace and quietness. The case is very different now; she is still a poker—but a poker of whom every one is afraid. It must be confessed that this silent observation from such an observer is rather formidable. Most writers are good-humoured chatterers—neither very wise nor very witty. . . . But a wit, a delineator of character, who does not talk, is terrific indeed!

"After all, I do not know that I can quite vouch for this account, though the friend from whom I received it is truth itself; but her family connections must render her disagreeable to Miss Austen, since she is the sister-in-law of a gentleman who is at law with Miss A's brother for the greater part of his fortune." This account is entertaining but its accuracy has been questioned. Jane Austen, at Mrs. Mitford's marriage, was only ten years old, rather young to be husband-hunting. There is, however, no reason to suppose that the friendship ended then, for Alresford and Steventon are not far apart; and by the time Mrs. Mitford left for her first sojourn in Reading in 1791, Jane Austen would have been sixteen years old.*

In 1817, during a visit to London in the spring, she was

* Mr. Brimley Johnson (*Jane Austen*, p. 33, 1930) states "Mrs. Mitford's imagined recollections of 'the prettiest, silliest, most affected, husband-hunting butterfly' date from an acquaintance *concluded* when Jane was barely 10 years old;" but he ignores the fact that the friendship might well have been continued. M. R. M.'s use of the word "then" may have been due either to a slip of the pen or faulty recollection on the part of Mrs. Mitford. Dr. Chapman (*Jane Austen: Facts and Problems*, 1948) makes the same point, but he, too, ignores the fact that the acquaintanceship might have continued, especially as James Austen, Jane's eldest brother was at one time curate at Overton, but not, it would seem, when Mrs. Mitford's father was the Vicar. We are not, however, trying to establish the truth of this description, but merely that Mrs. Mitford was in a position to make it.

introduced to the painter Benjamin Haydon at his studio where she admired his picture, *Christ's Entry into Jerusalem*,* then in the course of production. A friendship was formed between them which ended only with the painter's death some thirty years later. Haydon was a strange and interesting character, a man whose ambitions were in excess of his talents, and who, in consequence, was doomed to failure and unhappiness. He was, nevertheless, well known during his lifetime, and was a friend of Wordsworth (who addressed a sonnet to him), Lamb, Keats, Leigh Hunt and all the eminent men of the time. It would seem also that it was during this year that she first made the acquaintance of the painter Hofland† and his novelist wife.‡ "It was that notable fool, His Grace of Marlborough,§ who imported these delightful people into our Boetian town," she wrote. "He—the possessor of Blenheim—is employing Mr. Hofland to take views of Whiteknights¶—where there are no views; and Mrs. Hofland to write a description of Whiteknights—where there is nothing to describe." This enterprise unfortunately brought nothing but disaster on the Hoflands, for the Duke, whose pecuniary affairs were in the utmost disorder, was unable to pay them and they were forced to meet all the costs of production themselves.

Towards the end of 1817, in a letter to Sir William Elford, there is a reference to Thomas Noon Talfourd, a man who was to have a considerable influence on her destiny. Talfourd, the son of a Reading brewer, was born in 1795, and was educated at Mill Hill and then Reading Grammar School, presided over by Dr. Valpy. On leaving school, he studied law, eventually becoming a Justice of the Common Pleas, and M.P. for Reading. The real interest of his life, however, was literature, and at sixteen

* Exhibited at the Egyptian Hall, Piccadilly in 1820.

† T. C. Hofland (1777-1843), landscape painter.

‡ Barbara Hofland (1770--1844), novelist.

§ George Spencer, 5th Duke of Marlborough, noted for his extravagance and bibliophilism.

¶ The Duke's estate outside Reading.

he published a volume of poems. When he was studying law, he wrote for the reviews and magazines, and it was through his connection in the literary world that Mary Mitford was able to establish her reputation. He was the intimate friend of many famous men, Wordsworth, Dickens (who dedicated *Pickwick Papers* to him), Forster, Browning, Macready and Charles Lamb, whose biographer he afterwards became. By nature, Talfourd was kindly, sympathetic and ever willing to help his friends; and even that embittered man Macready, who never erred on the side of generosity when delineating the characters of his friends, refers to "the gentle outpourings of his [Talfourd's] affectionate heart towards his friends and associates."* Although November 20th, 1817, is the first time his name appears in Mary Mitford's correspondence, she must have known about him for several years prior to that date, for Dr. Valpy is almost certain to have mentioned his talented pupil: henceforward, during the years 1819-1823, the period covered by her diary, his name appears in the entries almost as often as her father's and mother's. It was Talfourd who advised her over her articles and sketches; it was he who conducted the negotiations which eventually resulted in the representation of her plays at Covent Garden and Drury Lane, and it was he who advised her on the legal steps to be taken in the many difficulties which arose out of Dr. Mitford's extravagances. It was doubtless he, too, who introduced her to his great friend Charles Lamb, although we have not been able to trace when the introduction took place. The first recorded meeting was on 21st August, 1822, when there is an entry in her diary "Called at Talfourd's; saw Charles Lamb": but it is almost certain that they met several years earlier, for there is a reference to him in a letter dated September 13th, 1817, when she says: "The best estimate I ever met with of Wordsworth's powers is in Coleridge's very out-of-

* *Diaries of Macready*, ed. Toynbee, p. 227, 1912.

the-way, but very amusing *Biographia Literaria*. It is in the highest degree flattering, but it admits that he may have faults; and Mr. Lamb, who knows them both well, says he is sure Mr. Wordsworth will never speak to Mr. Coleridge again."

It is also probable, although there is no definite proof, that she met Hazlitt during this period. In a letter dated 28th December, 1818, she tells Sir William Elford that she was staying at Tavistock House when Hazlitt was writing his dramatic criticisms on Kean for the *Morning Chronicle*.* "I . . . well remember the doleful visage with which Mr. Perry used to contemplate the column of criticism, and how he used to execrate 'the d——d fellow's d——d stuff' for filling up so much of the paper in the very height of the advertisement season. I shall never forget his long face. . . . He had not the slightest suspicion that he had a man of genius in his pay—not the most remote perception of the merit of the writing—nor the slightest companionship with the author. He hired him, as you hire your footman; and turned him off (with as little or less ceremony than you would use in discharging the aforesaid worthy personage) for a very masterly but damaging critique on Sir Thomas Lawrence. . . ." Hazlitt, however, had his revenge, and the incident which she relates next must, presumably, have taken place in her presence: "Last winter† when his *Characters of Shakespeare* and his lectures, had brought him into fashion, Mr. Perry remembered him as an old acquaintance and asked him to dinner, and a large party to meet him, to hear him talk, and to show him off as the lion of the day. The lion came—smiled and bowed—handed Miss Bentley to the dining-room—asked Miss Perry to take wine—said once 'Yes' and twice 'No'—

* The first appeared on 26th January, 1814. There is no record of M. R. M.'s being in London at that date, but she was in town in June of that year, staying with the St. Quintins. However she saw a great deal of James Perry and may have dined at his house.

† She was staying at Tavistock House in February, 1818, when this incident presumably took place.

and never uttered another word the whole evening. The most provoking part of this scene was, that he was gracious and polite past all expression—a perfect pattern of mute elegance—a silent Lord Chesterfield; and his unlucky host had the misfortune to be very thoroughly enraged without anything to complain of."

Another event which took place during 1818 was the death of Lady Elford. Although Mary Mitford had never met her, this lady had exercised a considerable effect on her correspondence; and soon after her demise, a subtle change took place in the style of the letters to Sir William. They became gayer, more natural and free from that pedantry which spoils the earlier ones in the series. She now obviously feels that she can give full play to her wit, and that there is no longer any fear that her sentences will be read by a stranger. It is indeed an ill wind that blows nobody any good, and posterity is certainly the gainer on this occasion.

There was another visit to town in 1818, when she again stayed at Tavistock House with the Perrys. The most notable event of this sojourn was a dinner party attended by the Duke of Sussex, the sixth son of George III. The Duke took her into dinner and, she said, "Nothing could have exceeded his civility. He complained of want of appetite, but partook of nearly every dish on the table." There was, of course, the usual round of exhibitions and theatres, before she eventually returned to Bertram House early in March. That summer, there was an election in Reading. The Whig candidates were Shaw Lefevre, Dr. Mitford's friend, and Fyshe Palmer. The Doctor, of course, took part in it, and his daughter told Sir William Elford, "Papa is going to stay in Reading the whole election, and mamma is going to take care of him. Very good in her, isn't it? But papa does not seem to me at all grateful for this kind resolution, and mutters—when she is quite out of hearing—something about 'petticoat government.'"

Throughout these years the Chancery suit over the sale of Bertram House had dragged on without a decision being gained by either party. At the end of 1818, however, the Master of the Rolls referred the matter back to the Master in Chancery, who had already given a decision in Dr. Mitford's favour. After that matters moved with comparative speed, for Charles Elliott apparently judged it prudent to settle out of court. Some time in the late summer of 1819, he visited Bertram House, and Mary Mitford told Mrs. Hofland that "... this long affair, this Chancery suit of eight years, was settled in eight minutes. He takes possession at Michaelmas, though we may, perhaps stay a little longer, as he means to make many alterations, which are not to be begun until the spring. I have not a notion where we shall go. But for the ill-luck of Mr. Elliott's having a wife, I need not move at all, since, had it not been for that misfortune, he says he would certainly have had me himself. I wish you had seen him when he made this declaration. Imagine a mean-looking Bond Street shopkeeper of sixty-five, with a methodist face, all bile, and wrinkles, and sadness, and a spruce wig in fine curls, shining like a horse-chestnut. I would certainly have married him, though, but for the aforesaid impediment. I would take anybody that would marry me to these walls and trees. I shall certainly break my heart when I leave them."

To one so home loving, the thought of leaving Bertram House, where she had spent the sixteen years of her youth, must indeed have caused many pangs. And in addition, there was the uncertainty over their future residence. Mr. Elliott did not, after all, take possession by Michaelmas, for on the 26th September, the money for the house had not yet been paid, nor had the necessary documents been signed. As usual, Dr. Mitford kept his own counsel about his future plans, probably because they were non-existent; and his daughter expressed the fear that one day he would announce he had taken a house in Reading " which papa likes, for its newspaper and its justice-rooms and its elections ; and which I dislike for various negative reasons." What she and her mother would prefer, she said, was a cottage within walking distance of Reading ; and for once, their desires were granted, probably because Dr. Mitford had not the money to go anywhere else. This delay in making the necessary arrangements for a future home was typical of him : he would put off a decision to the last moment in case he could lay his hands on a sum which would enable him to do what he wanted. Then, the initial expenses secured, he would take some establishment without an idea as to how it was to be maintained. That, on this occasion, he did not do so is proof of his total lack of money at that time. By the end of November, still nothing had been settled ; and matters were further delayed by the sudden death of Charles Elliott's solicitor. " All however is once more *en train*," Mary Mitford wrote to Mrs. Hofland, " and in about six weeks after we shall probably move, but where, I know no more than you do." And by the end of the year, the position had not changed.

X

1820-1821

In the last chapter, we referred to Mary Mitford's diary: and it is perhaps apposite to interpolate here some account of this interesting document, since it is the principal source of information for the next few years which are some of the most productive of her life.* The diary itself is one of the Literary Pocket Books edited by Leigh Hunt and published annually for several years by C. and J. Ollier. It is a plain morocco leather pocket book, at both ends of which is information likely to be of interest to the user and containing several blank pages for personal memoranda. The only difference between it and a modern diary is that the spaces for the entries only occupy one side of the page; so that when it was full, Mary Mitford was able to utilize the blank pages for the following year. When these too were complete, she wrote on the memoranda pages and then covered the printed information with entries, which made the task of deciphering her handwriting a considerable strain on the eyesight. In all, the diary covers a period from 1st January, 1819, to 11th March, 1823. It is interesting inasmuch as it was never intended for publication; and its laconic entries (the space for each day was small) are a record of actions rather than thoughts. There are no impassioned outpourings of the writer's ideas on life, death, love and other interesting topics. Nor is there any acute portrayal of the people she met. The most she was prepared to admit, on such occasions, was "Met Mr. So-and-so. Did not like him." Towards the end, when

* So far as we are aware, the information contained in this diary has not been previously published. It is in the British Museum.

paper became scarce, the diary is merely a record of work achieved, which makes it possible to ascertain when most of the sketches in *Our Village* were written. It has previously been stated that they were first published in 1819, and therefore must have been written prior to that date. Neither of these statements is true, however, but this matter will be dealt with in the following chapter.

As we have seen, at the end of 1819, nothing had been settled about a future home, nor had the arrangements about Bertram House been completed. On 25th November, however, Charles Elliott's son came to inspect the house and timber; and early in 1820, the Mitfords began to look for another place of residence. A Mr. Body, who owned land and property in the vicinity and was probably a prosperous farmer, offered them a cottage at Three Mile Cross, a village on the Basingstoke road, three miles from Reading and about a mile from Grazeley. Mary Mitford when she first inspected the cottage, did not care for it; nevertheless the family decided to take it. On 17th March, Mr. Elliott came to take possession of Bertram House* and on Wednesday, 5th April, the Mitfords moved to their new home. The entries in the diary at this period, though terse, give some indication of the sadness she experienced at leaving Bertram House. *Saturday, April 2nd. At home. Went with dear Drum*† *to Farley Hill.*‡ *Came home to dinner, Probably my last ride in the dear old dog cart. . . . Monday. April 3rd. . . . A great deal of packing and moving going forward. . . . Went firtopping,*§ *I suppose for the last time. Tuesday, 4th. . . . My last day, I suppose, at that dear house. Mr Haydon sent me the* New Times *with a critique on his picture.*¶ *Went about very disconsolate. . . . Drew a plan of*

* He did not remain there long for the house changed hands three times in the three years subsequent to the Mitfords' removal.

†In the diary, her father is usually referred to as "Drum" and her mother as "Granny."

‡ Farley Hill Court, the residence of Mr. and Mrs. Dickinson.

§ Gathering fir cones.

¶ *Christ's Entry into Jerusalem.*

the place. . . . A very uncomfortable, melancholy day. Wednesday, 5th April. Heard from Sir William Elford. . . . Left Bertram House and went to live in Mr. Body's cottage at The Cross. Very sorry to go. In a great skirmish all day long. Very uncomfortable indeed. There is something pathetic, yet characteristic, in her drawing a plan of her old home so that she might be able to dwell on the familar features in the days when she was no longer among them; yet with her passion for accuracy she must be certain, when conjuring up visions of the past, that the details were correct.

The contrast between Bertram House, with its eleven bedrooms and the cottage at Three Mile Cross which, when she first went there had probably only four, must have been very marked; this contrast must have brought home to her most forcibly the decline in the family's financial position. Yet there were compensations. She had not been transported to the detested Reading, and she was still in the neighbourhood she loved so well. Besides, the cottage was only supposed to be a *pied-à-terre*, a temporary residence until Dr. Mitford's pecuniary situation became ameliorated. And it is a measure of his ruin that not only did he remain there until his death, but his daughter had the greatest difficulty in maintaining even this modest establishment. Her difficulties arose not from the day to day expenses of the household, but solely through the extravagance of her father. He still maintained his greyhounds; he still visited London frequently (the diary is revealing on this point), he still entertained lavishly; and although forced to sell his stable on leaving Bertram House, it was not long before he once again possessed other conveyances. And she, although she held the purse strings, was forced to acquiesce in this state of affairs, because she was unaware of his follies until they had been committed. Then she had to make the choice between repudiating his debts and allowing him to be imprisoned, or paying them: and she paid.

Three Mile Cross has changed very little since she went

to live there a hundred and twenty-eight years ago. The suburbs of Reading, it is true, have crept alarmingly near; there are a few red brick villas on the outskirts of the village; there is no longer a " cool, clear pond, overhung with elms "* at the cross roads at the bottom of the hill, but it remains, in essentials, as she described it in the first sketch of *Our Village*. There is still the Swan Inn† " a white-washed building, retired from the road behind its fine swinging sign, with a little bow window coming out on one side," and with the open space in front which in her day " was the constant resort of carts, waggons and return chaises," whose drivers, no doubt, refreshed themselves in the inn's oak-beamed parlour. There is still the village shop, next door to her own cottage, which was " like other village shops, multifarious as a bazaar "; and there is still the lieutenant's cottage, then red brick, but now white-washed, lying on the other side of the cross-roads a little way up the hill. And the view she described from this same hill, " the village street, peeping through the trees, whose clustering tops hide all but the chimneys, and various roofs of the houses, and here and there some angle of a wall; farther on, the elegant town of B——, [Reading] with its fine old church-towers and spires," is still much the same, although the countryside is less wooded and the suburbs of Reading more obvious.

Her own cottage, however, is not as it was when she went there. In 1820, it was red brick, in the traditional style, with the front door in the centre, two windows on the ground floor and two on the first. On the side of the Swan Inn was a stable, and on the other, next to the village shop, was an outbuilding which projected to the road and is now joined to the cottage. Mary Mitford describes the place as a " miniature house, with many additions, little

* This has only disappeared within living memory, probably when the road was made, for a gentleman long acquainted with the neighbourhood told us he could remember it.

† She called it the " Rose Inn."

odds and ends of places, pantries and what not ; all angles, and of a charming in-and-outness ; a little bricked court before one half, and a little flower-garden before the other ; the walls, old and weather-stained, covered with hollyhocks, roses, honeysuckles, and a great apricot-tree ; the casements full of geraniums ; . . . the closets . . . full of contrivances and corner cupboards ; and the little garden behind full of common flowers, tulips, pinks, larkspurs, pionies, stocks, and carnations, with an arbour of privet, not unlike a sentry-box, where one lives in a delicious green light, and looks out on the gayest of all gay flower-beds."

A print of the cottage as it was when she went there was published by Lovejoy, the Reading bookseller. This has been described as an artist's impression, an idyllic version of the original, because it does not correspond with the cottage as it is to-day. Constance Hill* states : " Curiously enough some early prints of the cottage are very misleading. A limner at a distance has evidently tried to make a pleasing drawing from some very imperfect sketch done on the spot, which did not reveal the fact that the right-hand portion of the house recedes, and that the front door is not in the middle but on one side.† Thus a report arose that the cottage had been rebuilt in later years. But happily we possess conclusive evidence to the contrary given by a gentleman still living who passed his childhood in the cottage almost as an adopted son of the household. When visiting the place a few years ago he declared that the cottage was unchanged, and recalled, as he passed from room to room, his happy associations with each spot." Nevertheless, we are afraid we must disagree with the assertion that " some of the early prints of the cottage are very misleading," for in a sketch taken on the spot

* *Mary Russell Mitford*, C. Hill, pp. 179-180, 1920.

† This print was from a sketch by Edmund Havell, to whom there are references in the correspondence of 1836, i.e. before the alterations took place.

and published in the *Mirror** the building is shown to be of exactly the same proportions as in Lovejoy's print. Therefore if the statement of the gentleman referred to be true (and we do not doubt it, for he must have been Henry Taylor, the son of one of Mary Mitford's maids, who as a small child, was in residence in the cottage in

The Cottage at Three Mile Cross, before the alterations
from *The Mirror* June 28th, 1834.

1845†) the building must have been altered during the Mitfords' residence. This we believe to be the case, for at the end of 1837, the workmen were in the place for some considerable time, undertaking alterations and repairs: and in a letter to Elizabeth Barrett, dated 15th December, 1837, she wrote " We are in the agony of moving ourselves

* *The Mirror.*, June 28th, 1834.

† In 1920, when Miss Hill's book was published, he would have been between 70-80 years of age. It is unfortunate that the author does not tell us whether this statement was made to her direct, or whether she obtained it secondhand.

and our goods and chattels to a cottage still smaller than this, two doors off, whilst this house proper is repaired and painted—the two ends which have been taken down and built up again being to be roofed in on Saturday night, which drives the saws and hammers forward to the interior, and we find that in these closets (by courtesy called rooms) the workmen and we cannot co-exist, manage how we will. . . . Did I tell you that I shall have a pretty upstairs sitting-room, thirteen feet square, with a little ante-room, lined with books, both looking to the garden ?" Thus it would seem that the additions to the cottage were carried out at that time; and that it is to-day essentially what it was during the last fifteen years of her occupation.*

The same, however, cannot be said of the garden which she loved so well and in which she entertained so many of her famous contemporaries. A corrugated iron hall has been erected on the site which, although it has ruined the view from the back of the cottage, is mercifully not visible from the front. Corrugated iron halls, wherever they may be erected, are usually an eyesore but not necessarily a desecration: unfortunately this one is both. The hall is, no doubt, dedicated to useful objects, but surely it could have been built on a less historic site ?

Mary Mitford's first impressions of her new abode were not unfavourable and three days after her arrival, she wrote a gay description of it to Sir William Elford: "It consists of a series of closets, the largest of which may be about eight feet square, which they call parlours and kitchens and pantries; some of them minus a corner, which has been unnaturally filched for a chimney; others deficient in half a side, which has been truncated by the shelving roof. . . . We are all beginning to get settled and comfortable and resuming our usual habits. Papa has already had the

* Additional confirmation is to be found in an undated letter to Talfourd, *circa* autumn 1837, in which she refers to the kitchen's being enlarged (i.e. one end of the cottage) and to a new bedroom for herself, probably at the opposite end of the cottage, over the outbuilding shown in the *Mirror* print.

satisfaction of setting the neighbourhood to rights by committing a disorderly person who was the pest of the Cross, to Bridewell. Mamma has furbished up an old dairy and made it into a not incommodious store room. I have lost my only key, and stuffed the garden with flowers. . . . Moreover, it is an excellent lesson of condensation—one which we all wanted. Great as our merits might be in some points, we none of us excelled in compression. Mamma's tidiness was almost as diffuse as her daughter's litter. Papa could never tell a short story—nor could papa's daughter (as you well know) ever write a short letter. I expect we shall be much benefited by this squeeze; though at present it sits upon us as uneasily as tight stays and is just as awkward looking. Indeed my great objection to a small room always was its extreme unbecomingness to one of my enormity. I really seem to fill it—the parlour looks all me. . . .

"... We are a mile nearer to dear Mrs. Dickinson; and, though I have no conveyance at present, yet I have in perspective a bright vision of a donkey cart. Last, and best of all, we are three good miles from Reading. You will easily understand, my dear friend, that I have been terribly afraid of being planted in that illustrious town, and am quite enchanted at my escape. . . ."

Indeed the uprooting did not prove so formidable as she had anticipated, for there were many compensations. One of them was that she saw a great deal more of Mrs. Dickinson whose carriage, no doubt, was frequently in the Basingstoke road, and who, she told Sir William "is rather a romantic lady, and has something of a fancy to be a cottager herself; so, as she can't compass that interesting character in her own person, she contents herself with achieving it by proxy in mine." Then she must have made the acquaintance, about this time, of Lady Russell* who would also frequent the main road on the way from

* Marie Clotilde, wife of Sir Henry Russell, 2nd baronet. She was a Frenchwoman.

Swallowfield Park to Reading. This friendship was to endure for thirty-four years and was to prove a great consolation, particularly in her declining years.

When the family moved to Three Mile Cross, Mary Mitford was thirty-two, her mother seventy and her father some ten years younger. Up till then, she had been a dilettante in the arts, a maker of verses ; and although she had acquired some reputation within a limited circle, it is doubtful whether she had derived much pecuniary advantage from her labours. Now, however, the need for money became acute, for all Doctor Mitford's sources of supply were at an end because he no longer possessed any property on which to raise funds. Before leaving Bertram House he had applied to his friend, the Count de St. Quintin, now living in Paris, in an attempt to recover some of the sums advanced to that gentleman and the Marquis de Chabannes ; and a passage from St. Quintin's reply to one of his appeals gives an indication of the Doctor's total ruin. "Your heartrending letter has overwhelmed myself and my wife with dismay," wrote the Count. "What is to be done? I really know not. You harrow up my very soul with the account of your distress." We can well imagine the outburst of self-pity penned by the Doctor which called forth this sympathetic reply. This correspondence, which was continued throughout the summer of 1820, sheds an interesting, but partial, light on the past transactions of the two men; but it is to be doubted whether it had any result beyond a promise from St. Quintin to try and obtain the money owed by Chabannes. It must, therefore, have been obvious to Mary Mitford that if money was to be found for the household, her father would not be the one to procure it. Thus she passed from the passive *rôle* of spectator of the family's tribulations to the active one of its breadwinner. Henceforth she, by her industry and talent, was to dominate the scene, although the forceful, reckless personality of her father was never entirely relegated to the background. He was always there to vitiate her efforts and to make her task doubly difficult.

Although she must have been cogitating on this problem ever since her arrival at the cottage, she did not at once take any practical steps in the matter. Her diary reveals that no literary work was undertaken during the summer and autumn of that year. On 27th June, she and her father, in a borrowed gig, drove to London. Their route was by Wokingham, where they breakfasted, Egham, Windsor Park to Richmond where they stopped for tea, eventually arriving at their destination, 50, Great Queen Street, at ten o'clock at night. It was, Mary Mitford records, "the hottest day I ever remember." During this brief visit, she called on Benjamin Haydon, the Perrys and went to the English Opera House* to see Miss Kelly.† On July 1st, her father returned home and she went to Richmond, to her friends the James'. "The house where I was staying," she told Sir William, "had a beautiful garden down to the river; and there, or on the water, I quite lived. We went to see Pope's Grotto, which is unchanged except in the addition of some china plates stuck about the wall; Strawberry Hill, which is likewise a sad china-shop, but where I walked about amongst the finery in a very pleasant reverie, thinking of Horace Walpole and his correspondents; Hampton Court, which I wonder to see so deserted." This last expedition was carried out by water, as was also a visit to Kew Palace, after which she returned to Wokingham on the outside of the coach. A few weeks later (8th August) Lucy, the maid who had come with them from Bertram House, and who was the sole survivor of the large retinue of servants attached to that establishment, was married to the village schoolmaster in Shinfield Church, an event which she has described in *Our Village*. But it was not until a later visit to London that an event

* Later known as the Lyceum.

† Fanny Kelly, to whom Charles Lamb wrote a proposal of marriage.

took place which, insignificant in itself, was to launch her on a literary career. On 6th December she went to Covent Garden to see William Charles Macready in a play entitled *Wallace* by a young and unknown author. She learned that this piece which was by no means first-class, had earned the author several hundred pounds, and she determined to emulate his example. No doubt she discussed this project with her friend Talfourd, for they met in London; and no doubt he encouraged and advised her. At any rate, a few days after her return to Three Mile Cross, on 20th December, there is an entry in the diary "... *Began Fiesco. God grant we may make money of it.*"

Although the motive which actuated this work was the urgent need for money, she had a very great love of the drama, which dated back to the early days of her childhood. The first theatrical performance she ever saw was in a barn at Alresford, at the age of four, when a company of strolling players acted *Richard III*, and from that time she attended the theatre whenever an opportunity occurred. At the beginning of the last century, the public had a taste for historical tragedies; and it was not satisfied until all the principal characters had met a violent and bloody death. It is strange to think of the witty, urbane, peace-loving Mary Mitford engaged in such productions, which must have been contrary to her nature; but it is proof of her versatility and talent that she was able to write four tragedies which met with the approbation of the greatest actors of the day, Macready and Charles Kemble, and one of which, *Rienzi*, achieved what was in those days a long run. It must be remembered that in 1820, no woman except Jane Austen (and her work had not yet received its due recognition) had reached the top rank of literary attainment. There were well known women writers, Amelia Opie, Joanna Baillie, Felicia Hemans, Maria Edgeworth, who had achieved fame; but their work was judged solely as the production of women and was not compared on any basis of equality (and it did not merit it) with the achievements of men. Mary Mitford was one of the first women to win an international reputation (her books were as popular in the United States as in this country) which was all the more remarkable since she never resorted to the arts and stratagems of publicity customary among other literary ladies of the day. She passed the greater part of her life quietly in the country, only coming to London when business demanded, and her position was acquired solely on the merit of her work; and while this could never be placed in the same category as Jane Austen's,* Emily Bronte's and Elizabeth Barrett Browning's, it was much superior to anything that had yet appeared. The fact that her tragedies are now forgotten does not detract from her achievements. They should be judged by the standards prevailing at the time, for few plays come down to posterity; and the majority of those which have had long runs to-day will be forgotten in fifty years' time.

The subject she chose for her first attempt was in the unsuccessful conspiracy organised in the fifteenth century by Giovanni Fiesco, Count of Lavanga, against the Genoese, Andrea Doria. Having made up her mind, she acted with commendable speed: by the second week in January, 1821, the rough draft was finished and at the end of the month the complete tragedy was despatched to Talfourd for criticism. He, who was theatrical critic for the *New Monthly Magazine* and had many contacts in the theatrical world, was fully qualified to give an opinion. In a few days the play was returned to her for alterations. On 9th February she wrote to Benjamin Haydon "I have been very busy—audaciously busy—writing a tragedy. We are poor, you know. . . . It is finished; that is, it was finished; but as I had unluckily slid my hero off the scene like a ghost, I am advised to

* Nevertheless, Sir John Squire (*Our Village*, vii, 1936), says: " . . . amongst essayists, recorders of character and custom, and sensitive painters of natural scenery, Miss Mitford ranks as high as Miss Austen ranks among novelists."

write the fifth act over again, which I shall do next week. It is terribly feeble and womanish, of course—wants breadth—wants passion—and has nothing to redeem its faults but a little poetry and some merit, they say, in the dialogue. I am afraid it will not be accepted and that you will never hear of it again; but I could not bear to make an attempt of the sort without confiding my many fears and my few hopes to one who will, I am sure, sympathize with both. My anxiety on the subject is not of vanity. It is not fame or praise that I want, but the power of assisting my dearest and kindest father."* She spoke truly when she said that she did not care for fame or praise. She was a woman who disliked the limelight and who held commendably modest views on her own talents and achievements. In later life, when an incident revealed her popularity with the public, she was astonished and bewildered, and could scarcely credit the outward manifestations of the esteem in which she was held.

Her fears for *Fiesco* were not without cause. It would have been nothing short of miraculous if her tragedy had been accepted, for to sell a play by an unknown author is a most difficult feat, in this or any age. The reason is that the transaction is not a simple affair between author and management. There are the actors to be considered. In those days, at any rate, the theatrical profession abounded in petty intrigues and personal jealousies, and what pleased one actor displeased another. So far as *Fiesco* was concerned, Mary Mitford was spared these experiences (they were reserved for her other plays), for the negotiations came to an end before there was any question of casting the tragedy. The MS., after it had been altered to Talfourd's satisfaction, was sent to his friend Macready, who had difficulty in making up his mind about its merits. He thought it lacking in action, but it had excellent dialogue. The only point on which he was emphatic was that the

* Reading Collection.

author's handwriting was illegible, and that the play must be copied before being submitted to the management. This opinion was given at the end of March, 1821. She was kept in suspense for some months more, however, for the final rejection was not received until the end of June. In a letter to Sir William Elford, dated 1st July, she wrote "*Fiesco* has been returned on my hands as I foresaw, and I am now knee-deep in another tragedy on the subject of the Venetian Doge Foscari, who was obliged to condemn his own son. . . ."* Thus ended her first attempt at play writing.

* Reading Collection.

XI

1821-March, 1823

Plays, however, were not her only interest at this period, for her diary shows that early in 1821 she was also writing for the reviews and magazines. This again was probably on Talfourd's suggestion, for he was a contributor to them himself, and in a position to advise on the marketing of her work. She told Sir William Elford, " . . . I am writing for the magazines—poetry, criticism and dramatic sketches. I work as hard as a lawyer's clerk; and besides the natural loathing of pen and ink which that sort of drudgery cannot fail to inspire, I have really at present scarcely a moment to spare, even for the violets and primroses."* What were the articles she was writing at this time? The diary, unfortunately, is not very revealing on this point, for she refers to her work merely as " sketches," " prose articles " or " dramatic sketches," and does not, as a rule, specify the subject or title. Her first article, however, was one on wild flowers, and towards the end of March, 1821, she wrote a dramatic sketch entitled *Emily*, which was published in the May issue of the *London Magazine*.†

There is no doubt, however, that throughout 1821, she was writing the sketches which were later to constitute the first volume of *Our Village*; but before we proceed further in this matter, it is necessary first to examine previous statements on the subject. In *A Gallery of Illustrious Literary Characters*, published in 1873, the editor William Bates, in his notes on Mary Russell Mitford (No. 12 in the

* Reading Collection.

† Her fellow contributors to the *London Magazine* were Lamb, Hazlitt and de Quincey.

series) stated "The papers known in their collected form as *Our Village* were offered to Campbell, the poet, for publication in the *New Monthly Magazine*, but were unaccountably rejected by him as unsuitable; and the *Ladies Magazine* (1819) had the honour of giving them to the world. . . ."* It is always difficult to trace the origin of an incorrect statement which, when once in print, is repeated by subsequent writers on the subject; but Bates evidently obtained his facts from an obituary notice on Mary Mitford which appeared in the *Gentleman's Magazine*.† It has therefore been presumed, in the absence of other evidence, that the sketches were written in 1818 or 1819. The diary, however, provides evidence to the contrary, and furthermore, reference to the volumes of the *Ladies Magazine* shows that they were not published in 1819, but in 1823, 1824 and possibly 1822.‡ Again Mary Mitford, in a letter to William Harness, states that the first two or three articles she ever wrote were not rejected, but accepted by Campbell, the editor of the *New Monthly Magazine*, although one or two subsequent papers were returned to her.§ Therefore it is unlikely that Campbell ever saw more than a small proportion of the papers in *Our Village*. The first indication in the diary that the sketches were being written is under the date Tuesday, March 27th when the entry reads: ". . . *went*

* *A Gallery of Illustrious Literary Characters* (1830-1838) drawn by the late Daniel Maclise, R.A., and accompanied by notices chiefly drawn by the late William Maginn, LL.D. Edited by William Bates, B.A., pp. 35, 36, 1873.

† *Gentleman's Magazine*, Vol. 43, p. 428, 1855: "It is mentioned as an instance of lack of editorial discernment, that these papers were originally offered to Thomas Campbell for the *New Monthly Magazine*, and rejected by him as unsuitable. The *Ladies Magazine* had the honour of first bringing these charming papers before the public, about the year 1819."

‡ The B.M.'s volumes of the *Ladies Magazine* were destroyed by enemy action, but the Bodleian Library has the volumes for 1823 and 1824 which contain the majority of the sketches.

§ Reading Collection, 29th July, 1824: "I ought to tell you that two or three very trifling articles, the very first prose I ever attempted in my life and bad enough of all conscience, were inserted in that magazine [*New Monthly*] three or four years ago, and one or two longer and better subsequently rejected. . . ." We have been able to identify two: *Richmond*, Vol. II, No. VII, pp. 56-59 and *On Letters and Letter Writers*, Vol. II, No. VII, p. 144 ff.

violeting. Worked at my sketch." It is probable that this relates to the article entitled *Walks in the Country—Violeting*, which is dated March 27th.* The first sketch about which there is definite proof of its being written that year is *Lucy*.† On Thursday, 30th August, the diary records "Finished my article on Lucy." Additional confirmation is provided by the opening phrase of the article, "About a twelvemonth ago we had the misfortune to lose a very faithful and favourite female servant"; for Lucy, as has already been stated, was married in Shinfield Church on August 8th, 1820. Up to the end of June, 1821, Mary Mitford was working nearly every day on articles for the magazines; and it is interesting to note that the idea of *Our Village* as a central theme for the sketches was even then in her mind, for she wrote to Talfourd "What you say of *Our Village* is exceedingly encouraging and comfortable. I had looked on prose composition as a thing not difficult merely, but impossible. I shall now take heart."‡

Although she was unknown as a writer of prose, she does not seem to have experienced much difficulty in selling her work. It is surprising, for instance, that the first article she ever wrote should be sold to the *New Monthly Magazine*; but it is probable, in this instance, that Talfourd's influence was wielded in her favour. It was certainly he who sold her dramatic sketches, for she told Sir William Elford, on 4th April, "I am now occupied in dramatic sketches for Baldwin's magazine§—slight stories of about one act, developed in fanciful dialogues of loose blank verse. I have written two—and suppose they will appear in May or June. By the way Mr. Baldwin has not heard a word of the felicity that is to befal [*sic*] him, for they are upon circuit with my young barrister friend;

* *Our Village*, Walks in the Country, p. 100, 1824.
† Idem, Lucy, p. 58.
‡ MSS. John Rylands Library, June 21st, 1821.
§ *The London Magazine*, edited by John Scott, published by Baldwin.

but as he is a great literary man, and undertakes for their insertion, I have not much doubt about the matter."* It is impossible to over-estimate the help which Talfourd gave her at this time; for although, had she been without talent, the temporary benefits gained by his influence would have proved ephemeral, it is certain that his help, combined with her gifts, enabled her to make a name, and what was more important to her, money, much more quickly than if she had struggled alone. It must, for instance, have been a great relief when her father, during a short visit to London in July, was able to collect £19 as the proceeds of some of her magazine contributions.† It must, also, have been a pleasant surprise for him, for here was a source of income which did not necessitate any effort on his behalf. Not, of course, that he ever consciously contemplated living on his daughter's earnings; but the idea must have sunk deep into his subconscious mind, for from that year onwards, he never made any attempt, so far as can be ascertained, to contribute to the family's income.

Mary Mitford does not appear to have considered her magazine articles as anything more than a side-line, a means to obtain much needed money. She certainly never dreamed it would be through them that her fame would descend to posterity. Her principal preoccupation at this time was with the theatre; and as soon as *Fiesco* was rejected, she began another drama. This was on the subject of the Venetian Doge, Foscari, who was forced to condemn to death his own son. It is an interesting psychological point that in two of her plays (*Foscari* and *Julian*) the principal theme is the conflict—and its concomitant suffering—between parent and offspring. Even in *Rienzi*, where the plot is more involved and there is consequently more action, the quarrel between Rienzi and his son-in-

* Reading Collection, 4th April, 1821.

† Diary, 11th July, 1821, "Drum received 19 pounds for my writings in the magazines."

law, and its reactions on Rienzi's daughter, is the central theme. Such romantic interest as there is in all three tragedies is entirely subsidiary to this conflict. Perhaps being deficient in imagination, such a clash unconsciously appealed to her because it was one which she could envisage. Was not her whole life a struggle, in a sense, with her father? She never admitted it, for she was far too devoted to him ever to contemplate such a disloyalty: nevertheless the conflict existed, and she was not unaware of it.

Foscari was begun on 20th June, 1821.* After consultation with Talfourd, she had decided that it should be written so as to provide parts for Macready, Charles Kemble and Young, then all members of the company at Covent Garden. This decision, which was designed to facilitate the play's presentation, was in fact a potential source of trouble, owing to the internecine jealousy between the leading actors. Mary Mitford, however, was fortunately oblivious of this state of affairs; and buoyed up by the encouragement she had received over *Fiesco*, worked ceaselessly on her new drama. Every day in her diary has an entry at this time, "Worked on *Foscari*." It was not to be expected that the first draft would be accepted, but it is doubtful whether any play has undergone such vicissitudes as *Foscari* before its presentation. It was bandied about between Talfourd, Macready and Charles Kemble, each of whom suggested alterations and improvements. The harassed author confided to her old friend Sir William Elford, ". . . if you have a mind to take a perfect hatred of pen and ink you have nothing to do but to write a tragedy, as I have done, three times over in two months. It is finished now, thank God! all but another copying; and my oracle Mr. Talfourd thinks it will do."† This statement, however, proved unduly optimistic, for the play was once again returned to her.

* Diary, Wednesday, 20th June, ". . . Began *Foscari*."
† Reading Collection, 30th August, 1821.

Throughout September and early October, she was engaged in further alterations, and it was not until the 18th of that month that she recorded triumphantly in her diary "Finished *Foscari*."

Talfourd was then in Reading, drawn thither by the presentation of a Greek play by the boys of his old school, under the auspices of the headmaster, Dr. Valpy. These plays were given triennially, when the principals of some of the Oxford Colleges visited the school to hold scholarship examinations; and they caused something of a stir in the quiet old town. Mary Mitford has left a most entertaining account of them in *Belford Regis*. "Besides the excellence of the theatre," she says, "the audience, another main point in the drama, was crowded, intelligent, and enthusiastic. The visitors from Oxford, and the mayor and corporation of Belford (in their furred gowns—poor dear aldermen, I wondered they survived the heat!—but I suppose they did, for I never remember to have heard of any coroner's inquest at Belford, of which the verdict was 'Died of the Greek plays,'), these, the grandees of the University and the Borough, attended *ex-officio*; the parents and friends of the performers were drawn there by the pleasanter feelings of affection and pride, and the principal inhabitants of the town and neighbourhood crowded to the theatre for a double reason—they liked it, and it was the fashion." The play chosen that year, the *Orestes* of Euripides, was performed twice, on the 13th and 17th October, and she attended on both occasions, afterwards writing an account for the Reading paper. It is pleasant to be able to record that although she was as yet unknown to the general public, she was not a prophet entirely without honour in her own country. At a festive supper party after one of the performances, held at Dr. Valpy's house, the amiable Doctor gave her name as a toast; and at a public dinner the following day, given by the mayor (no doubt the aldermen, poor dears, again attended in their furred gowns !) to the distinguished visitors, Talfourd again proposed her health, which was, as she recorded with gratification in her diary, a " Very Great honour."

During this visit to Reading, Talfourd called twice at the cottage at Three Mile Cross, and no doubt *Foscari* formed the principal topic of conversation. No doubt, too, they were both now optimistic about its chances of acceptance. But she was to receive yet another blow over this ill-fated play : on the day it was sent to the management of Covent Garden, Lord Byron published his tragedy on the same subject. " I am so distressed at the idea of competition," she told Haydon, " not merely with his lordship's talents, but with his great name . . . that I have written to Mr. Talfourd requesting him to consult another friend on the propriety of entirely suppressing my play. . . . I rather think now that it will not be offered—that Mr. Talfourd will suppress it ; and I heartily wish he may." It was, however, offered if not to the management, at any rate to Macready, for on 9th November she received a letter from Talfourd enclosing a note from the actor suggesting still further alterations. Anyone less pertinacious, or perhaps less in need of money, would by now have lost all interest ; but although she entertained misgivings as to the eventual outcome, she nerved herself to undertake further changes, and on 16th November, she wrote to Talfourd, " Here is another catastrophe, my dear Sir, for Mr. Macready's consideration. I only wait hearing from you to finish the poisoning scene, which I shall send up as soon as I can consistently with my natural slowness. If you like none of them I shall be quite ready to try another—or to alter any of these. Of course they are submitted to you with most full and perfect liberty to cut and alter and *add* whenever you think proper. . . ."* Talfourd was not long in making up his mind over these proposals, for by the 22nd, she had despatched the

* MSS. John Rylands Library.

completed manuscript. But by now Charles Kemble, owing to quarrels with Macready, had seceded from Covent Garden, so that *Foscari* had had to be altered to provide two, instead of three principal parts. Such a radical change did not, of course, improve its chance of acceptance, and on 15th December, she wrote in her diary, " Heard from Mr. Talfourd with an account of the rejection of Foscari."*

It might be thought that this was the end of the matter, and she was certainly of that opinion, for on 30th December, she began another tragedy entitled *Julian*. Macready, however, having eliminated his great rival Charles Kemble, had taken a fancy to *Foscari*, and in conjunction with the manager of Covent Garden, urged the harassed author to undertake still further changes. These involved " a new fifth act, nearly a new fourth and a change from first to last of one of the principal characters."† She was not anxious to undertake this work, but nevertheless agreed to do so, for " it seems to me that my interest, and therefore my duty, requires me to attempt this alteration."‡ In the meantime, she had been reading Byron's play, and she told Sir William Elford " . . . he [Byron] has taken up the business just where I left it off, so that his play does not at all clash with mine. The Doge is well executed, I think; but young Foscari notwithstanding good speeches, is utterly imbecile—an ultra-sentimentalist, who clings, no one knows why or wherefore, with a love-like dotage, to the country which has disgraced and exiled and tortured, and finishes by killing him; and his wife, Marina, is a mere scold." To verify that this criticism was an honest opinion and not actuated by professional jealousy, it is only necessary to read Byron's play. It is totally lacking in action, and, as Jeffrey says " the interest . . . is founded upon feelings so peculiar or overstrained, as to engage no

* Talfourd's letter is in the John Rylands Library.
† Reading Collection, Feb. 9th, 1822. Letter to Sir William Elford.
‡ Ibid.

sympathy ; and the whole story turns on incidents that are neither pleasing nor natural."*

Henceforth it is not easy to follow the fortunes of Mary Mitford's much mutilated play. It seems that when the alterations demanded by Macready had been made, Charles Kemble took over the management of Covent Garden, and the negotiations had to start all over again. She confessed that she was so "thoroughly out of heart" about it that she could not bear even to think or speak of it. In the meantime, she worked steadily at her articles for the magazines—*A Great Farm House*, one of the *Our Village* sketches, was finished on 19th April, 1822—and on her new tragedy *Julian*, which she sent to Macready in May. Charles Kemble, however, once more interested himself in *Foscari*, and the diary mentions "a very hopeful letter" from Talfourd on the subject. On 20th May, Dr. Mitford went to London to conduct negotiations which were evidently successful, for a few days later his daughter went to town and interviewed Charles Kemble at Covent Garden. She told Haydon, on 13th June that *Foscari* was accepted, "and that Mr. Charles Kemble, whose conduct has really been very kind, promises certainly to bring it out next season. But there must be another alteration in the catastrophe—which as well as the delay, exceedingly provokes my still kinder, though unknown, friend Mr. Macready. I must alter it, however, as well as I can. A manager has certainly a right to require that. . . . But you may imagine what a job it will be when I tell you that this fifth act has already been remodelled six times ! The Doge has died of joy—and his son has died of joy ; there have been two poisonings (the one by the bye worse than the other—I am a sad hand at the fatal draught) two assassinations, and now I am going to kill my hero by fair fighting."† These alterations were finished in July and on

* *Complete Works of Lord Byron*, with all the notes by Sir Walter Scott, Francis Jeffrey, Professor Wilson, etc., p. 549, A. & W. Galignani & Co., 1837.

† Reading Collection, 13th June, 1822.

13th August, Charles Kemble wrote to confirm that the play would be presented as early as possible in the coming season. At last it seemed as though all her toil was to be rewarded, and she wrote to her friends to tell them the good news. The diary states: "One of the happiest days of my life. . . ."

Unfortunately Charles Kemble, although the manager of Covent Garden, still had to obtain the consent of his rival, Macready, to play the part of the Doge, for there were no other actors in the company capable of performing the part. Macready was that autumn in Italy, so that nothing could be settled until his return. Thus the matter was still further delayed. As was only to be expected, Mary Mitford, after her previous experiences, felt some uneasiness, and she told Sir William Elford in November, "As to *Foscari*, I have not yet heard anything and am in a state of anxious expectation. . . . But I am hoping to hear that it is in first rehearsal, and do all I can not to think of it. . . ."* But the fact that everything depended on Macready's good will made the play's chances extremely slender. He was a man who, although an admirable artist, never forgot a quarrel. Born of comparatively humble parentage, educated at Rugby and destined for the bar he was nevertheless obliged, through his father's loss of fortune, to enter the theatrical profession, which as it carried no social status at that time, he despised. He considered himself a man ill used by fate and consequently bore a grudge against his social superiors. He was—it is almost needless to say—a violent radical in politics, envying and hating those whom he considered more fortunate, but not more worthy, than himself, thus providing the most potent argument for the existence of the aristocracy he so much despised: for men born into high positions, as a general rule, are fortunately lacking in that most unlovely quality, envy and its concomitant jealousies and

* Reading Collection, 16th Nov., 1822.

hatreds. He was not, however, deficient in some of the more sterling virtues. He was frank and honest and, as his diary reveals, made the most superhuman efforts to overcome his cardinal faults of jealousy and envy, although he was too narrow-minded ever to realize that they sprung from his overwhelming sense of inferiority and ill-usage.

When one's fate depends on the caprices of such a man, it is apt to be a little precarious; and in this instance, the wretched author's "state of anxious expectation" was so prolonged that it affected her health. ". . . I am worn out with mental labour and hope deferred," she wrote to Sir William on 13th January, 1823, "and begin, for the first time in my life, to know what the ladies' complaint called *nervous* means. You must not for a moment blame Charles Kemble. He is true and kind and good as ever man that lived. Blame nobody: blame only the anomalous and extraordinary state of the theatre in which the two great actors do not even speak to each other. Charles Kemble means to bring out *Foscari* in about six weeks, and has no doubt of doing so. He looks upon it as the main prop of his theatre for the season. This I know, but I dread the time, for I know—or at least deeply fear—that Macready will not play the Doge, and that it will occasion another tremendous feud and end, probably, in the abandonment of the tragedy."* Her fears were only too well founded. On 5th February, Talfourd wrote to say that Macready had refused the part of the Doge, and that the play could not therefore be performed.

But Macready, although he would not act with Kemble in *Foscari*, had no feeling of enmity, on this occasion, towards its unfortunate author; and he was perfectly willing to appear in a new play in which he would have the principal part. In May 1822, as has already been stated, Mary Mitford had sent him her tragedy, *Julian*, and although this had not satisfied him at the time, it had, as *Foscari*, undergone many

* Reading Collection, 13th January, 1823.

radical alterations and was now pronounced suitable for presentation. This news was conveyed to her in a letter from Talfourd on 27th February, 1823; he announced that *Julian* had been read in the green room at Covent Garden (the preliminary step to a performance) and that it would be played shortly.

It can well be imagined that this letter was the cause of great relief and excitement in the cottage at Three Mile Cross. At last the two years of unremitting toil, disappointment and anxiety were to be rewarded, and what was more important to her, there was a chance of making a substantial sum of money. Mary Mitford who, in addition to her nervous complaint, had been suffering from a bad feverish cold (she was bled twice) for the greater part of February, made a quick recovery, to which Talfourd's letter doubtless gave impetus. Visitors called at the cottage (among them Mrs. Dickinson) to offer their congratulations; and in preparation, no doubt, for her forthcoming visit to London, she went into Reading one morning "to buy" the diary informs us "a black satin gown" and "net for a cap." Talfourd was also in Reading, and she saw him twice. From the laconic entry on 5th March "nothing ever like Mr. Talfourd's kindness," it can safely be assumed that, apart from discussing theatrical concerns, she took the opportunity of expressing her gratitude for his help and kindness.

On Wednesday, 12th March, she went to town to stay with her friend Mrs. Hofland, then living in Newman Street, to attend the rehearsals of her play. She has given an account of the bewilderment she always experienced at these theatrical preliminaries in the preface to her *Dramatic Works*. "And those rehearsals, where for noise of every sort nobody can hear himself speak, where nobody is ever to be found where he is wanted, and nobody ever seems to know a syllable of his part; those rehearsals must have some good in them notwithstanding. In the midst of the crowd, the din, the jokes, and the confusion, the business must somehow have gone on; for at night the right scenes fall into the right places, the proper actors come at the proper times, speeches are spoken in due order, and, to the no small astonishment of the novice, who had given herself up for lost, the play succeeds."*

Julian was produced at Covent Garden on 16th March, 1823, with Macready in the leading *rôle*. The author was too nervous to attend the first night, but remained throughout the performance in a small room near by, while her friends brought her news of the play's reception. On this occasion, she had no cause to be nervous, for the play, whilst not being the dramatic success of the season, was certainly not a failure. It had what was for those days a reasonable run, eight days, and it brought her in £200. In judging the merits of the play, the current theatrical taste must be borne in mind. This was for high flown historical tragedy, preferably with a continental setting; and judged by those standards, *Julian* did not fall short of what was required. Nevertheless the play did not receive a good press, which both Macready and the author attributed to the influence of Charles Kemble and his wife. It is indeed a curious commentary on the state of the theatre that a manager should inspire adverse criticism of one of his own productions simply through jealousy of his leading actor. The play was violently attacked in *John Bull* and *The Examiner*, and the dramatic critic of the powerful *London Magazine* wrote with playful patronage: ". . . There has been much promise held out in the newspapers of the surpassing excellence of a production from the pen of Miss Mitford; and much as we are in general inclined to believe in the unprejudiced report of the newspapers—and confident as we must of course feel in the tragic powers of any lady, who can spare time from her muslins to devote herself to the muses—we must say

* *Dramatic Works*, Vol. I, p. xxvi, 1854.

we had fears—no—not fears—apprehensions—faint misgivings, that our lady authoress would not altogether drown the stage with tears, and turn us Londoners into dramatic Deucalions. We thought, by the help of many handkerchiefs and some philosophy, to be able to keep our head above water. As we, therefore, went to the theatre with amiable hopes and tempered expectations—we have much pleasure in honestly confessing that we came away with a respect for Miss Mitford, and with a faint surprise at the effort which a ladye pen had made. The truth is . . . no lady has ever yet succeeded in tragedy: and, from the powers which are absolutely necessary for a grand success, we shall be pretty safe in asserting, that no lady ever will be splendidly triumphant.

"The plot of *Julian* is, perhaps, the worst thing Miss Mitford has to answer for; and, indeed, its unnatural and improbable exaggeration goes very near to the distraction of several of the leading characters towards the end of the play. They have difficulty to keep their senses in the *situations*. . . .

"The tragedy, in our opinion, was very indifferently acted. . . . To Mr. Macready the authoress appears to have entrusted all her hopes; and, by a copy of the tragedy, which has just been put into our hands,* we perceive that her sense of his merits and his kindness is higher than any modern dramatist has hitherto ventured to express.† In our opinion, Mr. Macready never played worse. He outraged all discretion—and maddened those fine tones of his in a way to distract all lovers of good sensible acting. . . . In the last scene of the tragedy, he lashed himself into a fearful fury. Quieter acting would have done Miss Mitford more service; and we are only surprised she should be so misled as to fancy that five acts of noise can be good in any actor. . . ."‡

* It was published in 1823, and went into at least three editions.
† She dedicated the play to Macready.
‡ *London Magazine*, April, 1823.

Hazlitt, however—perhaps a better judge than this ponderously playful gentleman—approved of the tragedy :* and although Macready many years later, after he had quarrelled with the author, recorded " that the performance made little impression and was soon forgotten,"† there is no doubt that, at the time, he thought highly of it, for he wrote to the author " Depend upon it, I shall neither be inactive in thought or effort until I see *Julian* fairly established, which I am *confidently persuaded* it will be."

* Reading Collection, *circa* April, 1823. In a copy of a letter to Macready, she says " . . . Mr. Haydon wrote me word that Mr. Hazlitt applied to Mr. Jeffrey for his sanction to review *Julian* in the *Edinburgh*. This is a great compliment, and will be, if the request be granted, a great advantage. . . ." Apparently Jeffrey did not consent, for we have been unable to trace the review. In another letter dated 23/24 March to Haydon she says " After all whilst Mr. Macready acts and Mr. Hazlitt approves, I may well consent to a little abuse from such as they [the other reviews]."

† Macready's *Reminiscences*, Chap. XVIII, p. 278, 1875.

XII

1823-1825

It was now slightly more than two years since she started to make money by her literary work; and there is little doubt that her earnings were the sole income (apart from the interest on the trust funds which was mortgaged to Dr. Mitford's creditors*) of the family at Three Mile Cross. Under any circumstances, the support of ageing parents is a heavy burden, but when one of them is the extravagant, foolish Doctor, the burden becomes well nigh intolerable. Only those who have had experience of dealing with an individual totally lacking in money sense can have any idea of the utter hopelessness of her task. No matter what economies she might make; no matter what small sums she might accumulate against emergencies—saved, perhaps, over months through self-sacrifice and self-denial—her efforts would be dissipated over night by some reckless expenditure of her father's. It would not have mattered how much she had earned. If she had made vast sums the result would have been just the same, for supplying money to a gambler is like pouring water down a pipe—the aperture is never filled.

It is not possible to estimate, with any degree of accuracy, how much money she was making at this time, but the sum cannot have been negligible. Throughout 1823, she was a regular contributor to the *Ladies' Magazine* with the sketches which were later to constitute the first volume of *Our Village*. One, and sometimes two, articles appeared each

* This money seems always to have been used in this fashion, for many years later she told Talfourd (MSS. J. Rylands Library, 22nd May, 1837) " . . . I am quite sure that the pittance in William Harness's hands would be found to be mortgaged for different debts. My father does not tell me so—but I feel that it is so. . . ."

month. She was also contributing to other periodicals. Rates of payment in those days varied from ten to thirty guineas a sheet, but it is difficult to ascertain exactly what constituted a sheet. It might have been four, eight, twelve or sixteen pages, according to how the magazine was printed.* In a letter to Dr. Mitford in 1825, she mentions that eleven pages were worth seven guineas; if we assume, therefore, for the purposes of a rough computation, that she sold three articles a month (she wrote more than that) at this price, then her income from this source would be about £260, to which must be added the £200 she obtained from *Julian*. Therefore her total income in 1823 must have been somewhere in the region of £500; and this was before she published *Our Village*, and had become one of the highest paid writers of the time. As the pound was worth considerably more than its present value, and as the rent of her cottage was only £20 a year,† it is obvious that her income was sufficient to keep the household, if not in affluence, at least in comparative comfort. But when we consider that Dr. Mitford, in the past, had been in the habit of losing the equivalent of one year's income in one night at cards, it is not difficult to understand how she was never able to make income balance expenditure. It may well be that his gambling propensities were now somewhat subdued; that instead of losing £500 he contented himself with a modest and occasional £50; but even this would be more than she could afford. There is not even any evidence that he gambled at all at this time, although it is difficult to believe he would abandon the habit of a lifetime merely because his daughter could not make sufficient money to pay his debts. There is, however, plenty of evidence that his habits of extravagance persisted; that he entertained his friends on the same lavish scale as before

* In 1814 the *Edinburgh Review* paid, to ordinary contributors, 20 gns. per sheet of 16 pp. Special contributors were paid at the rate of 30 gns. or more per sheet.

† In a letter to Talfourd, which from its contents must have been written in the autumn of 1837, she says " . . . for seventeen years and a half we have given for this poor cabin (without the garden) £20 a year." MSS. John Rylands Library.

and that he bought—or rather obtained on credit—anything which would contribute to his material comfort.

In theory, it should have been possible for her, as the breadwinner, to have forced him to behave in a reasonable fashion by threatening his expulsion from the family circle. But theory and practice are unfortunately two different matters, and such an idea never entered her head. In the first place, a dispute of this nature would have upset her mother, whose health was now declining: then it was obvious that if her father still maintained his adolescent mentality at sixty-three, no threat was likely to change it. But the overriding factor was that she, loving him, was incapable of uttering a threat, still less of carrying it out. Thus she was in the unenviable position of being responsible for matters over which she had no control: the most she could hope for was to earn enough money to reduce the gap between income and expenditure to reasonable dimensions. Small wonder is it that, many years later, she was to tell Elizabeth Barrett Browning "I may truly say that ever since I was a very young girl I have never, although for some years living apparently in affluence, been without pecuniary care—a care that pressed upon my thoughts the last thing at night, and woke in the morning with a dreary, heavy sense of pain and pressure of something which weighed me to the earth—which I would fain cast off, but could not."

The urgent need to her, therefore, was to earn more money. It was not sufficient to reap a steady income from the magazines, which would increase as she became better known, for a few hundreds a year would never be sufficient to meet the demands of her rapacious father. Only a large sum could do that, which, in turn, could only be earned from the theatre. There is a letter to Macready, written during April, a few weeks after the first performance of *Julian*, in which she mentions *Rienzi*, the 14th century Governor of Rome who was assassinated for his cruelties, as a possible subject for a new play. This shows that she was determined, very wisely, to follow up her success. In the meantime, the ill-fated *Foscari* was again causing her anxiety. Owing to the success of *Julian*, Elliston, the manager of Drury Lane, applied for permission to perform it at that theatre. Although she was anxious to withdraw the play from Covent Garden, in order that Macready might not be called upon to play the Doge, she thought it prudent to consult Charles Kemble before making a decision. He, however, was determined, perhaps not unnaturally, that no-one else should benefit from the new dramatist he had discovered, and he threatened her with a law suit if she withdrew the play. In the quarrel between the two actors, she was a mere cat's-paw, "affronting both parties and suspected by both, because I will not come to a deadly rupture with either." Notwithstanding all the difficulties with which she knew she would have to contend, she did not relax her efforts, and on May 13th she told Sir William Elford "I intend . . . to write a tragedy on a very grand historical subject (Rienzi, *vide* Gibbon, vol. xi or xii). . . . At the same time I go to the work as a victim to the altar, so much do I dread the scenes which I know, first or last, I must encounter. But it is my duty and that settles all. You have yourself no notion how unfit I am for the terrible struggles amongst which I have been placed. Macready says that my character is a complete counteraction to my genius,* and perhaps he is right. I literally cannot scold and squabble and bargain and hold and threaten as he would have me. I can neither resist kindness, nor bear up under hard usage, and this feebleness and want of moral courage will not do for a theatre. But I must try once again. It is my duty. There is no other way in which I have a fair prospect of making so much money." † It is certain that she, who was never able to resist the

* She uses the word to denote talent rather than extraordinary creative abilities, as is the fashion to-day.

† Reading Collection, 13th May, 1822.

extortions of her father, was totally unfitted to battle in the world of sordid intrigue that was the theatre; but this inability is rather to her credit than otherwise. Those who can threaten, bargain and bludgeon their way through opposition may be strong, but they are not, as a general rule, particularly lovable or admirable characters.

To add to her troubles, in the spring of this year the editor of the *Ladies' Magazine*, S. J. Hamilton, absconded, owing her £40. But her sketches were so popular (they had increased the sales of the magazine from 250 to 2,000 a month) that the journal survived this disaster and was taken over by a Mr. Davidson, who promised her "security for the future." In order to fulfil all her magazine engagements at this time, she was chained to her desk eight to twelve hours a day, she told a friend, but this "sort of drudgery is heaven when compared with Covent Garden." She was, indeed, so worn out with fatigue that even her insensitive and self-centred father noticed her decline in health and resolved to find some remunerative employment in order to lighten her burden. But though his spirit may have been willing, his flesh was lamentably weak, and in August of that year (three months after this noble resolution) his daughter recorded "My dear father, relying with a blessed sanguineness on my poor endeavours, has not, I believe, even enquired for a situation." It was perhaps a little late, at sixty-three, to change the habits of a lifetime; and it must be admitted that of all the Doctor's habits a natural aversion to any sort of work was one of the most deep-rooted.

She was thus burdened with the entire support of her small household; and while, in normal circumstances, this should not have been beyond her powers, it developed into a grim struggle which took great toll of her health and which, while it did not break her spirit—for she knew how to bear suffering with fortitude and dignity—certainly impaired her enjoyment of life. A study of the documents chronicling her life at this time reveals the astonishing amount of work she undertook, which must have placed a great strain on her physical resources, particularly as most of it was done late at night when her domestic and social duties had been fulfilled. In addition to her magazine articles, she appears to have begun two tragedies, at the instigation of Macready—*Rienzi* and *Charles I*—neither of which, owing to theatrical squabbles, was performed for several years. The negotiations over *Rienzi* were even more tortuous and complicated than those connected with *Foscari*; and were to result, through no fault of her own, in a breach between Macready and herself. In the autumn of 1823, however, while they were still on terms of friendship, Macready's quarrel with Charles Kemble reached a climax in the cancellation of his contract at Covent Garden. He then joined the rival company at Drury Lane, making his debut there in October, 1823.* Any hopes that Mary Mitford may have entertained of *Rienzi's* production at Covent Garden were therefore at an end. She seems, temporarily, to have lost interest in the play for it was not until August, 1824, that negotiations were once more begun with Macready.

In the meantime, she was forced to rely upon her magazine work as her principal source of income. This perhaps was fortunate, for it resulted in the publication of *Our Village* in the latter part of May or early June, 1824.† The book would have appeared sooner, but for the serious illness of Mrs. Mitford that winter, which, owing to the constant nursing it necessitated, delayed the negotiations with the publisher, George Whittaker. She gave the first news of this venture in a letter, dated 18th January, to her old friend Sir William Elford. The book was to consist, she said, "... of essays and characters and stories, chiefly of country life, in the manner of the *Sketch Book*,‡

* In Sheridan Knowles's *Virginius*.
† See *Notes and Queries*, Vol. 146, p. 90.
‡ *The Sketch Book*, by Washington Irving, 1819.

but without sentimentality or pathos—two things which I abhor." On 5th March she reported it would be out in three weeks or a month, and that "Charles Lamb (the matchless 'Elia' of the *London Magazine*) says that nothing so fresh and characteristic has appeared for a long while. It is not over modest to say this," she added, "but who would not be proud of the praise of such a *proser*?" Who, indeed? And posterity has endorsed Lamb's verdict. The book had an immediate success, and was well received by the literary journals. The *New Monthly Magazine* referred to it as "an engaging volume, full of feeling, spirit and vivacity"; and the *Quarterly Review*, which had dealt so severely with her poems, made the *amende honorable* by a long and exhaustive article which, if it did not display unqualified enthusiasm (for it was only when attacking that its myrmidons could feel really enthusiastic) at least demonstrated its patronising approval of the modest little work. "We have no passion for 'Breaking a butterfly upon the wheel'," said the reviewer, with untruthful condescension, "and should not notice this little volume, if we were not on the whole pleased with its contents. The sketches of country scenery, in which it abounds, have such a convincing air of locality; the human figures, interspersed among them, are touched in such a laughter-loving, good-humoured spirit of caricature, innocent, and yet often pungent withal, that we scarcely know a more agreeable portfolio of trifles for the amusement of an idle hour." But it would not have been in the true tradition to have continued in this strain, and the next sentence—"Abundant matter for small criticism, indeed, might be found in the details of the work" —is the prelude to several pages of admonition in which the author is accused of coarseness of expression, and is informed that she should "record with fidelity the peculiarities of uneducated society, without identifying herself too closely with them." She is also exhorted not "to clothe her ideas in the phraseology of the dog-kennel and the kitchen." Nevertheless, despite these strictures, which to-day seem ridiculous, the reviewer is warm in his praises of the country scenes and sketches, and we are in full agreement with his final remarks: ". . . we would direct the reader's notice to . . . *Modern Antiques* and *The Talking Lady*—both abounding in arch and amusing touches of character, which prove that Miss Mitford has observation and tact, and playful *badinage*, to catch higher follies as they fly, than the whims and eccentricities of village life. We hope she will employ these qualities for the future gratification of her readers; and we part from her in her own good-humoured mood, and with no disinclination to be her debtors for another smile."*

The *Talking Lady*, an account of a loquacious woman's visit to the cottage at Three Mile Cross is one of the most perfect sketches of its kind ever written. One can sense the boredom experienced by the Mitford family as they listened, hour after hour through four long tedious days, to their guest's incessant monologue; and one can picture their sigh of relief and their first tentative breaking out into speech after four days of silence, when she eventually departed on the coach. There have been many authors who have dealt with the same theme—talking ladies abound in fiction—but we cannot recall another character who so makes us gasp when we read of her exploits, or who so appals us by the monotonous persistence of her quiet monologue. This effect of persistence is obtained by the author's skill in linking one phase and phrase with another. Subject follows subject, each only dealt with in a few lines, so that before we have grasped its significance, another is before us. The whole description is welded into one long paragraph of incisive and corruscating prose which flows easily and effortlessly, but which cost the author infinite pains, for as she told Talfourd "what looks like ease in my style is labour."†

* *Quarterly Review*, December, 166 ff, 1824.
† MSS. John Rylands Library, 21st December, 1825.

From the first *Our Village* proved popular with the public. By August, the first edition was sold out, and a second was going through the press; and its popularity has persisted to this day. In the British Museum's catalogue, thirty-one editions are listed up to the year 1942 (these include the selections made from the five volumes eventually published), and this list is by no means complete. It only includes two editions published during her lifetime, the first (the five volumes appeared in 1824-26-28-30) and one in 1852, whereas by 1835 there were fourteen editions of the first volume alone. It is only natural, perhaps, that the hundred and twenty-four sketches presented in the five volumes should prove an irresistible lure to editors, publishers and illustrators; but in our opinion there has yet to be a selection which is truly representative of the author's work. There appears to be an overwhelming tendency to concentrate on the country scenes and characters and to exclude the more subtle and worldly characterisations, possibly because these do not lend themselves so well to the art of the illustrator. This, in our opinion, is a pity, for wit is a scarce commodity and should consequently be cherished.

With the publication of *Our Village*, Mary Mitford found herself, if not famous over-night, at least well known among the reading public, then far more limited than it is now. Her readers wanted to know where "Our Village" was situated, and whether the characters were drawn from life, and not the least curious was her old friend Sir William Elford, to whom she wrote in June: ". . . I proceed to answer your question, 'Are the characters and descriptions true?' Yes! yes! yes! As true as is well possible. You, as a great landscape painter, know that in painting a favourite scene you do a little embellish, and can't help it; you avail yourself of happy accidents of atmosphere, and if anything be ugly you strike it out, or if anything be wanting, you put it in. But still the picture is a likeness; and that this is a very faithful one, you will judge when I tell you that a worthy neighbour of ours, a post captain, who has been in every quarter of the globe, and is equally distinguished for the sharp look-out and the *bonhomie* of his profession, accused me most seriously of carelessness in putting 'The Rose' for the 'Swan,' as the sign of our next-door neighbour; and was no less disconcerted at the *misprint* (as he called it) of B. for R. in the name of our next town. *A cela près*, he declares the picture to be exact.* Nevertheless, I do not expect to be poisoned. Why should I? I have said no harm of my neighbours, have I?" Perhaps not; but we feel that the Talking Lady might have had something to say on this matter. Let us hope, however, that she was too busy talking ever to glance at her young friend's composition.

With the success of her book, it is to be presumed that the financial situation of the family at Three Mile Cross was temporarily alleviated. At any rate, in July she referred to the recent acquisition of a pony and pony-chaise which had enabled her mother and father to take several drives. Although Mrs. Mitford had made a good recovery from her asthmatic complaint, her state of health still remained delicate; and to add to her daughter's anxiety, Dr. Mitford also fell seriously ill that year and did not make a complete recovery until the autumn. These two illnesses took great toll of Mary Mitford. She was worn out by mental and physical fatigue and was incapacitated from working for some considerable time. By the autumn, however, she was once more writing for the magazines, and her publisher had asked her to undertake two more volumes of *Our Village*. In addition, she was again working on *Rienzi* which she hoped would be produced, under Macready's auspices, at Drury Lane in the coming season. In

* So accurate, indeed, are her descriptions that it is possible, with the aid of a map, to trace the itinerary of many of her walks and expeditions. Also the names of some of her village characters are on the tombs in Shinfield Churchyard (*Notes and Queries*, 8th August, 1936).

November, she went to London with the MS. and Macready informed her that certain alterations must be made. There must be a new first act, the second and third acts must be amalgamated and the fifth act entirely re-written; and all these alterations must be carried out in a fortnight so that the play could be produced immediately. She hurried home in order to do the work in the stipulated time—no mean undertaking—and while she was carrying out the alterations she received a letter from Talfourd, written at Macready's instigation, asking her to bring up the MS. personally, so that if further changes were necessary, they could be carried out at once. Some time early in December, therefore, she was back in London, for Crabb Robinson met her at the Lambs' in Islington on the 5th.* Her hopes must have been high, for she had received the following letter from Macready:

"10, Conduit Street, Dec. 7th.

Mr. Macready presents his compliments to Miss Mitford; begs to inform her that he has presented the play of *Rienzi* with his opinion of its merits—that Mr. Elliston† thinks the play possesses great merit; and desiring a card of his terms to be sent to the author, has acquainted Mr. Macready that he will read it again, and wishes to have a personal interview with the author to give a final decision, or make an arrangement respecting it."

When, however, she saw Macready, he received her coolly and remarked "that there was no great hurry for her play. The managers had another piece at the theatre which must at all events be produced first: and it was very improbable that her play could be acted at all."‡ What happened next is a matter for conjecture; but there was

* *Diary of H. C. R.*, ed. Sadler, 1872, "Sunday, Dec. 5th, 1824. Walked back to Islington, and met there Mr. & Mrs. Talfourd and Miss Mitford, the dramatist and poet, a squat person but with a benevolent and intelligent smile. Scarcely any conversation. Lamb merry."

† Manager of Drury Lane.

‡ *Blackwood's Magazine*, Vol. 17, June, 1825.

undoubtedly a dispute in which she expressed herself forcibly as, under the circumstances, she had a perfect right to do. It is difficult, indeed, not to believe that Macready was at fault. It may well be that in the first interview he exceeded his instructions from the management; that he gave the impression the play would definitely be produced when the matter was only under consideration. He may well have believed—being a vain and autocratic man—that if the alterations met with his approval, this was sufficient to ensure the play's production. Alternatively, another play may have come along in the interim in which he thought he would appear to a better advantage. At any rate, the fact that he felt himself in the wrong would account for his coolness and lack of manners at the second interview. Nevertheless, whatever interpretation may be placed upon the facts, it cannot be denied that he had led her to believe the play would be accepted and caused her to do a great deal of unnecessary work: and it can well be imagined that when, later, she referred to the incident as "a bitter disappointment," she did not exaggerate.

It must therefore have been with a heavy heart that she once more returned to Three Mile Cross towards the end of December. A letter to Haydon on the 29th reveals that after Macready's rejection, she offered the play to Charles Kemble for production at Covent Garden. He accepted it, and Young agreed to play the principal part; but for some unknown reason Kemble advised her to withdraw it from the theatre, which she accordingly did. "I must try to forget that the play was ever written," she added bitterly, "and all that happened in London except the kindness I received there."* She was not to be allowed to forget, however, for this incident had important repercussions. In June 1825, a letter addressed to Charles Kemble and R. W. Elliston "on the present state of the

* Reading Collection, 29th Dec., 1824. This refers to the portrait painted of her by Haydon during this visit and which is now in the Reading Museum. It was not, however, considered a good likeness and was much disliked by her friends.

stage," signed Philo-Dramaticus, appeared in *Blackwood's Magazine*. The author, after deploring the dearth of good plays, stated " I am aware that the imputation of loving a paradox, will immediately be cast upon me, when I attribute the present depressed state of the national drama to the fault of your *great actors*—I mean your *soi-disant great actors*—of Messrs. Kean, Young and Macready. The arrogant pretensions of these gentlemen, as unwarranted by any extraordinary merits of their own, as injurious to the interests of you their employers, are gradually completing the work which Mr. Harris* and his pantomimes began." As an example of the " arrogant pretensions " of Macready, the writer then cited the alterations to *Rienzi* which the actor had insisted upon, stating that these were not necessary for dramatic effect, but were made solely to enhance the principal part. He also gave a detailed account of the cavalier treatment received by Mary Mitford, and demanded, with fine scorn, " Now, gentlemen, do you suppose that persons of real poetic genius—persons respectable from their station in society and their intellectual cultivation, will dedicate their time and talents to the labour of writing for the stage, if they are to be subjected to such impertinence? . . ."

The effect of this article on a man of Macready's temperament can well be imagined. He believed, not unnaturally, that if it was not written, it was at least instigated by Mary Mitford, as no-one else could have supplied the information. In later life, he asserted that it had ruined his reputation, caused a great loss of income and nearly resulted in his retirement from the stage. Such an assertion is, however, absurd, for although the article was a personal attack on him, it was not nearly so virulent, nor so scurrilous as many others appearing daily at that time in the press and literary journals. Public figures must expect to be criticized, and if they do not care for criticism, they

* The previous manager of Covent Garden.

should retire into private life. Macready, however, was hypersensitive, and moreover vindictive; and he never forgave Mary Mitford to whom he referred, in his diary, as "base and worthless." She was not, however, the author of the article, nor had she any idea of its being written. The first indication she received of its appearance was from Haydon to whom she wrote, on 7th June: "Having left off reading magazines. . . . I had not seen *Blackwood* till you mentioned it. Of course I sent for that. It is a very able article and written with very kind feelings towards me. Nevertheless I regret it as tending to provoke fresh disputes."* The real culprit, however, was William Harness, to whom she had confided the whole story, possibly during her visit to London at the end of the previous year. He had communicated the details of the transaction to a friend, and together they had concocted the *Blackwood* article. That he should have betrayed her confidence and published the facts without her sanction seems to us—however well meaning may have been his intentions—a grave breach of trust. On July 28th, she wrote to him: "If you happen to know anything of the author of a very clever letter in *Blackwood's Magazine* you may tell him, with my compliments, that he put the authoress of *Rienzi* into a sound fright. I expected nothing less than a long pompous article in the next number, holding forth that unlucky authoress by name; so I wrote to Mr. Talfourd to find out if he could, whether Mr. Macready did mean to write to the Editor. Mr. Talfourd sounded him accordingly and discovered that he had formed the wise determination never to look at anything against himself— so *me voilà quitte pour la peur*. Pray don't put this into print. Of course I did not tell Mr. Talfourd that I had any suspicion of the author, nor shall I. I found you out partly by a letter containing pretty much the same opinions which I had received from you before, partly by its exceeding

* Reading Collection, 7th June, 1825.

manliness and spirit, and partly (prepare for a grand compliment) partly by a little bit of bad English which had crept in, you know how, in altering the construction of a sentence."*

Macready, however, seems to have changed his mind, and he demanded a complete denial from her of the facts contained in the *Blackwood* article. She was ill in bed when she received his letter, suffering great pain from an abscess in the side: and she was sorely perplexed as to how to answer him. She did not wish to offend still further the enraged actor (for she regretted the publication as much as he did), yet she was not prepared to deny the truth of Harness's statement about the negotiations over *Rienzi*. Her reply was therefore scarcely calculated to be satisfactory to Macready. In it, she maintained that the facts given in the article were true, but that she deplored their publication, and added: "I can safely assure you that no event of a life singularly unprosperous has ever given me greater regret than this affair of *Rienzi*—especially the article in the magazine. You could not imagine that I knew of it!" This reply was evidently based on suggestions from her friend and counsellor Talfourd, for on 12th August she wrote to him: "I hope you will approve of the enclosed.† *They*‡ do not—but it satisfies my own feelings, and surely he will not and cannot make an ill use of it. Pray tell me if you approve it for I am very anxious till I hear. You see that I have committed no-one. . . ."§

This incident had a curious sequel fourteen years later. On 3rd January, 1839, Macready and Harness were both guests at an evening party, and on being alone together Macready, who had long regarded the clergyman as the author of the article, tackled him on the subject. He has given an interesting account of their conversation in his

* Reading Collection, 28th July, 1825.

† A copy of her letter to Macready. This can be found both in the Reading Collection and among the MSS. in the J. Rylands Library.

‡ Harness and his friend, presumably.

§ MSS. John Rylands Library.

diary : " I then mentioned to him the libellous article which in June, 1825, had been written against me in *Blackwood's Magazine* ; the effect it had had in raising the *press* against me ; the partial contradiction that Miss Mitford had given it ; the strong and loud *lie* that Procter* gave to it ; that it had driven me to leave the stage, on which resolution I was only deterred from acting upon by the birth of my children ; that I had suspected him of being the author, and had mentioned the suspicions ; that it had nearly driven me to extremities which it is dreadful to think of. He was evidently much embarrassed and seemed to suffer much ; his mode of expressing himself was confused and *rambling* ; he said that he must acknowledge he was inculpated so far as that he had heard the story told by Miss Mitford, and had communicated it to the writer of the article, but that he had not written it, nor anything in periodical literature of a critical kind except, etc. I told him that I was very glad to hear that he was not the author, as I was happy to think well of all men, and was very sorry that I had suspected him of the fact. He was going away, when he turned back, having passed the door, and said : 'I think we ought to shake hands.' I gave him my hand saying, 'I was very happy to do so,' and we parted. My heart was much lighter, and I fear his was *much*, *very much* heavier, as it is evident, though not the author, that he was deeply implicated in that shocking transaction—that assassination of my character."† More deeply implicated, we feel, than he cared to admit ; for there is no doubt that as Mary Mitford recognized his phraseology in the article, he must have contributed some of the matter.

* Barry Cornwall.
† *Diaries of Macready*, ed. Toynbee, Vol. 1, p. 486, 1912.

XIII

1825-1828

The year 1825 was assuredly not a lucky one, despite the fact that by April *Our Village* had gone into a third edition. If she had concentrated on prose, which all her friends except Harness advised, she might have been more fortunate; but being in perpetual need of substantial sums of money, she refused to abandon the theatre. And in her theatrical ventures she was singularly unfortunate. Apart from *Rienzi*, she had, early in the year, once more taken up her tragedy of *Charles I.* This was finished and sent to Kemble by the autumn who pronounced it "admirable though somewhat dangerous" and despatched it to the licenser, George Colman. Colman felt unable to take the responsibility of sanctioning its performance and passed it on to the Lord Chamberlain. It seems strange now that there should have been any doubt about the licensing of a play on such a subject, especially as the author's sentiments were very much in favour of Charles and against the dictator; but in 1825 the monarchy was not so well established, nor was it in such good repute, due to the unsavoury private life of George IV and his attempts to divorce his wife. Therefore the Lord Chamberlain, the Duke of Montrose, thought fit to uphold Colman's ruling, with the result that, on October 17th, she received the following letter:

"My dear Madam,

I regret to say that I have this day received the Lord Chamberlain's refusal to license the representation of *Charles the First*. Under the circumstances, it is unnecessary to bore you with remarks upon the piece. We will talk it over when next I have the pleasure of seeing you. In the meantime, I beg you to believe that I am, my dear madam,

most faithfully yours,

C. Kemble."*

Then in addition to this catastrophe, George Whittaker, her publisher, stopped payment at the end of the year ; and although she had fortunately not parted with the copyright of her book, she lost the profits of her last edition. Perhaps her greatest misfortune was that the mental powers of her mother, who was now seventy-five, were beginning to fail. Mrs. Mitford had always been dearer to her than her father. They had so often been left together to face the consequences of his irresponsible conduct, that there was a bond of sympathy and understanding between them which was lacking in the relations between father and daughter. The waning mental powers of her mother must therefore have added considerably to her already overwhelming anxieties and sorrows. "Poor mamma's failure of faculty is very peculiar," she told Harness. "You might see her twenty times for twenty minutes, and yet not perceive it ; or, on the other hand, she might in one twenty minutes show it a hundred times. She mistakes one person for another—one thing for another—misjoins facts—misreports conversations—hunts for six hours together after a pincushion which she has in her pocket, or a thimble on her finger—and is totally absorbed in the smallest passing object. *This* is, in one respect, fortunate, since it prevents her from foreseeing greater evils. But then again, it deters her from supporting me in any effort to mitigate them. So that, from her incapacity, and the absolute inertness of my father in such matters—an obstinacy of going on in the same way which I cannot describe—I find myself compelled to acquiesce in a way of living which, however inexpensive, is still more so than we can afford, for fear of disturbing, and perhaps killing her." *An obstinacy of going on in the*

* Reading Collection.

same way which I cannot describe : this was one of the few occasions when she permitted herself to comment, even in this restrained fashion, on her father's conduct. Now that she had lost the moral support of her mother, her troubles increased tenfold ; and until Dr. Mitford's death, seventeen years later, the references in her correspondence to pecuniary difficulties, and her own resultant ill health through anxiety, become more and more frequent.

Nevertheless the year 1826, which started unpropitiously by an unsuccessful visit to London to collect moneys due to her from publishers and booksellers, was not, from a material point of view, unsatisfactory. She was busier than ever on work for the magazines (she was actually being " dunned ", she says, for contributions), she had started a novel, and in March, in conjunction with Harness, was writing charades, then a very popular form of entertainment. These subsequently appeared in *Blackwood's Magazine*, and as the sale was negotiated by Harness, this is additional proof of his connection with that journal. Nevertheless she considered that ten guineas a sheet, the price offered by Blackwood, was bad pay, and told Harness that she had frequently received twelve guineas from other magazines, and twenty to thirty from annual publications. In April, she was busy preparing the second volume of *Our Village* which her father sold to George Whittaker (whose brother-in-law seems to have come to his rescue) for £150. She could have obtained £200 elsewhere, but in view of the extreme depression in the book-selling trade, she considered the price to be a fair one. This sum included the copyright of the first volume, an unwise move as it afterwards turned out, for as we have already stated, this had gone through fourteen editions by 1835. But she could not resist the lure of the theatre, and in March asked Harness to sound Kemble about an opera on the subject of Cupid and Psyche, and to find out whether the actor could induce Weber to compose the music. A few weeks later she reported that Mrs. Trollope and Mr. Milman* had both read *Rienzi* and were most enthusiastic about its merits. Mrs. Trollope, who was friendly with Kean and Macready, was most anxious that either one or other of these two actors should immediately produce the tragedy; and so far as Macready was concerned, she did her best to persuade him to reconsider the matter. She was not successful—he was still smarting under the *Blackwood* article—but it was probably due to her influence that he took both *Rienzi* and *Charles* with him on his American tour that year.

Although none of these projects matured, Mary Mitford had a theatrical success in the autumn of that year; for Charles Kemble decided, at long last, to produce *Foscari* at Covent Garden. At the end of October, she and her father went to London to attend the rehearsals, and took lodgings at 45, Frith Street. Of course there were the usual alarms connected with a theatrical venture—Kemble was so hoarse that he could scarcely speak; the Duke of York was seriously ill, and it was feared he might die and the theatre have to be closed—but fortunately nothing occurred to prevent the production. She was extremely nervous about the play's reception for so much, she told Harness, depended upon it. If it were a success, Macready would undoubtedly produce *Charles I* and *Rienzi* in America, and the latter might eventually be performed in England; Charles Kemble would look with much more favour on a new play she had just written, *Gaston de Blondeville*,† and in, addition she would be able to sell a volume of *Dramatic Scenes* which she had recently begun. *Foscari* was produced at Covent Garden on Saturday, 5th November, and had a good reception. In a hasty note scribbled after the performance to her mother, she said: "It was received, not merely with rapturous applause, but without the slightest symptom of disapprobation from beginning to end." She was not present in the theatre, but remained throughout the

* Afterwards Dean Milman, who then had the living of St. Mary's, Reading.
† Founded on the posthumous novel of that name by Mrs. Radcliffe.

performance in a room near by belonging to George Robins, of the firm of Messrs. Robins, the Piazza, Covent Garden, the auctioneers who had effected the sale of Bertram House. Mrs. Trollope, however, was in the audience, and the gratified dramatist recorded that her friend, " between joy for my triumph and sympathy with the play, has cried herself half blind." She herself attended the theatre on the following night, and Dr. Mitford reported to his wife " . . . you will rejoice to hear that although the night was unfavourable, the pit was a bumper before the rising of the curtain, and Mr. Kemble, Mr. Fawcett, etc., admitted that it was the best house they ever saw upon the second performance of a tragedy. It was a real money house, and at the dropping of the curtain, three distinct vollies of cheers from every part of the house, not one note of disapprobation was to be heard."*

She certainly deserved this success, and it must have compensated, in some degree, for all the disappointments she had suffered. As she had anticipated, it brought others in its train, for her father sold the copyright of the play and the volume of *Dramatic Scenes*† for £150; so that with the £200 she received from the theatre, this visit to London enriched the family's exchequer to the extent of £350. *Foscari* had a run of fourteen nights, which was considered excellent in those days; and as it was not performed on consecutive nights, it was still in the repertoire of Covent Garden in December. It was only then suspended because the principal actress, a young married woman, was going to have a baby. Had it been played once more, she would have received a further £100, for the agreement was for £100 for the 3rd, 9th and 15th nights; but as it was put on again in the spring of 1827,‡ it is to be presumed that she eventually received this sum. She was now overwhelmed

* Reading Collection, 7th Nov., 1826.

† A copy of the *Dramatic Scenes* is in the Richmond Public Library. There is not one in the British Museum.

‡ Reading Collection, to Sir W. E., 12th May, 1827, " My father is gone to town to see *Foscari*, which they are doing to-night at Covent Garden."

JANUARY, 1 to 3, 1819.

January the 1st we were living at Ber-
-tram House - dear [illegible] dear
Mama & I - Our servants poor Lucy
Jane (who is going away) & George
Our pets - Dear Mossy - his sister Tiny
Fly - Kelly - Moses - (greyhounds) Moss
a borrowed greyhound - Whim our
springing spaniel who came from
Lockinge - Miranda our dear beauti-
-ful greyhound puppy - Zelie our Puss
Cat & Polle a tabby do - & 22 Bantams - the
3 Doves given me by poor Jesse Cliff.

Dec. 31st Went with Papa & Eliza
Webb to a dance at Mr. Dickinson's
- very splendid - very delightful - much
laughing - Mr. Crowther not to be forgotten

1 Friday
At Farley Hill - Happy day - Mrs D [illegible]
singing - Whim on your walk - Mr D
reading - Count Ugolino -

2 Saturday
Another happy day - at Farley
Hill - Reading & home -

3 Sunday
At home - told dear Mama
all about the Ball - read
Burke & the Reviews of the E. R.
& the Q. R.

A page of the Diary
by courtesy of the Trustees of the British Museum.

Mary Russell Mitford, aged three.

Mary Russell Mitford
by John Lucas
(by courtesy of the National Portrait Gallery) see Appendix IV.

Mary Russell Mitford, 1824
by B. R. Haydon
(by courtesy of the Reading Museum and Art Gallery).

with offers of work from the two principal theatres. Charles Kemble pressed her to write both a tragedy and a comedy; and the management of Drury Lane offered her five hundred guineas for any play she might choose to write. She refused this offer, however, considering that she was bound to Covent Garden. In addition, the first edition of the second volume of *Our Village*, which was published in October, was sold out in a fortnight, and another was going through the press. The reviews were exceedingly favourable, particularly that of the *New Monthly Magazine*.

It might be thought that with these well merited successes (well merited in the sense that her talents justified her fame rather than her motive in exploiting them) there would be some relief from the relentless pressure of pecuniary anxieties: and in normal circumstances, this would undoubtedly have been the case. But while Dr. Mitford remained alive, her circumstances were never normal, and we find her admitting, only a few months later, that "we are as poor as poor can be . . . and are ourselves living on credit." Her success and growing literary reputation brought her little pleasure or gratification: indeed in some ways it was a burden, for having received ample proof of her ability to make money, she felt unable to relax for a single moment. It is indeed remarkable, in view of the strain imposed on her powers, that the quality of her work did not suffer. It is not difficult, from the available material, to reconstruct the circumstances of her life at this time. Since her mother's mental faculties had begun to fail, she and her father made a point of never being away from the cottage at the same time, unless they were both forced to go to London on business. As Dr. Mitford was still a magistrate, and as he had never relinquished his habits of entertaining and being entertained or his coursing and political activities, it is safe to assume that the onus mostly fell on her. Then, since

Mrs. Mitford was now incapable of attending to the management of the household, this duty also became her responsibility. Her ailing mother must, indeed, have been a cause of endless anxiety, for apart from the physical effort of looking after her, there was the mental agony of watching the decline of the person she loved best in the world. How she found time to write, in view of the multifarious calls upon her, is something at which to wonder; and her work was achieved only by the total exclusion of all personal pleasure. She made herself a prisoner in the cottage, never stirring from the place unless to take exercise, scarcely seeing a soul unless a visitor chanced to call; and she worked far into the night, when her domestic duties were over, when it was no longer necessary to read to her mother or supervise the affairs of the household. Is it to be wondered, therefore, that she refers to the loneliness of her existence, or that this unnatural way of life, particularly so to one of her sociable tendencies, undermined her health and spirits? Her only relaxation and indulgence was her garden, of which she had given this charming description to Haydon: "My little garden is a perfect rosary—the greenest and most blossomy nook that ever the sun shone upon. It is almost shut in by buildings; one a long open shed, very pretty, a sort of rural arcade, where we sit. On the other side is an old granary, to which we mount by outside wooden steps, also very pretty. Then there is an opening to a little court, also backed by buildings, but with room enough to let in the sunshine that comes aslant in summer evenings, through and under a large elder tree. One end is closed by our pretty irregular cottage, which, as well as the granary, is covered by cherry trees, vines, roses, jessamine, honeysuckle, and grand spires of hollyhocks. The other is comparatively open, showing over high pales the blue sky and a range of woody hills. All and every part is untrimmed, antique, weather-stained, and homely as can be imagined—

gratifying the eye by its exceeding picturesqueness, and the mind by the certainty that no pictorial effect was intended—that it owes all its charms to 'rare accident.' My father laughs at my passionate love of my little garden—and perhaps you will laugh too; but I assure you it's a 'bonny bit' of earth as ever was crammed full of lilies and roses. . . ." Here in the few moments she could spare from her manifold duties, she would plant and weed, or read and work in the open shed, "the rural arcade"; and here, perhaps, among the flowers she tended so carefully, she found a few moments' oblivion from the cares with which she was so heavily burdened.

These interludes of relaxation, at any rate during the next few years when so much work was achieved, must have been rare. Early in 1827, she was writing another tragedy for Covent Garden, *Inez de Castro*; but the work, she told Sir William Elford, only proceeded slowly because she was "perpetually hindered by applications from magazines and annuals—which, however, is not quite time thrown away, since besides the present pay, I reserve the copyright, and shall collect the papers next year into another volume of *Our Village*."* The sales of that book continued to be excellent, and in May an artist came down to Three Mile Cross to take views of the village for yet another edition, which were to be "executed in a newly invented sort of lithography on transfer paper, which is said to have nearly the effect of a line engraving. . . ."† Indeed, had the present day arrangements between author and publisher been in force, and payment been on a royalty basis, she would have become a rich woman from the sales of this book alone. As it was, she must have made a considerable sum, for she was paid twice over, by the magazines and by the publisher. In 1828, a third volume of this popular book was published, but the most important

* Reading Collection, 12th May, 1827.
† Ibid.

event of the year was the production of *Rienzi* at Drury Lane with Young in the principal part. This was the most successful, from the point of view of construction and plot, of all her plays; and Talfourd writing to her a short time before its production says: "... the Lambs called here yesterday. ... They are so very much interested for *Rienzi*, which they read, you may remember, with great pleasure, and thought very far above *Foscari*."* From a pecuniary point of view, too, it was the most profitable, bringing in at least £400. There seems to have been some suggestion of producing it at Covent Garden in April, for she hurried to London to see Charles Kemble. But the arrangement did not materialize, and it was not actually performed till October. She wrote the joyful news to Sir William:

"Three Mile Cross,
Sept. 23, 1828.

My dear Friend,

My tragedy of *Rienzi* is to be produced at Drury Lane Theatre on Saturday, the 11th October; that is to say, next Saturday fortnight. Mr. Young plays the hero, and has been studying the part during the whole vacation; and a new actress makes her first appearance in the part of the heroine. This is a very bold and hazardous experiment, no new actress having come out in a new play within the memory of man; but she is young, pretty, unaffected, pleasant-voiced, with great sensibility, and a singularly pure intonation—a qualification which no actress has possessed since Mrs. Siddons. Stanfield† is painting the new scenes, one of which is an accurate representation of Rienzi's house. This building still exists in Rome, and is shown there as a curious relique of the domestic architecture of the Middle Ages. They have got a sketch which they sent for on purpose, and they are hunting up costumes

* MSS. John Rylands Library, 19th Sept. 1828.
† Clarkson Stanfield, A.R.A.

with equal care; so that it will be very splendidly brought out, and I shall have little to fear, except from the emptiness of London so early in the season. If you know anyone likely to be in that great desert so early in the year, I know that you will be so good as to mention me and my tragedy. . . ."

There is an account of her, during this visit to London, by Mrs. S. C. Hall, herself a writer and wife of Samuel Carter Hall, a well known journalist of the time.* Mrs. Hall was a friend of Mrs. Hofland's, and the encounter took place at the latter's house in Newman Street. "I was certainly disappointed," wrote Mrs. Hall, "when a stout little lady, tightened up in a shawl, rolled into the parlour in Newman Street, and Mrs. Hofland announced her as Miss Mitford; her short petticoats showing wonderfully stout leather boots, her shawl *bundled* on, and a little black coal-scuttle bonnet—when bonnets were expanding—added to the effect of her natural shortness and rotundity; but her manner was that of a cordial country gentlewoman; the pressure of her 'fat' little hands (for she extended both) was warm; her eyes, both soft and bright, looked kindly and frankly into mine; her pretty, rosy mouth dimpled with smiles that were always sweet and friendly. At first, I did not think her at all 'grand or stilted,' though she declared she had been quite spoilt—quite ruined since she came to London, with all the fine compliments she had received; but the trial was yet to come. 'Suppose—suppose *Rienzi* should be——' and she shook her head. Of course, in full chorus we declared that impossible. 'No! she would not spend an evening with us until after the first night; if the play went ill, or even coldly, she would run away and never be again seen or heard of; if it succeeded——' She drew her rotund person to its full height, and endeavoured to stretch her neck, and the expression of her beaming face assumed an air of unmistakable triumph.

* He was supposed to be the original of Pecksniff.

She was always pleasant to look at, and had her face not been cast in so broad—so 'outspread'—a mould, she would have been handsome; even with this disadvantage, if her figure had been tall enough to carry her head with dignity, she would have been so; but she was most vexatiously 'dumpy' . . . but when Miss Mitford spoke, the awkward effect vanished—her pleasant voice, her beaming eyes and smiles, made you forget the wide expanse of face; and the roly-poly figure, when seated, did not appear really short. . . .

"She kept her promise to us, and after *Rienzi's* triumph spent an evening at our house—'the observed of all observers.' She did not, however, appear to advantage that evening; her manner was constrained and even haughty. She got up tragedy looks, which did not harmonize with her naturally playful expression. She seated herself in a high chair, and was indignant at the offer of a footstool, though her feet barely touched the ground; she received those who wished to be introduced to her *en reine*; but such was her popularity just then, that all were gratified. She was most unbecomingly dressed in a striped satin something, neither high nor low, with very short sleeves, for her arms were white and finely formed; she wore a large yellow turban, which added considerably to the size of her head. She had evidently bought the hideous thing *en route* and put it on, in the carriage, as she drove to our house, for pinned at the back was a somewhat large card, on which were written, in somewhat huge letters, these astounding words 'very chaste—only five and threepence.' I had observed several of our party, passing behind the chair, whispering and tittering, and soon ascertained the cause. Under the pretence of settling the turban, I removed the obnoxious notice; and of course she never knew that so many wags had been merry at her cost."*

We find difficulty in crediting this account; not the

* *Book of Memories*, by S. C. Hall, p. 438 ff, 1871.

details of her wardrobe nor the anecdote of the turban (although we think it significant that the writer, knowing Mary Mitford to be miserably poor, should have commented upon them), but the description of her haughty and constrained manner. In the first place, she was singularly modest about her work,* and to imply that the success of *Rienzi* had gone to her head was absurd. She was not a young girl (she was forty) and this was not the first success she had obtained. Then she was a woman of breeding, and many witnesses have testified that her manners were those of a woman of the world, easy and polished, which perhaps was the reason for this feline attack. The Halls, who were Irish, mixed in the dubious—in those days—circles of journalism. They were pretentious snobs and social climbers; and it is possible that Mary Mitford, unintentionally, gave them a feeling of inferiority, for she possessed in her natural good manners what they would have given much to achieve.

Rienzi set the seal on its author's reputation. Not only did it earn her a large sum of money, having by December 16th passed its twentieth night, but it was loudly acclaimed by both the public and the press. The critics, indeed, endorsed Macready's opinion that it was a "wonderful tragedy," and George Daniel, editor of Cumberland's British Theatre wrote: "In a drama founded on history, some allowance may be made for a departure from facts, when the interest of the scene demands it. Shakespeare never has recourse to invention when history is sufficient for his purpose: but, when its details prove tedious and unimportant, he augments or diminishes at his pleasure; still keeping in view the leading incident, and preserving, as regards fable and character, the truth and spirit of his original. Miss Mitford has done no more than this: and, had she done less, her tragedy had been deficient in interest and effect. The female characters are entirely her own: the

* In a letter to Sir W. E., 26th Dec., 1825, she says "I am at present over rated."

wiley imperious Lady Colonna, the delicate impassioned Claudia. The latter conception is eminently beautiful, and in perfect harmony with the elegant mind from whom it emanated. . . . If, in the character of Rienzi, Miss Mitford has shown that she can write with masculine energy, let Claudia bear witness that her wonted dominion over the heart is still in full force."*

No doubt she was gratified by her success, and no doubt, for a short period, she had some relief from her many worries, for in addition to the money accruing from the theatre, the tragedy was published and had sold eight thousand copies by December.† But as she had probably sold the copyright, these large sales would not have benefited her. In addition, the play was popular in the United States, for she told Sir William that "*Rienzi* has been received rapturously all over America."‡ But here again, she would not benefit, for there was no law of foreign copyright in those days, and the works of English authors were pirated all over the North American continent.

* *Remarks on Miss Mitford's Tragedy of Rienzi*, by the Editor of Cumberland's British Theatre, 1828. This pamphlet was issued separately, but was a reprint from the *British Theatre, with Remarks, Biographies, and Criticisms, printed from the acting copies as performed at the Theatres Royal, London.*

† It must have been put into the repertory of the theatre for it was played again in October, 1829.

‡ Mrs. Trollope saw it in New York in 1831.

XIV

1829-1831

Despite these successes, she dared not relax, and soon after the production of *Rienzi* she was working on another tragedy, this time on a German story, *Otto of Wittelsbach*. By her situation, her residence in the country, she never experienced to the full the effects of her success. This was the era of literary lionism when, with the extension of popular education and the consequent demand for " literature " of every kind, writers became so numerous that they formed a class of their own. Their popularity, and the interest they aroused were comparable to the interest shown nowadays in a film star, and the means they adopted to publicise themselves were almost as vulgar. They showed themselves in public places, no party was complete without them and they employed a system of puffing each other in the press and literary journals which ensured that their names were always before the public. Mary Mitford took no part in such proceedings, and her popularity with the public was entirely spontaneous and due to the quality of her work. On the other hand, she never adopted the precious attitude of disdain for popular success, for one of the most pleasant aspects of her character was an aristocratic lack of self-consciousness which made her free from all affectations. It would have been physically impossible, of course, for her to have become a literary lion, for living in the country, she was cut off from all literary society. This, perhaps, was one of the principal causes of her loneliness, for it was an extreme deprivation to be denied all such contacts for long periods at a time: and to be obliged to spend her days among those whose interests differed from her own. It was not that she had a taste for

Bohemian society, but merely that she craved the companionship of her intellectual equals.

It was during her visits to London that she renewed her literary and artistic connections, at the Lambs', the Hoflands', the Kembles', at Haydon's and in the many other circles which she frequented. But although her father was proud of her fame, these contacts were, on occasions, only maintained with difficulty ; for he belonged to a generation which considered men of letters—indeed all those who practised their art in a professional capacity—as little better than adventurers. Something of the tribulation she experienced is expressed in a letter to William Harness on the subject of an actor, Cathcart,* in whom she was interested :

" . . . But—to you—I confess that this measure [going to London on Cathcart's behalf] would be attended with great personal difficulty. My father—very kind to me in many respects, very attentive if I'm ill, very solicitous that my garden should be nicely kept, that I should go out with him, and be amused—is yet, so far as art, literature, and the drama are concerned, of a temper infinitely difficult to deal with. He hates and despises them, and all their professors—looks on them with hatred and scorn ; and is constantly taunting me with my ' friends ' and my ' people ' (as he calls them), reproaching me if I hold the slightest intercourse with author, editor, artist, or actor, and treating with frank contempt every one not of a certain station in the county. I am entirely convinced he would consider Sir Thomas Lawrence, Sir Walter Scott, and Mrs. Siddons as his inferiors. Always this is very painful—strangely painful ; but sometimes, in the case . . . of Mr. Cathcart, it becomes really hard to bear.

* She took a great deal of trouble to help this man (who afterwards played the lead in *Charles I*), so much so that it was rumoured her feelings towards him were something more than those of a friend. This allegation is absurd. He was several years her junior, and in addition had a wife, or mistress, and several children, of whom she was fully aware. The correspondence in the John Rylands Library proves that she was actuated solely by kindness and generosity and pity for his dependants.

"Since I have known Mr. C. I can say with truth that he has never spoken to me or looked at me without ill-humour; sometimes taunting and scornful—sometimes more harsh than you could fancy. Now, he ought to remember that it is not for my own pleasure, but from a sense of duty, that I have been thrown in the way of these persons; and he should allow for the natural sympathy of similar pursuits and the natural wish to do the little that one so poor and powerless can do to bring merit . . . into notice. It is one of the few alleviations of a destiny that is wearing down my health and mind and spirits and strength —a life spent in efforts above my powers, and which will end in the workhouse or in a Bedlam, as the body or the mind shall sink first. He ought to feel this; but he does not.

"I beg your pardon for vexing you with this detail. I do not often indulge in such repining. But I meant to say that it will be a scene and an effort to get to town for this purpose. Nevertheless, *if you think I could do good I would most assuredly go.*"

She could, of course, have very well retorted that if she mixed with those whom he so much despised, it was because his reckless improvidence had forced her into their company: and it was probably only because he knew she would never do so that he dared to behave so outrageously. But we think that something more than mere snobbery actuated him. He was, by nature, a very possessive man; and once before, in an earlier letter, there is a reference to his jealousy of one of her women friends. In his egotistical vanity, he was not prepared to allow someone to loom so large in her life that attention was distracted from himself. If he had paused to think, he would have realized that she had given ample proofs of her devotion and sense of duty: but never in his long life had he indulged in ratiocination, for he was a mental adolescent, actuated by instinct rather than any process of rational thought. Nevertheless despite all these impediments, she could not escape entirely from the consequences of her fame; and at the end of 1828 a young artist, John Lucas, desired to paint her portrait.* He was at the beginning of his career, and it was thought that if he exhibited her portrait, it would attract attention and add to his reputation. She was a little alarmed lest this demand should offend Haydon, who had painted her previous portrait, and she wrote him a tactful letter on the subject. He, however, eventually raised no objections, and by the beginning of 1829 the portrait was finished. She told Sir William: "I never saw a more ladylike picture. . . . The face is thoughtful and placid, with the eyes looking away—a peculiarity which, they say, belongs to my expression."† Apart from the fact that she was dressed in the fashionable garb of a society woman, the picture seems to have been a good likeness. It is certainly pleasing to look at, and belies her oft repeated assertion that she was ugly.

While she was living quietly in the country, rumour had been busy with her name. On 3rd March her friend Mrs. Hofland wrote to Mrs. S. C. Hall with the news that she had been married to Bertram Mitford of Mitford, and had gone with him to Northumberland. This happy event, continued Mrs. Hofland, was a profound secret, "for what reason I do not know, but I conjecture that it may not interfere with the arrangements respecting her forthcoming tragedy." Then this enthusiastic matchmaker's imagination ran riot. Bertram Mitford had been attached to his kinswoman in youth, but could not then marry: now all difficulties were removed. "They are perfectly suited in age. He is a man of great ability and proud of her fame, so that there is every prospect of happiness." For a month rumours and counter rumours continued to circulate in Newman Street, and then Mrs. Hofland, unable to bear the

* It was Mr. Milton, Mrs. Trollope's brother, who introduced Lucas.

† Mrs. Hofland says of this picture "The figure is well managed, but the hat badly fixed; the likeness is unquestionably well preserved, and very agreeably given. . . ."

suspense any longer, wrote to Three Mile Cross and demanded "Are you married or are you not?" The astonished Mary Mitford replied: "Even at the certainty of not getting a frank, I must write to you, to put an end to this extraordinary mistake. It is perfectly true that my cousin Bertram Mitford, the head of the house, is married to another cousin of his and mine, Miss Frances Mitford, grand-daughter of Colonel Mitford, who wrote the *History of Greece*—and grand-niece to Lord Redesdale. It was a long engagement; everybody began to think it would never take place. He is a very pleasant Northumberland squire, not the least literary—the bride I have never seen, but she is well spoken of by everybody, and I have no doubt it will be a most happy and suitable marriage. . . . In real truth, my dear friend, it is most certain that I shall never marry; at my age it would be most foolish, even if any one were simple enough to desire so old and ugly a wife. . . . At present I have had my hands quite full without any such folly." Then she added that she had been ill, that her mother was suffering from asthma, "My father, too, has had the rheumatism—one horse is lame, and one of my dearest friends in the neighbourhood is dying; so that nothing on earth can be less like the gay bride that I have been thought. . . ."

It is probably due to all these illnesses that there is not much reference to her literary activities in the correspondence of 1829; but she was, as usual, writing for the magazines and was still working on her German play, *Otto of Wittelsbach*, about which she was not enthusiastic, being sure that Young would be incapable of playing the principal part. In September, William Harness came to stay at the cottage. It is not easy to deduce her real feelings towards this friend of her childhood. Her letters to him were always couched in warm terms, and there is no doubt that she showed, if she did not always feel, considerable respect for his judgment and opinions. But with an old friend, it is quite possible to entertain feelings of affection while yet being aware of certain flaws of character; and between herself and the clergyman there were deep grounds of dissension. In the first place, Harness hated Dr. Mitford and could not sympathize with her attitude of tolerance towards her father. He referred, in his letters, to the Doctor as a "hypocrite" and a "humbug," both of which terms were singularly inapplicable, for if anyone was blatantly egotistical, that man was George Mitford. As Harness was trustee for Mrs. Mitford's money, it can well be imagined that when financial matters were discussed, there was considerable constraint between them. Then again they were not in sympathy over their religious views. Harness was a rigid believer in dogma and ritual, and would not allow any deviation from the doctrines of the Church of England. She, on the other hand, showed a tolerance in her beliefs which could not but have dismayed him, and which she had expressed to him in a letter written during the early part of that year. "There would be a tacit hypocrisy, a moral cowardice, if I were to stop here [on her comments on a book of his sermons] and not to confess, what I think you must suspect, although by no chance do I ever talk about it—that I do not, or rather cannot, believe all that the Church requires. I humbly hope that it is not necessary to do so, and that a devout sense of the mercy of God, and an endeavour however imperfectly and feebly, to obey the great precepts of justice and kindness, may be accepted in lieu of that entire faith which, in me, *will not* be commanded. You will not suspect me of thoughtlessness in this matter; neither, I trust, does it spring from intellectual pride. Few persons have a deeper sense of their own weakness; few, indeed, can have so much weakness of character to deplore and to strive against. Do not answer this part of my letter. It has cost me a strong effort to say this to you; but it would have been a concealment amounting to a falsity if I had not, and falsehood must be wrong. Do not notice it; a correspondence of controversy could only end in alienation. . . . Do not notice what I have said, and yet write soon. There is no cause why you should not. I occasion no scandal either by opinions or by conduct. . . ."

This confession is interesting for several reasons. In the first place it is the only occasion, so far as we have been able to ascertain, on which Mary Mitford refers to the opinions which she held for the greater part of her life. The Mitfords were not, indeed, a religious family in the sense that they considered the subject suitable for comment in conversation or letters; and Harness remarks on the fact that in none of Mrs. Mitford's letters to her schoolgirl daughter is the question of spiritual beliefs ever mentioned. They must have attended, as was customary, church on Sunday, although references to such attendances in the correspondence are rare: nor is the diary more revealing, for although Mary Mitford noted the names of her visitors and the literary work she carried out on the Sabbath, she never once recorded a visit to church. Nevertheless, as this letter proves, she was not an irreligious woman, and her want of faith was in the tenets of one particular sect and was not a total lack of spiritual belief. Again, her letter shows that she was not in the habit of discussing those subjects which touched her most deeply. Few complaints about her father's conduct ever escaped her—"I do not often indulge in such repining"; and she kept silent about her religious doubts—"by no chance do I ever talk about it." Such an attitude was inherent in her, by taste and by breeding; and her silence was not due, as has been suggested, to unawareness of the objects of contention, but to an inborn dislike of discussing them. There is no doubt that Harness was profoundly disturbed by her confession. It is not practicable for a minister of religion to tolerate disbelief in the doctrines of his church, for that would imply a lack of faith on his own part. Therefore he reverted to the subject again ; and he had the satisfaction of knowing that Mary Mitford, before she died, acknowledged herself to be a member of the Church of England, although one of the reasons she gave was so typical of her own tolerant outlook, that it can scarcely have afforded him much consolation.

Towards the end of 1829, she was interesting herself in astrology, and had her horoscope cast ; and then an event occurred which drove all other matters from her mind. Her mother whom, she had told Harness, "few things touch now," had a paralytic stroke on the day after Christmas. For a week she lingered in the valley of the shadow and then, at nine o'clock on the morning of January 2nd, 1830, she died as she had lived, gently and unostentatiously, in the presence of her husband and child. Her grief-stricken daughter gathered chrysanthemums and other flowers which, with a sprig of rosemary, she placed in the coffin. Mrs. Mitford was buried in Shinfield Church on January 8th. Many persons, friends, neighbours and village folk were present at the service, which was conducted by the Rector, Mathew Fielde ; and her pall-bearers were farmers and local tradesmen. During her last brief illness, the consummation of the decay which had been creeping on for the past few years, she was devotedly nursed by her husband and daughter, and Mary Mitford has left a touching account of her mother's last illness, which, however, is too long to quote here. But at the moment of death she "looked sweet, and calm and peaceful ; there was even a smile on her dear face"—a fitting passing for one who had never harmed a living soul and who, within her limited circle, had set an example of courage, unselfishness and loyalty.

It was perhaps as well that, at this time of sorrow, Mary Mitford had much to do, and that she had little leisure in which to grieve over her loss. She was now alone with her father, and lacked even the gentle support of Mrs. Mitford in any measures she might take to combat his recklessness and extravagance. Her life was indeed hard and wretched, and with the exception of brief intervals of relaxation, was to become more so as the years passed. Even at this period of grief, she still had to earn the money for the household expenses, and for her mother's illness and funeral; and at the end of January, she sold a fourth volume of *Our Village* to Whittaker for £150. She was also approached to edit two volumes of American stories for a fee of £200. The details of this transaction are obscure, but she was visited at Three Mile Cross by a man "a deaf and disagreeable scarecrow" who, it would appear, was prepared to pay her and to make suitable arrangements with a publisher; but unexpected difficulties intervened and a few weeks later she thought the matter might fall through, after she had done the not inconsiderable work of editing and selecting the material. However, as usual when in distress she consulted Talfourd, who intervened effectively on her behalf, and the book was eventually published that year under the title of *Stories of American Life by American Writers*. Thus the output of work was maintained despite the tribulations and anxieties to which she was subjected. But her health, never very robust, began to decline. That winter, she suffered from bronchial trouble, and she complained of a cough which "nothing silences but opium —a remedy which, whilst it pacifies the nights, stupefies the days." It has been stated that, as her health deteriorated and her anxieties multiplied, she resorted to opium as a perpetual stimulus,* but we can find no evidence to support this statement. In those days laudanum was frequently and freely used to alleviate pain, and its sale was not controlled. That she resorted to it in times of illness, we do not doubt; but that she became a permanent addict, who could only carry on her work by means of the drug, we find hard to believe.

She had now reached that stage of her career when her

* *Biographical Sketches*, Harriet Martineau, p. 386, 1885.

work was not only popular and in great demand in England, but also in America—a position which she was certainly one of the first women to attain. Besides the success of *Rienzi*, which had been played all over the United States, *Our Village* was also well known and appreciated. As a result, she began to make American friends. In her youth she had once boldly asserted "I never saw an American gentleman in my life," but with the riper wisdom of maturer years, she changed her mind. "Depend on it," she told Haydon, "that America will succeed us as Rome did Athens; and it is a comfort to think that by their speaking the same beautiful language, Shakespeare and Milton will not be buried in the dust of a scholar's library, but will live and breathe in after ages as they do now to us." One of her early American acquaintances was Catherine Sedgwick, the novelist, who wrote to her in June, 1830, and sent her a copy of her latest work. Mary Mitford was much gratified by the attention, and replied: ". . . I should have written instantly to thank you for your most kind and flattering letter, had I not waited for *Clarence*, the valuable present which you announced to me. It has not yet arrived, but I will no longer delay expressing my strong feelings of obligation to the writer, since having read *Redwood* and the *New England Tale*, I know how much pleasure I shall derive from the later production, which is no doubt waiting at some London bookseller's till they shall send a parcel to Reading. . . ." Miss Sedgwick's young niece Kate had written a postscript to her aunt's letter eagerly demanding information about the various characters in *Our Village*. This was rather a precocious effusion, and despite her aunt's assertion that it was "neither dictated nor retouched by an older hand," we find difficulty in crediting a small girl with such a vocabulary and such a knowledge of punctuation. However, Mary Mitford, whatever she may have thought, replied amiably to her youthful correspondent:

"My dear young Friend,

I am very much obliged to you for your kind inquiries respecting the people in my book. It is much to be asked about by a little lady on the other side of the Atlantic, and we are very proud of it accordingly. May was a real greyhound, and everything told of her was literally true; but alas! she is no more; she died in the hard frost of last winter. Lizzy was also true, and is also dead. Harriet and Joel are not married yet; you shall have the very latest intelligence of her: I am expecting two or three friends to dinner, and she is making an apple tart and custards—which I wish, with all my heart, that you and your dear aunt were coming to partake of. The rest of the people are doing well in their several ways, and I am always, my dear little girl,

Most sincerely yours,
M. R. Mitford."

In December of 1830, *Inez de Castro* seems to have been in rehearsal at Covent Garden, with Fanny Kemble in the principal female role. "I have never seen Fanny Kemble act," she told a friend, "but I am well acquainted with her off the stage, and know her to be a girl of great ability. The difference of age makes it singular, that she in Paris and I in London, should have been educated by the same lady."* *Inez*, however, was destined not to be performed, for although it was twice in rehearsal, for some reason or other Fanny Kemble was not able to play the principal part.† Theatrical matters, however, continued to engross her attention. In March, 1831, she wrote to the Duke of Devonshire, now Lord Chamberlain, in an attempt to obtain the lifting of the ban on *Charles I.* Notwithstanding her plea that it was free from any political allusions, the

* Fanny Rowden, who started a school in Paris, and afterwards became the second wife of the Count de St. Quintin.

† Possibly the Kembles' departure for America in 1832 had something to do with its postponement.

Duke felt unable to reverse the decision of his predecessor. He paid her the compliment, however, of asking for a copy of the play to add to his collection of dramatic manuscripts. At the end of that year she was writing an opera *Sadak and Kalasrade* in conjunction with a young musician, Charles Parker.*

Her position was now so well established that there were frequent laudatory references to her in the press; and if she had been less modest about her achievements or more preoccupied with self, she might well have become exalted through excessive adulation. But it was one of the most pleasing facets of her character that she never valued her work at its true worth; and while she took a natural, but modest, pride in her achievements, her success never ceased to astonish her. On the other hand, she was not indifferent to complimentary references, for she knew their value as regards the sales of her books. She must, therefore, have derived considerable satisfaction from an article which appeared that year in *Fraser's Magazine*.† It was written by William Maginn, one of the most brilliant journalists of the day, and was one in a series of pen portraits of literary figures, illustrated by Maclise, which was appearing in the magazine at that time.

"In our village," wrote Maginn, "we have an authoress, too, and her name is Mary Mitford. Now, let nobody suppose that Mary, on account of the pretty alliteration of her name, is one of the fine romantic young ladies who grace pastorals in prose or verse. On the contrary, our Mary is a good-humoured spinster of a certain age, considerably inclined, we do not know whether with her own consent or not, to *embonpoint*, and the very reverse of the picturesque. There are, however, few girls in our village, or twenty villages beyond it, that can dress up so pretty a basket of good-looking and sweet-smelling natural flowers, all of the true English soil, not foreign and

* Then a "master at the Royal Musical Academy, London."

† May, 1831.

THE AUTHOR OF "OUR VILLAGE".

Reproduced from the drawing by Maclise in *Fraser's Magazine*, May, 1831.

flaunting like the flaming dahlias that one class of bouquet-gatherers thrust under our noses with so much pretence, nor smelling of turf and whiskey like the strong-scented bob-lilies which are offered to us by the basket-women of the provinces ; nor yet at all resembling the faded imitation roses picked up in second-hand saloons, and vended as genuine posies of quality by draggletail damsels, who endeavour to pass themselves off as ladies' maids, generally without character. And Mary's basket is arranged in so neat, so nice, so trim, so comely, or, to say all in one word, so very English a manner, that it is a perfect pleasure to see her hopping with it to market. We say nothing as to the way she applies the profits of her business, though, if we did, it would redound to her praise and honour, because, in these our sketches, we have always looked at the subject before us only as it comes before the public.

"We are afraid, however, that if we attempt to write any longer in this style, our prattle will be voted tedious ; our imitations must partake of the vice of the original, and the only defect in Miss Mitford's own style of writing is its mannerism. . . . Dropping all metaphor, then, we have only to remark, that it is impossible that any thing can be cleverer or racier than Miss Mitford's sketches, and if she has not made so much noise in the literary world as other ladies far more slenderly qualified, why, the battle is not always to the strong, nor the race to the swift ; and, moreover, a lady who does not write politics or *double entendre*, or make herself a lioness, or enlist with the honourable corps of the puff-mongers, throws away a great many chances of renown, which are eagerly caught at by less scrupulous adventuresses.

". . . Miss Mitford, in the plate, is attended, not by Eros, but rather Anteros ; not by love's god, but by a printer's devil, to whom she is delivering copy, as they perversely call our original MS., for some of the thousand annuals, perhaps, which she ornaments. As one of the same diabolic breed is at our own elbow, we must finish our page by our wish that,

> Still may her picture, when she's pleased to sit for't
> Show her the same good-humoured Mary Mitford."

XV

1832-1835

The year 1832 opened with the fifth, and last volume of *Our Village* going through the press. "For ten long weary years, for five tedious volumes," she wrote in the Introduction, "has that most multifarious, and most kind personage, the public, endured to hear the history, half real, and half imaginary, of a half imaginary and half real little spot on the sunny side of Berkshire; but all mortal things have an end, and so must my country stories." Unfortunately she had miscalculated the amount of copy required to fill the volume, and was forced to work feverishly to keep pace with the printer. "You cannot conceive," she told a friend, "the miserable drudgery it is, to pass one's time in writing gay prose whilst in such bad spirits." This final volume, the longest in the series, shows unmistakable signs of the weariness and lassitude under which she was labouring. It contains several charades which, though entertaining, are out of place in such a volume; and some of the characterisations lack the naturalness and spontaneity of those in the earlier volumes. There are, however, two capital stories, *The Freshwater Fisherman* and *The Fisherman in his Married State*.

That year there appears to have been some question of the production of her opera; but with the uncertainty which pertained to all matters theatrical, its performance was postponed. This delay caused her great financial inconvenience, and at the end of September, Dr. Mitford went to London to collect moneys due from the magazines and journals. These amounted to nearly £70, and she asked him whether this sum, with the dividend from the trust fund, would be sufficient to last until Christmas. If not he must obtain an advance from his friend, the invaluable George Robins. Her financial situation, however, must have been alleviated a few weeks later, for the first edition of the fifth volume of *Our Village*, which had been recently published, had sold out in a day, and in October the third edition was going through the press. In addition, during this year, a further three volumes of American tales *Lights and Shadows of American Life* were published. But although she was overwhelmed with work for the theatre and the magazines, her health had so far deteriorated that she felt unable to carry it out. There was the first reference that autumn, to the gastric complaint from which she suffered for the remainder of her life, and which was brought on by worry, overwork and anxiety. She was also much bothered by the many visitors who came to the cottage. " Every idle person who comes within twenty miles gets a letter of introduction," she told Harness, " . . . and comes to see my geraniums or myself—Heaven knows which! I have had seven carriages at once at the door of our little cottage; and this sort of *levée*—bad enough in health—is terrible when one is not well. Mr. Milman, who has established for himself a character for inaccessibility, is a wise person. I wish I could do the same; and I would have done so had I ever thought it possible that the mere fact of being a writer of books would have brought such a torment in its train." She would have gone to London to be quiet, she added, but that her father " would lose much of happiness in relinquishing his country habits; and he must always be my first object." Even at this stage, however, she could have terminated her material troubles by accepting the offer of a home from a rich relative in Hampshire; but here again her father was the obstacle. She could not ask him to leave his friends or to abandon his position as a magistrate to which he attached so much importance. " Besides," she commented, " *he* would have felt himself dependent, though I should not." He did not, of course, object to dependence on her, whom he knew would never thwart him; but he would never consent to be under an obligation to someone who, paying the piper, might call the tune. The selfishness of this man, unpleasant in youth, becomes horrible and revolting in old age when there is nothing to divert the eye and the senses from its unlovely manifestations. And she, with her broken health, her grim struggle for existence, was paying the terrible price which is inexorably exacted for weakness.

In the spring of the following year, her health improved slightly, and she wrote that she was "better, but not well." She was much bothered, however, on the question of a novel which her friends and publishers were pressing her to write. She dreaded the task, knowing instinctively that her talents were not suited to it. She only wrote one full-length novel in her life, *Atherton*, and such was her distaste for the work that although the plot was conceived in 1825, the book was not published until 1854. Although it had much success, it was, in comparison with her other books, a very inferior piece of work. That year she made an acquaintance who was to have an important influence on her life. One day, probably in October, a parcel arrived at the cottage containing a little book entitled *The Rhymed Plea for Tolerance*. On the title page was a short inscription expressing the pleasure which the author had derived from her "tolerant and humanizing pen." Not unnaturally, she was pleased at the compliment, and a correspondence ensued. The donor of the book was John Kenyon,* a wealthy dilettante in the arts, the friend and correspondent of Wordsworth and other literary men; and, what was more important, a distant relative of Elizabeth Barrett's. It was through him that a meeting took place between the two women. Kenyon belonged to that class of persons

* Two interesting articles on Kenyon appeared in the *Temple Bar Magazine* in April, 1890 and May 1892.

which to-day is nearly extinct. He was a rich man who could afford to indulge his taste for literature and literary society, and Crabb Robinson recorded that "he delights in seeing at his hospitable table every variety of literary notabilities, and therefore he has been called 'the feeder of lions'," and added, "He is more bent on making the happy happier, than in making the unhappy less unhappy—a distinction I do not remember to have seen noticed."* When the first meeting between Kenyon and Mary Mitford took place is not known; but the acquaintance soon ripened into a warm friendship, and she became intimate with both him and his wife.

Although she made a new friend, she unfortunately quarrelled with an old one. One of her neighbours was a Mr. Merry, who, some time in October of that year, conducted himself badly towards Talfourd, then her guest. At an unexpected meeting between Mary Mitford and Mr. Merry at Bearwood, the home of John Walter, proprietor of *The Times*, she lost her temper. "I resented the thing, certainly with too much violence," she told Harness, ". . . Mrs. Walter having, with the kindest meaning, but very injudiciously brought us together in the very moment of anger and without warning." Although she immediately regained her self-control and made an unqualified apology, Mr. Merry would not be placated. For six weeks he kept up the quarrel and spread the story all over the neighbourhood, while she, characteristically, kept silent. But although she confided to Harness that "the friend who rejects an immediate and ample apology, and perseveres for six weeks in the bitterest enmity, is not worth any deep regret," she evidently repented of her conduct, for she wrote to Mr. Merry: "I cannot suffer you to leave our neighbourhood for weeks . . . without making one more effort to soften a displeasure too justly excited—without once more acknowledging my fault, and entreating your forgiveness.

* Diary of H. C. R., Vol. II, p. 360, ed. Sadler, 1872.

Do not again repulse me—pray do not! Life is too short, and too full of calamity, for an alienation indefinitely prolonged—a pardon so long suspended. I know you better, perhaps, than you know yourself, and am sure that, were I at this moment suffering under any great affliction, you would be the first—ay, the very first—to soothe and succour me. If my father (which may God in his mercy avert!) were dead; if I myself were on a sick bed, or in prison, or in a workhouse (and you well know that this is the destiny to which I always look forward), then you would come to me—I am sure of it. You would be as ready to fly to my assistance then as the angel of peace and mercy at your side. But do not wait for that moment; do not, for an error which has been sincerely and severely repented, deprive a melancholy and a most anxious existence of one of its few consolations. Lonely and desolate as I am—with no one belonging to me in the world except my dear father—poor in every sense, earning with pain and difficulty a livelihood which every day makes more precarious, I cannot afford the loss of your sympathy. I say this without fear of misconstruction. You will understand that what I regret is the friendship and intimacy, the every-day intercourse of mind and of heart, on which even you yourself—so much more happily placed—did yet set some value. You did like me once; try me again. You will find me—at least I hope so—all the better for the rigorous discipline which my mind has lately undergone; the salutary and unwonted course of self-examination and self-abasement.

"At all events, do not go without a few words of peace and kindness. I send you the last flowers of my garden. Your flower seems to have continued in blossom on purpose to assist in the work of reconciliation. Do not scorn its sweet breath, or resist its mute pleadings, but give me in exchange one bunch of the laurustinus for which I used to ask you last winter, and let it be a token of the full and perfect reconciliation for which I am a suppliant; and then I shall cherish it—oh, I cannot tell you how much!

Once again, forgive me—and farewell,
M. R. Mitford."

The forgiveness she solicited was granted, for few could have resisted such an appeal. This is surely one of the most gracious apologies in the language, and it proves that when sincerely convinced of her error, no false pride prevented her from acknowledging it.

Although we have not much evidence at this period of Dr. Mitford's activities, there is no doubt that his extravagances were the sole cause of her anxieties; and she must have lived in a perpetual state of suspense, never knowing when the results of some irresponsible action would tax her slender resources to the uttermost. It must have been something of this nature which caused her to write, on Christmas Eve, 1833, to Harness:

"My dear Friend,

I write in great haste, just to caution you in case you should receive any authority, or pretended authority, from any quarter, to sell out our money in the funds, not to do so without communicating with me. I have no doubt of my father's integrity, but I think him likely to be imposed upon.

The post is at the door. With every good wish of this season and of all seasons,

Yours ever,
M. R. Mitford."

Harness, however, needed no prompting from her to withhold his sanction. "Depend upon it," he wrote, "the money shall *never* be touched with my consent. It was consideration for your future welfare which prevented my father's consenting to its being sold out some years ago, when you had been persuaded, and wished to persuade him to your own utter ruin." This sum, he said, must be considered as a sheet anchor of her independence in old age, and after her father's death, he would take steps to have it invested profitably. "Till then," he continued, "from whatever quarter the proposition may come—I have but one black, blank unqualified *No* for my answer. I do not doubt Dr. Mitford's integrity, but I have not the slightest confidence in his prudence; and I am fully satisfied that, if these three thousand and odd hundreds of pounds were placed at his disposal *to-day*, they would fly the way so many other thousands have gone before them, *to-morrow*. Excuse me saying this; but I cannot help it."

This plain speaking, however, in no way impaired their friendship, though it must have emphasized to her their divergence of opinion. But she was sufficiently tolerant to agree to differ, and so far as he was concerned, being of a narrow and less liberal outlook, he was sustained by the conscious rectitude of his views and the necessity for emphasizing them on every occasion. Although she did not object to the expression of his opinions, she maintained the right to state her own; and early in the following year, she commented freely on one of his sermons dealing with the establishment of the Church. She believed in the establishment, but she thought the Church should be wisely tolerant. "Generally speaking, moreover, I think the Church of England is *tolerant*—incomparably more so than the sects that assail her—and, therefore, if for no other reason, ought to be protected." Although a nominal Whig, she was, at heart and by conviction, a traditionalist: she believed that the institutions of a country were evolved as the result of the collective experience of mankind, and should not therefore be lightly cast aside or exchanged for the untried systems and rhetorical speculations of the theorist. She believed in reform and amendment, but not in radical changes lest the last state should be worse than the first.

In May of 1834, owing to pressing pecuniary difficulties, Dr. Mitford visited London in an attempt to sell the copyright of her play *Charles I*, or to procure its representation. He obtained an introduction to Mr. Abbott, manager of the Victoria Theatre which, being on the Surrey side of the river, did not come within the jurisdiction of the Lord Chamberlain. Abbott immediately accepted the play, and offered liberal terms—£200 to be paid at once and a fourth share of the profits for a specified number of nights. Unfortunately there was the usual delay: the negotiations were protracted until June and it was not till the end of that month that Mary Mitford went to London to supervise the rehearsals. She stayed at 35, Norfolk Street, Strand, and spent four to six hours each morning in the theatre, coaching the actors in their parts. The play had a large cast and its production must have taxed the resources of a minor theatre to the utmost. Abbott played Charles while the part of Cromwell was taken by Cathcart, the young actor in whose welfare she had interested herself and about whom Dr. Mitford had been so absurdly jealous.

It is pleasant to be able to record that the tragedy was a success, and had a good press, despite the fact that Macready, who visited the theatre on July 12th, recorded in his diary: "The play is wretchedly constructed, with some powerful scenes, many passages of power and considerable effect in the sketch of Cromwell's character, which, deserving first-rate support, was consigned to the murderous hands of Mr. Cathcart—a very poor pretender indeed. There was so little plot in it that I could not remember the order of the scenes."* There is so much of personal rancour and professional jealousy in this entry (Macready rarely praised any of his fellow players) that, in view of the tragedy's success, it can be dismissed as serious criticism. Except when his own personal prejudices were involved, however, Macready was an excellent critic; and there is no doubt

* *Diaries of Macready*, Vol. I, p. 164, 1912.

that his conscientious work as an artist, and his very considerable talents, did much to maintain the great traditions of English drama.

This visit to London, with its concomitant entertainments and work in the theatre, put a great strain on Mary Mitford's already overtaxed strength, and she had several fainting attacks which warned her that she must return quickly to the country " to write another play, and run again the same round of fatigue, excitement and pleasure." Indeed a stronger woman than herself might well have collapsed under the strain, for sixty or seventy visitors called daily upon her, and she attended numerous parties. It was on this occasion that she met the American writer Nathaniel Parker Willis—" a very elegant young man "—and Harriet Martineau " who is cheerful, frank, cordial and right minded in a very high degree." The latter, however, did not reciprocate these sentiments. " I must say that personally I did not like her so well as I liked her works," wrote that austere lady. " The charming *bonhomie* of her writings appeared at first in her conversation and manners ; but there were other things which presently sadly impaired its charm. It is no part of my business to pass judgment on her views and modes of life. What concerned me was her habit of flattery, and the twin habit of disparagement of others. I never knew her respond to any act or course of conduct which was morally lofty. She could not believe in it, nor, of course enjoy it. . . ."* It is not difficult to believe that fundamentally these two women had little in common, although Mary Mitford always harboured pleasant thoughts about the writer—if not the works—of these caustic comments ; indeed when Harriet Martineau went to America, she gave her an introduction to the Sedgwick family. But she was a traditionalist in outlook, and for the " morally lofty " schemes of regeneration of the human race through the

* *Autobiography of H. Martineau*, Vol. 1, p. 419, 1877.

The Cottage at Three Mile Cross, circa 1836
from a lithograph from a sketch by E. *Havell.*

The Cottage at Three Mile Cross, circa 1896. *This is how it must have appeared after the structural alterations in* 1837.

The Cottage at Swallowfield.

advancement of scientific knowledge, Harriet Martineau's pet theory, she may have expressed a certain scepticism. And we, who live in the shadow of the atomic bomb, can scarcely gainsay her; but no doubt to the didactic reformer of Fludyer Street she must have appeared a worldly woman, lacking in ideals.

On her return to Three Mile Cross she must have concentrated on *Belford Regis*, the sale of which Dr. Mitford negotiated with Richard Bentley some time during the autumn. He made, however, such a "wretched bargain," that she sent him back to have it amended. He also seems to have been in contact with other publishers at this time, probably over her *Tales for Young People* which appeared in 1835. On neither of these occasions did he act with his usual astuteness, for she wrote angrily to Talfourd that she was "determined never again to trust my father with any matter of business."* The final negotiations with Bentley took place in February, 1835, and the book appeared in the spring of that year. There is little reference in her correspondence to this work, except that in the previous August she asked Sir William not to write to her, lest she should be tempted to reply, for she was overwhelmed with business. It is therefore to be presumed that it was written in the autumn of 1834 and finished early in the following year.

Belford Regis, as is *Our Village*, is a collection of sketches and stories with the theme of the country town, Belford Regis (Reading) as the connecting link. Elizabeth Barrett wrote that it "should probably take rank as her best work: it has most power and most character; and is somewhat less uniformly soft and green than Our Village."† She added, however, that the latter was her favourite. The author herself preferred it to all her other prose, although she admitted that it was "too full of carelessnesses and trifling repetitions." The work was intended to be in one volume, but it eventually expanded to three; and it is

* MSS. John Rylands Library, 24th Sept., 1834.

† *Letters of Elizabeth Barrett Browning to R. H. Horne*, Vol. I, p. 149, 1877.

possible that it was written more speedily (for her financial anxieties were acute at this period) and with less attention to detail, than her other books. Nevertheless it contains many excellent characterisations, of which Stephen Lane, the jovial butcher, and Mr. Singleton, the curate of St. Nicholas', are by no means the least admirable; and it provides a vivid picture of life and manners in an English country town at the end of the eighteenth century. Those who seek for realism, that is to say the less endearing aspects of human nature, will look in vain. But those who care for scenes painted by a kindly, tolerant and cultivated artist, will find much that is pleasing in the book. One quality, in comparison with *Our Village*, it lacks—wit. The humour is there, the skill in depicting details which, a hundred and fifty years later, prove so absorbing; but there are none of those incisive, rapier-like thrusts, those faint touches of satire which give to *Our Village*, despite the rural background, its polish and worldliness. She was sad at this period, and her vitality was low; wit does not flourish in such circumstances.

Nevertheless *Belford Regis* abounds in vivid and vital portraits of men and women which, in their familiarity with their modern counterparts, emphasize the immutability of human nature. Who, for instance, has not met Mrs. Hollis, that repository of local knowledge, whose fruiterer's shop, with its plate glass windows, was such a conspicuous feature of the Butts over a hundred years ago? "There was not a bolder talker in all Belford than Mrs. Hollis, who saw in the course of the day people of all ranks, from my lord in his coronet carriage, to the little boys who came for ha'porths or penn'orths of inferior fruits . . . from the county member's wife to the milk-woman's daughter, everybody dealt with Mrs. Hollis, and with all of them did Mrs. Hollis chat with a mixture of good humour and good spirits, of perfect ease and perfect respectfulness, which made her one of the most popular personages in the town.

As a gossip she was incomparable. She knew everybody and everything, and everything about everybody; had always the freshest intelligence and the newest news; her reports, like her plums, had the bloom on them, and she would as much have scorned to palm upon you an old piece of scandal as to send you strawberries that had been two days gathered. Moreover, considering the vast quantity of chit-chat of which she was the channel (for it was computed that the whole gossip of Belford passed through her shop once in four-and-twenty hours, like the blood through the heart), it was really astonishing how authentic on the whole her intelligence was; mistakes and mis-statements of course there were, and a plentiful quantity of exaggeration; but of actual falsehood there was comparatively little, and of truth, or of what approached to truth, positively much. If one told a piece of news out of Mrs. Hollis's shop, it was almost an even wager that it was substantially correct. And of what other gossip-shop can one make a similar declaration?" That type of shop keeper, despite the omnipotence of the chain store, exists to-day, and there can be few people who, having entered the modern equivalent to Mrs. Hollis's emporium, have not emerged wiser (but not sadder, for local gossip is so stimulating!) for the visit. The book received a good press, and the *Athenæum* gave it two notices, the second of which appeared in the issue of May 16th. "We acknowledged in our former brief notice, that we liked these volumes well," wrote the reviewer, "for the matter they contain and the mind they display. Both are thoroughly English—in the best sense of the word. If (to be hypercritical) the pictures they contain be a trifle too sunny and too cheerful to be real . . . we love them none the less, and their authoress the more. Her style, too, leaves little to be desired; she has read, and recurs to our sterling true-hearted old authors, with an intelligent delight which does her honour. . . ."

In the spring of that year, George Baxter, the famous colour printer, came down to take views of Three Mile Cross for a special edition of *Our Village*,* and in April, her opera *Sadak and Kalasrade* was performed at the Lyceum. This was her first theatrical failure. The opera was played only once, and Henry Chorley, the music critic of the *Athenæum* states : " Wretchedly played and sung as it was, it hardly deserved a better fate. . . . The music, by a now forgotten pupil of our Academy of Music, was heavy and valueless, and the dramatist, though graceful and fresh as a lyrist, had not the instinct, or had not mastered the secret of writing for music."† Although Chorley was not a great critic, on this occasion his judgment seems to have been correct. The opera was played only once, and apart from a brief mention of it in the preface to her *Dramatic Works*, it seems to have sunk quickly into oblivion.

At this period, there are frequent references in her letters to her garden and plants. Her love of flowers was so well known that ardent gardeners frequently called new specimens after her, and there were several species of geranium which bore the name *Miss Mitford* and also a new dahlia, of which she had been sent a cutting. Many of these horticultural details were confided to her friend Emily Jephson, who lived mostly in Ireland and had been brought up by the Edgeworth family, and who—since a good correspondent chooses his subject to suit the taste of the recipient—must also have been a keen gardener. " I send you, my dearest Emily," she wrote in September, " the four white œnotheras, the blue pea, the *Salpiglossis picta*, the white Clarkia, a new lupine, the most beautiful I have ever seen, similar to the *Lupinus mutabilis*, in kind and fragrance, but a clear lilac and clear white, and of far larger spikes of flowers (I enclose a flower), a new annual chrysan-

* This is a very rare edition, and there is not a copy in the British Museum. The woodcuts reproduced in this volume are from the copy in the Reading Public Library, and are views taken on the spot while Baxter was staying at the cottage at Three Mile Cross.

† *Letters of M. R. M.*, 2nd Series, pp. 8, 9, 1872.

themum (Cape marigold) with yellow outer leaves, and two little packets of seeds from Madeira, sent me by a gentleman whom I have never either seen or even heard of till now, but who, having been ordered there for his health, took my books with him, and found them of so much amusement to him that he sent me some seeds on his arrival by way of return, and we are likely to become great friends." She was, without doubt, an accomplished gardener, and her letters reveal a most intimate knowledge of the subject. Most of her plants came from seed, and in view of modern horticultural practice, it is astonishing to learn of geraniums, chrysanthemums and other flowers usually propagated by cuttings, being raised in this manner. It was due to this that she was able to keep the ground stocked with flowers for the greater part of the year at little expense. When the family first arrived at Three Mile Cross, she described the garden as being "about the size of a good drawing room," but many years later she says it consisted of about an acre of ground. It is probable that further land was acquired, possibly in 1834, when the entire garden was re-made. Geraniums were her favourite flowers, and on one occasion she refers to three hundred varieties. William Howitt, the Quaker author, who visited the garden in the summer of 1835, writes: "Look on all those noble plants [geraniums] that form . . . the grand pile before the conservatory. Mark well their number, their splendour, their rarity. . . . Let me lead you forward into the second garden, and show you others by dozens, and scores and hundreds, seedlings, cuttings, first flowers, new varieties, by whole colonies. . . ."*

This "grand pile" was the cause of an act of kindness on the part of Captain Gore, one of her neighbours.† One afternoon, he and his wife were sitting in the garden at Three Mile Cross, watching this pyramid of geraniums

* The *Athenæum*, 7th July, 1835.

† Capt. the Hon. Edward Gore, brother to the Earl of Arran, whom he succeeded. He lived at Bertram House, the Mitfords' old home.

wilting in the sun. Everyone was lamenting that no way could be devised of erecting a canvas awning over the plants, when the Captain, a naval man, exclaimed "Can't it be done in wood? Anything may be done in wood. We must stop a week and build a roof to let up and down by blocks, sailor fashion. I'll come to-morrow and see what we can devise—to-morrow or Tuesday." "Not Tuesday, dear Captain Gore," replied Mary Mitford, "for I am going out as early as twelve o'clock." On the morrow, however, there was no sign of the gallant captain, and she assumed that the matter had been forgotten; but on returning from her round of visits on the Tuesday, she found him, with six men, erecting the wooden canopy. It was a marvellous affair, highly ornamental, and so easy to work that a child could let it up and down. He had designed it himself, and had made most of it with his own hands. "Now don't you like Captain Gore?" she exclaimed. It was incidents such as these which revealed how much she was beloved by her neighbours: and it is pleasant to dwell on the fact that her grim struggle for existence was lightened by many similar acts of neighbourly kindness.

XVI

1836-1837

With the publication of *Belford Regis*, her best work was done. Her subsequent productions were eminently readable, and contained much that was interesting: but the work which has given her name to posterity, in which she might be said to have initiated a literary tradition, was now accomplished. From 1836 onwards, there was a steady decline in her physical health, which progressively reduced her literary output and consequently increased her pecuniary anxieties.

At the beginning of that year, however, she signed a contract for a novel with Saunders and Otley, for the sum of £700. It was intended that this should be printed in September, but it was many years before she completed the work for, as we have already stated, she shrank from a task which was uncongenial to her talents. There is little reference in her correspondence of this period to her literary activities. At the end of 1835, however, she was writing for *Chambers's Edinburgh Journal* which, although the first number had only been issued in 1832, had already reached what was then the phenomenal circulation of 80,000 a week.* She must also have been working on her volume of *Country Stories* which was published in 1837; but after the failure of her opera and her inability to procure the production of her tragedy *Otto of Wittelsbach*, she seems to have lost interest in the theatre. It is possible that she felt physically incapable of dealing with the disputes, jealousies and postponements which were the inevitable corollary to a theatrical production.

She had a brief moment of relaxation on a visit to

* *Memoir of Robert Chambers*, p. 242, 1872.

London for the purpose of attending the first night of the tragedy *Ion*, by her friend Sergeant Talfourd, when she spent ten days with him and his wife at their home, 56, Russell Square. This performance, and the supper party which followed, was a memorable one, for among the guests were Wordsworth, Landor, Clarkson Stanfield, Browning, Forster, Jeffrey, Rogers, Procter, Milman and John Lucas, the painter; and in addition to her own account, Macready* and Crabb Robinson† also referred to it in their diaries. *Ion* was produced at Drury Lane on 26th May, with Macready in the principal rôle, supported by Ellen Tree. It met with an enthusiastic reception, the audience calling for Talfourd, who acknowledged the plaudits of the crowd from his box. Both Macready and Ellen Tree were also warmly applauded, and the actor recorded in his diary that he "acted the character [of Ion] as well as I have ever played any previous one, with more of inspiration, more complete abandonment, more infusion of myself into another being, than I have been able to obtain in my performances for some time." Afterwards at the supper party held at Russell Square, he found himself seated between Wordsworth and Landor, with Browning on the opposite side of the table: he pointed out to Wordsworth a passage in *Ion* which had been suggested by some lines in a tragedy of the poet's, and the old man replied characteristically: "Yes, I noticed them," and quoted,

> "Action is transitory—a step—a blow,
> The motion of a muscle—this way or that—
> 'Tis done; and in the after vacancy
> We wonder at ourselves like men betrayed."‡

Toasts were proposed to the author, the actors and the principal guests, including Mary Mitford. Macready whose

* *Daries of Macready*, Vol. I, p. 318 ff, 1912.
† *Diary of H. C. R.*, Vol. I, p. 413, 1877.
‡ *The Borderers.*

customary defensive attitude was mellowed by the gaiety of the occasion, suggested with a heavy jocosity that she should emulate Talfourd and write another play, to which she replied swiftly, " Will you act in it ? "—and Harness, who was near, added " Aye, hold him to that." But the spectre of his wrongs rose up between them, and he turned away and scowled. He never forgot an injury, real or supposed. The party went on until the small hours—Macready did not arrive home till two—nevertheless Mary Mitford found time to scribble a note, after it was over, to her father. " I like Mr. Wordsworth of all things ; he is a most venerable-looking old man, delightfully mild and placid, and most kind to me. Mr. Landor is a very striking-looking person, and exceedingly clever. Also we had a Mr. Browning, a young poet (author of *Paracelsus*), and Mr. Procter and Mr. Chorley, and quantities more of poets, etc. . . . I am tired to death, and must go to bed."

This event, although it occasioned her trip to London, was by no means the only festivity she attended, for the entire visit was a succession of entertainments. Kenyon gave a dinner, at which were Landor and Wordsworth—" You cannot imagine how very, very, very kindly Mr. Wordsworth speaks of my poor works. You, who know what I think of him, can imagine how much I am gratified by his praise "—and Lady Dacre, a sister of Sheridan's second wife, invited fifty people to meet her. Among the guests was Edwin Landseer who expressed the wish to paint her dog, Dash. Then the Duke of Devonshire called at Russell Square, and brought her a nosegay of lilies of the valley and moss roses. " You can't imagine how well the Duke and I got on," she told her father. " He is a first-rate talker —he *must* be—for I am living in the midst now of all that is best of London conversation, and I have not met with any one who exceeds him : there was not a moment's pause." A conversation with the Duke was something of an achievement, for he was exceedingly deaf. Her hostess,

Mrs. Talfourd, was unable to make him hear; but there must have been something in the timbre of her own beautiful voice which overcame his affliction. He begged her always to keep him informed of her visits to London, so that they might meet again; and gave her an order to visit his house at Chiswick. She seems, during these hectic ten days, to have seen a great deal of Kenyon, for besides their meetings on formal occasions, they went together, on 27th May, to the Zoological Gardens to inspect the giraffes. "A sweet young woman," she told her father, "whom we called for in Gloucester Place,* went with us—a Miss Barrett—who reads Greek as I do French, and has published some translations from Æschylus, and some most striking poems. She is a delightful young creature;† shy, and timid and modest. Nothing but her desire to see me got her out at all, but now she is coming to us to-morrow night also." They met again at Kenyon's dinner party, where the charming Miss Barrett told her new acquaintance, with the deference due to the other's position, that it was like a dream that they should be talking together, and that she knew all Mary Mitford's works by heart. A few days later the new friends visited Chiswick together, accompanied by Wordsworth. "I went with him [Wordsworth] and Miss Mitford to Chiswick," wrote Elizabeth Barrett to a friend, "and thought all the way that I must certainly be dreaming. I saw her almost every day of her week's visit to London . . . and she, who overflows with warm affections and generous benevolences, showed me every present and absent kindness, professing to love me, and asking me to write to her."‡ Thus began what was, from every aspect, a most remarkable friendship.

Several years later, Mary Mitford wrote a description of her young friend as she was at this time: ". . . a slight, girlish figure, very delicate, with exquisite hands and feet,

* The Barretts were then living at 74, Gloucester Place, W. 1.

† Elizabeth Barrett was 30 at the time of this meeting, and Mary Mitford 49.

‡ *Letters of E. B. B.*, Vol. 1, p. 43, 1897.

a round face, with a most noble forehead, a large mouth, beautifully formed, and full of expression, lips like parted coral, teeth large, regular, and glittering with healthy whiteness, large dark eyes, with such eyelashes, resting on the cheek when cast down ; when turned upward, touching the flexible and expressive eyebrow ; a dark complexion, with cheeks literally as bright as the dark China rose, a profusion of silky, dark curls, and a look of youth and of modesty hardly to be expressed. This, added to the very simple but graceful and costly dress by which all the family are distinguished, is an exact portrait of her some years ago. . . . When I first saw her, her talk, delightful as it was, had something too much of the lamp—she spoke too well—and her letters were rather too much like the very best books. Now all that is gone. . . ."

This visit, therefore, must have been a pleasant experience, an oasis of gaiety in her lonely existence ; but as is the way with all human affairs, its joys were not unalloyed, for a coolness sprang up between her and her old friend and host, Talfourd. It would seem that the success of *Ion* had given him exaggerated notions of his literary merits and that, for the time being, his vanity became insufferable. "You have no idea of our poor friend's tremendous inflation," she wrote to Dr. Mitford. "It is specimen enough to say that he actually expressed to me great wonder that Lord Lansdowne* did not put off a dinner, which he is to have next Wednesday, and for which tickets have been out these six weeks, because *Ion* is to be played a second time that night ! Of me he is furiously jealous, so he is of Wordsworth ; but more of me, because people come to his own house to see me, and walk up to me and crowd about me whilst he is in the room :" and on another occasion, "Talfourd is so devoured by jealousy at my reception that he does not even speak to me, and *to my*

* Henry Petty-Fitzmaurice, 3rd Marquis of Lansdowne. After holding various political appointments, he subsequently served as President of the Council in Melbourne's two administrations.

certain knowledge concealed from Lord Holland (Miss Fox told me so*) that I am in town, and from Lord Lansdowne where I am. . . . Mr. Sergeant would not go to Lady Dacre's to-night, because it was a party made for me. He is really so inflated with vanity, and so bitter with envy, that you would not know him. He told me (when I said that the papers had been very far more favourable to him than to my plays) that I forgot *the difference !*† And if you had seen the scorn with which he said it ! He said worse to Jerrold.‡ . . . We have had no quarrel—no coolness, even, on *my* part. I behaved, at first, with the warmest and truest sympathy, until it was chilled by his bitter scorn ; and since, thank Heaven ! I have never lost my self-command. . . . But Mr. Kenyon observed the thing, and so did William ; and he must change very much indeed before the old feeling will come back to me."

As she was not given to exaggeration, we do not doubt that these remarks give a fair and truthful account of Talfourd's lapse ; but we cannot help wondering how she could allow herself to cherish, if only for a short period, feelings of irritation towards someone to whom she was so much indebted. That she acknowledged this debt, and was fully aware of her obligations, is proved by this passage in a letter written two years later : " During a long and arduous struggle your friendship has been my support and consolation—almost my only one : to your public praise I owe what little reputation I may have acquired and to your private encouragement the power of writing—of earning money—in a word, of living. No human being perhaps in the world owes so much to another as I to you, and the gratitude which, unless you think me intolerably wicked you must know that I feel, has always been so

* Lord Holland's sister.

† Talfourd's vanity over his tragedy was so excessive that he went to see it whenever it was performed, which made a wit exclaim, after he had been elevated to the Bench, " Surely he does not go to see '*Ion*' *now that he has become a judge ?*" *Some Literary Recollections*, James Payn, p. 77, 1884.

‡ Douglas Jerrold (1803-1857) journalist and dramatist.

lightened by your own delicacy, and so elevated by the admiration and respect inspired by your thousand splendid qualities, that the burthen has been turned into a pleasure."* We feel, therefore, that she could well have afforded to overlook what can only have been a temporary lapse in an otherwise kindly and generous man, and that this was one of the few occasions when her conduct could be condemned. Vanity and conceit are excessively irritating, but then kindness and generosity on the scale shown to her by Talfourd are excessively rare, and should not be forgotten in a moment of temporary exasperation. Whether she was able, as she stated, to conceal her annoyance—for she was quick-tempered on occasions—is doubtful; for on the 1st June, Macready, who had been playing in *Ion* went round to Mrs. Talfourd's private box, where the matter was under discussion. "They are much displeased with Miss Mitford," he recorded in his diary, "who seems to be showing herself *well up*. She was bad from the beginning. How strange with so much talent!"† It needs great self-control indeed to resist the temptation of saying "I told you so!" and self-control was not one of Macready's more salient qualities.

On her return home, her new friend Henry Fothergill Chorley, whom she had met at Talfourd's,‡ came to stay at the cottage for a few days. He was a young man of Quaker stock, the son of an unsuccessful manufacturer, who a few years previously had been appointed to the staff of the *Athenæum*. He was upright and sincere, but narrow minded and conventional, and he lacked the breadth of vision necessary to a great critic. It was he who, after her death, edited the second series of her letters and prefaced them by a biographical note which is not remarkable for its psychological insight. "The sorrow—the disadvantage—the mistake of Miss Mitford's life should

* MSS. John Rylands Library, 26th May, 1838.
† *Diaries of Macready*, p. 323, 1912.
‡ She had previously been in correspondence with him over a *Life* of Mrs. Hemans, which he was writing at that time.

be clearly unfolded," he wrote sententiously. "Hers was the story of a credulous woman sacrificing herself to an utterly worthless idol. . . . Dr. Mitford . . . was a robust, showy, wasteful profligate—a man whose life was a shame; whose talk was too often an offence, not to be tolerated in our days. . . ." After giving details of the fortunes Dr. Mitford had squandered, he continued "And from that time forth, to the end of his days, Miss Mitford was the 'breadwinner'—had to provide the funds required to satisfy her parent's sensual rapacity, and to uphold him among those who knew, from intimate contact, how gross, how worthless, was her idol—with something of defensive perversity and more of blind credulity. On the delusion, trenching on moral obliquity, of such a devotion as hers, there can hardly be two opinions. But the discredit too heavily fell on the woman: because she struggled for, and obtained, literary notoriety, and thereby was marked before the world." This seems to us a ridiculous over-simplification of the case. Dr. Mitford, though selfish and extravagant, was not entirely "profligate;" and while we do not doubt his eighteenth-century outlook and frankness of speech shocked Chorley's Victorian prudery, we are not prepared to say that this constituted an "offence." And once again we must ask, what else could Mary Mitford have done under the circumstances? Would there not, for instance, have been more "moral obliquity" if she had announced to the world that her father was a spend-thrift and a gambler, and that she had decided to turn him out of her home, than, as was actually the case, concealing his habits and bearing the burden, both moral and financial, herself? We do not doubt, as Chorley makes clear, that some of the discredit deriving from her father's actions fell on her;* but we should have thought that those who

* Harriet Martineau states that he borrowed from all M. R. M.'s influential friends; and in the *Gentleman's Magazine* (Vol. 43, p. 428, 1855), it is stated "Her father . . . was a sanguine, cheerful and speculative man, who . . . played at whist, spent every one's money, and something more . . . and made every living creature love him, lend to him and forgive him."

knew the truth would, if not have honoured her, at least have commiserated on her martyrdom. Chorley, in the course of years, paid many visits to Three Mile Cross to what he described as the "insufficient, meanly furnished labourer's cottage:" and although the feeling was stronger on his side than hers—once, in a moment of temporary irritation she referred to him as a "presumptuous coxcomb"—their friendship endured to the end of her life.

On this occasion, he left Three Mile Cross with a letter from his hostess to Elizabeth Barrett in his pocket, and a bouquet of flowers from the garden. And from henceforth the two women were in constant communication. This was, without doubt, a truly remarkable friendship, for although there was considerable affection—far greater on one side than the other—it is obvious, from the events which occurred, that neither ever understood the other's real character. The difference in age and experience would, in some measure, account for this lack of understanding; but it was, above all, due to a divergence of character so wide that it was almost impossible for one to conceive of, let alone comprehend, the other's point of view. In our opinion, the romance of Elizabeth Barrett's marriage to Robert Browning, and the unusual circumstances of her family life, tend to obscure other aspects of her character. But to the student of her letters it is obvious that hers was a subtle, determined nature, with something of intellectual arrogance—too much for one of her genius—and a morbid sensitivity, due in part to the life she had led, and to her tubercular tendencies. By birth and upbringing, she was a nonconformist, and in her earlier letters there is more than a little of intolerance and cant. These qualities, to a certain extent, were hidden beneath a shy and modest manner, which she retained to the end of her life. This is not to disparage her noble qualities, of which she had many, but merely to point out that although a superbly clever woman, she was but human; and that these frailties must be taken into account if her relations with Mary Mitford are to be understood.

To the weary woman at Three Mile Cross, this friendship brought immense consolations ; and it is no exaggeration to say that her affection for Elizabeth Barrett was greater than for anyone else, with the exception of her parents. Her letters, couched in intimate and affectionate terms, make this plain. This modest young woman, with her good looks and elegance, her intelligence and great gifts, was irresistibly attractive to the lonely, sad spinster, and aroused feelings which were of far greater emotional depth than those she usually experienced for others, warm-hearted and kindly though she was. At first their relationship was as near perfect as any which rests on such a transitory basis as human nature. Mary Mitford, from the start (at a time when few others had done so), discerned her friend's genius and was generous with her encouragement and praise. Within a few weeks of their meeting, she wrote to Harness : "I think, after all, that you will come round to us in the matter of Miss Barrett. To say nothing of the sweetness and feeling of some of her former poems (the *Stanzas to a Poet's Child*, for instance, and those called *The Sea Mew* in Miss Courtenay's Album), as well as their wonderful clearness and transparency of diction, there is a force, a vigour, and a tension, about the preface to the *Prometheus*,* which seems to be unmatched in modern prose. Depend upon it that, putting the learning out of the question, she is a most remarkable young woman." On her side, Elizabeth Barrett was at first delighted and perhaps a little flattered by the attentions of one so eminent. She had an indiscriminating adulation of genius, inasmuch as she was prepared to worship the man as well as the talent ; and this led her, on occasions, into some equivocal situations. But in the matter of the affections, there is nearly always one who gives and one who receives ; and

* *Miscellaneous Poems* (*Promethus Bound*), 1833.

in the relationship between these two women, Mary Mitford poured out her love and tenderness while the other, more self-contained and with many more outlets for her affections, came in time to the point where familiarity bred contempt and something akin to dislike. In mitigation, it must be said that having led a sheltered existence, with no experience of searing responsibilities or pecuniary troubles, it was almost impossible for her to conceive of the circumstances of Mary Mitford's life, nor the loneliness and desolation of her existence.

But that was for the future. At the beginning of their friendship, their relationship was that between the eminent woman of letters and the talented aspirant to literary fame. Elizabeth Barrett must have begged her to come to Gloucester Place, for in the letter of which Chorley was the bearer, Mary Mitford wrote, "To be sure I will come and see you when I next visit London, and I shall feel to know you better when I have had the pleasure of being introduced to Mr. Barrett; to be better authorized to love you and to take a pride in your successes—things which, at present, I take the liberty of doing without authority." Then she made some remarks on lucidity of style and added, "This is a terrible liberty from me to you, but I have seen so much high poetical faculty lost and buried for the one fault of obscurity, that I would impress upon every young writer the paramount necessity of clearness." And a few weeks later, she wrote "You should take my venturing to criticize your verses as a proof of the perfect truth of my praise. I do not think there can be a better test of the sincerity of applause than the venturing to blame." Few of Elizabeth Barrett's letters during this period have survived, but it would seem that literary matters, as was only to be expected, loomed largely in their correspondence. On one occasion Mary Mitford asked whether her new friend was a reader of the old English drama, and if she were familiar with Victor Hugo's plays, "the power and the pathos are to me indescribably great ;" and on another, "Let me say, my sweetest, that the *Romaunt of the Page** (which is a tragedy of the very deepest and highest order) always seems to me by far the finest thing that you have ever written ; and I do entreat and conjure you to write more ballads or tragedies. . . ."

It is doubtful, however, whether the new friends saw much of each other that year, for Mary Mitford was chained to her desk, working on the novel and her *Country Stories*. But visitors came to her. As the result of her correspondence with American friends, she was visited that autumn by the brother and nephew of Catherine Sedgwick, the novelist, both of whom stayed at Three Mile Cross. "They are gone now," she wrote in September, "to the great benefit of my book, but to my own personal sorrow." Her works were so well known in the United States that distinguished Americans usually made a pilgrimage into Berkshire. In the previous summer, she had been visited by George Ticknor, the historian, who was touring England with his wife and child ; and armed with an introduction from John Kenyon, spent a few hours at Three Mile Cross. Ticknor has recorded this visit in his journal : "We found Miss Mitford living literally in a cottage, neither *ornée* nor poetical†—except inasmuch as it had a small garden crowded with the richest and most beautiful profusion of flowers—where she lives with her father, a fresh, stout old man who is in his seventy-fifth year. She herself seemed about fifty,‡ short and fat, with very gray hair, perfectly visible under her cap, and nicely arranged in front. She has the simplest and kindest manners, and entertained us for two hours with the most animated conversation and a great variety of anecdote, without any of the pretensions of an author by profession,

* Published in *Finden's Tableaux of the Affections*, 1838.

† These remarks about the cottage seem strange nowadays, when many a middle-class family would be thankful to have the cottage. It has six bedrooms.

‡ She was forty-eight

and without any of the stiffness that generally belongs to single ladies of that age and reputation. . . ."*

Not only did she receive visitors, but she also received invitations. The Duke of Devonshire asked her to go to Chatsworth, and she indulged in dreams of a tour through England and Scotland, about which she would write a book to pay the expenses. But she doubted whether she could bear the fatigue, and also the problem of what to do with her father proved, as usual, insuperable: she had therefore to abandon the plan. That autumn, too, John Lucas, now a fashionable portrait painter, spent a week at the cottage. He wished to paint her again, for he had never been satisfied with the likeness taken several years previously. But she refused, and instead he painted her father. She was delighted at the result. "It is as like as the looking-glass; beautiful old man that he is! and is the pleasantest likeness, the finest combination of power, and beauty, and sweetness, and spirit, that ever you saw. Such a piece of colour, too! He used all his carmine the first day, and was forced to go into Reading for a fresh supply. He says that my father's complexion is exactly like the sunny side of a peach, and so is his picture." It was also during this year that she corresponded with George Darley, the author of *Sylvia* and *Nepenthe*. Darley† was a poet of some ability, who suffered from neglect; and her praise of his work gave him great pleasure. It is, indeed, one of the most laudable aspects of her character that she was always willing to help those whom she felt had not obtained their due recognition.

Such diversions, pleasant though they be, do not bring in money; and as usual, this was her urgent need. It seems that she planned to go to London early in 1837, in connection with theatrical matters, for Elizabeth Barrett told a friend: "I shall at least see dear Miss Mitford, who wrote to me not long ago to say that she would soon

* *Life, Letters and Journals of George Ticknor*, Vol. I, pp. 418, 419, 1876.
† Poet, novelist and critic.

be in London with *Otto* her new tragedy, which was written at Mr. Forrest's* own request, he in the most flattering manner having applied to her a stranger, as the authoress of *Rienzi*, for a dramatic work worthy of his acting. . . . She says her play will be quite opposed, in its execution, to *Ion*, as unlike it 'as a ruined castle overhanging the Rhine, to a Grecian temple.' And I do not doubt it will be full of ability, although my own opinion is that she stands higher as the authoress of *Our Village* than of *Rienzi*, and writes prose better than poetry, and transcends rather in Dutch minuteness and high finishing, than in Italian ideality and passion."† Whether this visit ever eventuated is doubtful, for Dr. Mitford was in London early in February, and it was probably he who attended to the negotiations over the play. In any case, these were unsuccessful, and she was obliged to withdraw the tragedy because, it would seem, Forrest was unable, through lack of money, to produce it.‡

Country Stories was published in the early part of the year, and she dedicated it to her old friend, William Harness. She had been unwilling to dedicate a play to him, for fear of injuring him in his profession; but she felt that "this slight testimony of a very sincere affection" could not harm him. She had no great opinion of the work and told Elizabeth Barrett "I speak the real truth in saying that I do not like it. If ever I did like any of my prose works it was *Belford Regis*, and this is more in the way of *Our Village*." We cannot, however, concur with her opinion. This little volume of stories and sketches demonstrates once again her inimitable skill in depicting the English country scene in what a modern critic has called her "poetically written prose."§ *Country Stories*

* An American actor who took Drury Lane for a season.

† *Letters of E. B. B.*, Vol. 1, p. 47, 1897.

‡ MSS. John Rylands Library, Letter to Talfourd, 10th June, 1837. ". . . and I have no doubt that his [Forrest's] not having furnished the money was the ultimate cause of his leaving D. Lane."

§ *Lif of George Crabbe*, by his Son, introduction by Edmund Blunden, p. XXIV, 1947.

really constitutes a sixth volume in the series of *Our Village*, and some of the stories, *Country Lodgings*, *The Lost Dahlia* and *The London Visitor*, are as good as anything she had previously written. There is, indeed, a quality of purity in her prose which is comparable to the limpid streams she so often described. At times it flows serenely, without a ripple on the surface; at others it bubbles and sparkles as a brook on a summer's morning.

The price she obtained for this volume was £100, but she was in such need of money, owing to the failure to obtain the production of *Otto* that Harness suggested she should apply to Lord Melbourne, the Prime Minister, for a Civil List pension. Her application was successful, and on 31st May, she wrote joyfully to Emily Jephson, "I cannot suffer one four-and-twenty hours to pass, my own dearest Emily, without telling you, what I am sure will give you so much pleasure, that I have had to-day an announcement from Lord Melbourne of a pension of £100 a year. The sum is small, but that cannot be considered as derogatory, which was the amount given by Sir Robert Peel to Mrs. Hemans and Mrs. Somerville; and it is a great comfort to have something to look forward to as a certainty, however small, in sickness or old age, unlikely as it is that I should ever live to be old. But the real gratification of this transaction has been the kindness, the warmth of heart, the cordiality, and the delicacy of every human being connected with the circumstances. It originated with dear William Harness, and that most kind and zealous friend, Lady Dacre; and the manner in which it was taken up by the Duke of Devonshire, Lord and Lady Holland, Lord and Lady Radnor, and many others—some of whom I have never even seen . . . has been such as to make this one of the most pleasurable events of my life." She was, indeed, greatly beloved and the circumstances of her life aroused much compassion; and since she never had any idea of her own popularity nor considered her conduct in any way meritorious, these marks of approbation always came as a surprise. It was hoped that, later on, the sum would be raised to £200, but this hope was not fulfilled; and other attempts, a few years later, to obtain an increase were not successful. Even to this day the State assesses artistic merits at a singularly low figure.

Another source of revenue that year was her editorship of *Finden's Tableaux*, one of the many annual publications which were so popular at that period. The idea of the annual, or Christmas gift book, originated in Germany;* and the first produced in this country was in 1822. So popular were they with the public that by 1829, no fewer than seventeen were issued, and the number afterwards increased. These books were lavishly produced, lavishly, that is to say, by the execrable standards of Victorian book production. *Finden's Tableaux*, the proprietor of which was a Mr. Tilt, contained a number of engravings, which were sent to the editor, who in turn distributed them to her contributors; and these unfortunate individuals were obliged to write something—prose or verse—on the subjects suggested by the engravings. It is remarkable, indeed, that the contents were not a perpetual lament, for the engravings which graced Mr. Tilt's annual were not remarkable for their artistry. The new editor appealed for help to Elizabeth Barrett: "If you can give me time and thought enough to write me one of those ballad-stories, it would give an inexpressible grace and value to my volume. Depend upon it the time will come when those verses of yours will have a money value." And the poetess told a friend: "*Speaking of Homer and Virgil*, I have been writing a *Romance of the Ganges* in order to illustrate an engraving in the new annual to be edited by Miss Mitford, *Finden's Tableaux* for 1838. It does not sound a *very* Homeric undertaking . . . but from my wish

* For an account of the annuals, see S. C. Hall's *Retrospect of a Long Life*.

to please her, and from the necessity of its being done in a certain time, I was 'quite frightful,' as poor old Cooke used to say, in order to express his own nervousness. But she was quite pleased—she is very soon pleased—and the ballad, gone the way of all writing, nowadays, to the press."*

Apart from this, however, she can have accomplished little literary work for the remainder of the year. She was ill most of the summer—for two months she never left the premises—and in July her father had an attack of English cholera, which necessitated his being nursed night and day. To add to her difficulties, the cottage was badly in need of repair—there was a danger that the roof might fall in—and the owner refused to have any work carried out. Early in the autumn, she contemplated a removal to a farmhouse in the vicinity; but further negotiations with the landlord must have taken place, for in December, there were workmen in the cottage. It was on this occasion that the alterations were made which transformed the cottage into its present state.† She wrote a pathetic account of her misfortunes to Elizabeth Barrett.

" Three Mile Cross,
Dec. 2, 1837.

My dear Love,

My book‡ has been hindered by my ill health, by my many visitors, and lately by workmen. . . . All this makes it more wonderful that I should have done so much [written *Otto*, *Country Stories* and her contributions to *Finden's Tableaux*] than that I should not have done more. Even if I have not the nausea, the other fearful suffering is sure to come on every morning, sometimes at four or five o'clock, and last till noon. Think how it incapacitates! and think what it is to feel that more ought to be done,

* *Letters of E. B. B.*, Vol. 1, p. 52, 1897.
† See page 131.
‡ Presumably her novel.

and yet that I cannot do it! To feel incapacity as a sin! Latterly, the din and bustle of workmen have wholly hindered all composition. . . . We shall gain great comfort, and at comparatively small expense, though still far more than we can afford. But that expense was inevitable, for the house was falling in, and the cost will be less than that of moving would have been; but still far, far more than we can afford or ought to spend; and this frets and worries me past expression. I believe there is not a labourer's wife in the parish who thinks so much of spending a shilling as I do. . . ."

As a culminating blow, the MS. of a short story, sent to Edinburgh, disappeared *en route*, with a consequent loss to its wretched author of £70.

XVII

1838-1842

As she had only been able, when in comparatively good health, to earn enough money for current expenses, now that she was incapacitated from working for long periods, her position became desperate and she was deeply in debt. In her anxiety, her thoughts turned to the trust funds, and she wrote to Harness : " I am going to ask you a very great favour which, as it depends entirely upon yourself, and as there are many reasons for granting it, and none against it, I cannot doubt your complying with. It is that you will sell out our money, the funds being now so high, let me have £600, and buy an annuity on my life and my father's with the rest. This will bring us in more in income than we now have ; will relieve my mind from an insupportable weight ; and will make me from a most anxious and miserable, a comfortable woman. *My father has nothing to do with the matter.** If I had written the novel as agreed upon, it would not have been wanted ; but ever since the affair of *Otto* I have been a martyr to a most painful complaint, which, not confining me (except occasionally, in very violent attacks), has yet kept me in a state of constant suffering during many hours, either of the night or day.†

" This winter, luckily, it came on with a violence so dangerous, that my father was forced to send, at midnight, for a very clever Reading surgeon, and he has put me in such a train, that, though I can hardly expect a cure, the incapacitating pain is much abated, and even the exceeding inconvenience lessened. So that the £200 a year, which will be in future all that we shall need to go on as

* The italics are ours.

† This was, we believe, the *tic doulourex*.

we are going on, can be gained without inconvenience, if it please God to continue to me health and faculty. Even so ill as I have been this last year, I have gained that and more. . . ."

Harness acceded to this request: the debts were paid, the remainder of the money placed on mortgage and, for a short period, she was free from anxiety. But it was one of the ironies of fate that while she was always hard pressed for money, she received frequent applications from impecunious people for financial assistance. When she replied that she "wrote for bread," the reply was "I know this; but being yourself popular and well paid, of course your first pleasure is to assist obscure merit." Two hundred a year, she said, would not meet the direct claims made upon her generosity, nor would five hundred cover the subscriptions she was asked to raise from her influential friends, such as the Duke of Devonshire, Lady Dacre, Lady Sidmouth and others, whom these opportunists did not hesitate to name. And these requests came from people she had never heard of, or from those who, having once forced themselves upon her at the cottage, afterwards wrote begging letters. On one occasion, when she had sent a guinea to a poet to assist his sick mother, her thanks was a letter of vile abuse. Her old friend Mrs. Hofland, was even more badly treated by the same gentleman. She gave him money, food and clothing, raised a subscription and found him a position in an office at £80 a year. A few months later, he again applied to her for help, and when asked why he had left his job, replied insolently "How could a man of genius be fettered to a desk?" Such is the price of fame, and there can be few eminent persons who have not had similar experiences.

Nevertheless it had its compensations. Elizabeth Barrett, despite poor health which forced her to lead the life of a complete invalid,* published that year another volume of

* She broke a blood vessel early in 1838.

poems *The Seraphim and other Poems*, in which she paid this tribute to her eminent friend :

" To Mary Russell Mitford
in her garden.

What time I lay these rhymes anear thy feet,
Benignant friend, I will not proudly say
As better poets use ' These *flowers* I lay,'
Because I would not wrong thy roses sweet,
Blaspheming so their name. And yet, repeat
Thou, overleaning them this springtime day,
With heart as open to love as theirs to May,
—' Low-rooted verse may reach some heavenly heat,
Even like my blossoms, if as nature—true
Though not as precious.' Thou art unperplext—
Dear friend, in whose dear writings drops the dew
And blow the natural airs—thou, who are next
To nature's self in cheering the world's view—
To preach a sermon on so known a text !"

Throughout her correspondence there are references to various literary projects which never materialized. Her work was so popular that she had only to put a suggestion before a publisher for it to be accepted ; and that year she seems to have contemplated a volume entitled *The Miscellany*.* Her father went to London in August to negotiate its sale, but it seems never to have come to fruition. Possibly bad health prevented her from carrying out the work. A few weeks later she and Elizabeth Barrett experienced very cavalier treatment from Mr. Tilt, the publisher of *Finden's Tableaux*. The poetess had moved to Torquay—despite the fact that her father's house-hunting efforts had at last terminated in the acquisition of 50, Wimpole Street—because it was deemed advisable that she should spend the winter in a warmer climate. Although

* This may have been the book referred to in an undated letter published in the *Letters of M. R. M.* (2nd series, Vol. 1, p. 151). It was to be done in collaboration with a friend, but the scheme came to nothing.

her life was still hanging in the balance, she engaged in literary projects; and one of her ballads had appeared in the recent edition of the *Tableaux*. She was not at all pleased, however, at its appearance. "Think of Mr. Jilt's [*sic*] never sending me a proof sheet," she exclaimed with dismay to a friend. "The consequences are rather deplorable. . . . I . . . simply look aghast at the misprints and mispunctuations coming in as a flood, and sweeping away meanings and melodies together."* And Mary Mitford's contributions were equally maltreated. "By having been limited by Mr. Tilt to the exact number of pages of the former volume," she complained, "my own stories were cut up on the proofs—to use the printer's language—*Anglicé*, after they were actually set up in type—within an inch of their lives; so that I feared they would appear bald and thin, as well as brief."

Apart from this, she seems to have accomplished very little literary work at this period. In 1839, she again edited another volume of the *Tableaux*, and promised contributions to Douglas Jerrold, then editor of a Sunday newspaper. Also in a letter to Harness she mentions that she is correcting proofs of a book; but as no volume of hers was issued that year, this may have been the *Tableaux*. Indeed until his death in 1842, her time was almost entirely occupied in looking after her father. Dr. Mitford was now in his seventy-ninth year, and although he still attended to his magisterial duties, his tenure on life was weakening. Now that he was unable to indulge in his former pursuits with his friends, he became almost entirely dependent on her for his every day occupations, for it was characteristic of his adolescent mentality that he was unable to amuse himself. It was also characteristic of his egotism that, in his desire for extraneous solace, he did not hesitate to occupy her time, thus preventing her from earning their joint daily bread. In his old age, his childishness became more

* *Letters of* E. B. B., Vol. 1, p. 78, 1897.

apparent, and this only increased his stranglehold on her. She was a lonely, unhappy woman, with strong affections, and it was only natural that, in her need to love, she should turn to him. "If I could but give my whole life to him," she told a friend, "reading to him, dining out with him, playing cribbage with him, never five minutes away from him, except when he is asleep (for this is what makes him happy), it would be the breath of life to me; for the complete and child-like dependence which he has upon my love to supply him food and rest and amusement is the most endearing of all ties. I love him a million times better than ever, and can quite understand that love of a mother for her first-born, which this so fond dependence produces in the one so looked to."

These sentiments are creditable to her; but it is not to his credit that he monopolized her attention in this fashion. Any one less selfish would have reduced his demands to a minimum; but the virtue of self-abnegation was not one with which he was familiar. He liked being read to, and playing cribbage; therefore these wants must be satisfied. He liked entertaining, and therefore as many visitors as possible must be invited to Three Mile Cross. The only curb on his hospitable proclivities was the smallness of the cottage which was the principal reason, she told a friend, why they remained in a habitation otherwise so devoid of advantages and amenities. During the summer of 1839, even his abnormal craving for entertaining must have been satisfied. Apart from the usual crowd of sightseers and friends, there were visitors from America. Catherine Sedgwick, with whom she had been in correspondence for a number of years, landed at Plymouth that summer; and after visiting various places in the west and south of England, came through Three Mile Cross on her way to London and spent an evening at the cottage. Daniel Webster, the orator and lawyer, afterwards U.S.A. Secretary of State and candidate for the presidency, was another visitor. Both she and her father were charmed with their transatlantic guests; although she changed her mind later when the novelist published an account of her visit in *Letters from Abroad to Kindred at Home*.* "If you have a mind to see a specimen of the very coarsest Americanism ever put forth," she told a friend, "read the *Literary Gazette*† of this last week . . . when you remember that her [Miss Sedgwick's] brother and nephew had spent twice ten days at our poor cottage—that she had been received as their kinswoman, and therefore as a friend, you may judge how unexpected this coarse detail has been. . . . Of course its chief annoyance to me is the finding the aunt of a dear friend so grossly vulgar."

The offending passage in the book was expurgated, through the good offices of John Kenyon who, coming across the proofs in the publisher's office half an hour before they went to press, arbitrarily deleted it; but not before the review copies had gone out to the journals.‡ As a result, the *Literary Gazette* published the following extract from Miss Sedgwick's account: "Our coachman (who, after telling him we were Americans, had complimented us on our speaking English, 'and very good English, too') professed an acquaintance of some twenty years standing with Miss M., and assured us that she was one of the 'cleverest women in England,' and 'the Doctor' (her father) 'an 'earty old boy.' And when he reined his horses up to her door, and she appeared to receive us, he said, 'Now you would not take that little body there for the great author, would you?' and certainly we should have taken her for nothing but a kindly gentlewoman, who had never gone beyond the narrow sphere of the most refined social life. . . . Miss M. is truly a 'little body,' and dressed a little quaintly, and as unlike as possible to the

* The book was published in England by Moxon.

† *Literary Gazette*, 10th July, 1841.

‡ It was customary at that time to circulate the review copies in advance of publication.

faces we have seen of her in the magazines, which all have a broad humour, bordering on coarseness. She has a pale grey, soul-lit eye, and hair as white as snow; a wintry sign that has come prematurely upon her, as like signs come upon us, while the year is yet fresh and undecayed. Her voice has a sweet, low tone, and her manner a naturalness, frankness, and affectionateness, that we have been so long familiar with in their other modes of manifestation, that it would have been indeed a disappointment not to have found them. . . . In this [the cottage] very humble home she receives on equal terms the best in the land. Her literary reputation might have gained for her this elevation, but she started on vantage-ground, being allied by blood to the Duke of Bedford's family." In these days, when intimate details of the domestic life of the famous (and infamous) are to be read daily in the newspapers and journals, this racy account may not seem, despite its insistence on her aristocratic connections, so lacking in taste as it did to Mary Mitford. She had, however, a horror of personal publicity, and the reference to her father as "a 'earty old boy" and to herself as "a little body," however kindly meant, can scarcely have been acceptable to her. Another visitor that autumn may have been her old friend Talfourd, for he wrote her a note which "breathes more of the old spirit of intimacy and sympathy than any which I have received from him for years." Despite their estrangement they had kept in touch, and she, at all events, had made an attempt to heal the breach in 1838. They were never again on the same intimate terms, but from this time forth their relations were on an amicable basis, and she still consulted him on literary and business matters.

Creative work was becoming more and more difficult, owing to her circumstances—her father's domination, her increasing anxiety over his infirmities and her own shattered health—but there are occasional references in her correspondence to literary projects. In February, 1840, she was planning to publish her letters to Sir William Elford who had died in 1837.* Kenyon and Chorley were both enthusiastic over the project, but she did not proceed with it, probably through lack of leisure to do the necessary editing. About this time, too, there seems to have been some question of the performance of her tragedy, *Otto*, at Drury Lane with the American actor Wallack in the principal *rôle*; but a series of misfortunes unparelleled even in her experience of the theatre, prevented its production. She was still editing the *Tableaux*, and during 1842 she must have written the poems which appeared in the *Bijou Almanack for* 1843†; but it was many years before she again undertook any serious work. The preponderating factor in her life at this period was the demands made on her by Dr. Mitford, and her letters are very revealing on the extent of his exactions. "I am almost a prisoner in our little house and three miles round," she wrote; and on another occasion "Nobody can conceive how much my dear father misses me, if only an hour absent. He could read, I think; but, somehow, to read to himself gives him no pleasure; and if anyone else is so kind as to offer to read to him, *that* does not do. They don't know what he likes, and where to skip, and how to lighten heavy parts without losing the thread of the story. . . . So that I have been obliged to resume my old habits and to read to him and play cribbage with him, during more hours of each day . . . than you could well believe." Such a selfish individual could not, of course, support with fortitude the privations and infirmities of old age; and his moods seem to have alternated between excessive irritation, which he vented on his unfortunate daughter, and boundless self pity. ". . . He often moans for hours together," she told a friend. "Mr. May [his medical attendant] comforts me by

* He died on 30th November, 1837, in his ninetieth year.

† *Schloss's Bijou Almanack for* 1843. This curious publication is about the size of a postage stamp, and less than a quarter of an inch thick. It contains several poems by her, and an almanack.

saying that there is more of habit than of suffering; but what a trial it is to bear, and how difficult to bear up with undiminished cheerfulness. . . ." That Mr. May's diagnosis was correct, and that the old sinner, when it so pleased him, could exercise self-control, is evident from her subsequent sentence: "The entrance of the . . . few whom he likes to see . . . of course breaks this painful current of thought, and controls its expression; but *that* . . . occurs very rarely."

There is no doubt that during his last years, as was only to be expected, his constitution was failing. In the winter of 1839-40 he was seriously ill and in the following spring, when in London on literary business, he had an accident and broke his right arm and two ribs: but such were his powers of resistance that although eighty years of age, he returned home before receiving medical attention. This accident left no adverse effects, and except for the last year of his life, he seems to have escaped the major ills to which the flesh is usually heir at advanced age. But this immunity was no cause for thankfulness to him: on the contrary there were still his minor ills to serve as an excuse for monopolizing his daughter's attention. Scarcely a night passed, for instance, without her being called several times to his bedside, and the effect of this sleeplessness on her already over-taxed strength can well be imagined. He demanded constant attention, although his weaknesses never prevented his doing what he pleased. In January, 1841, his daughter recounted an incident to Elizabeth Barrett which proves that any thought of the consequences of his actions, the burden of which would fall mainly on her, never entered his head. "I write, my beloved friend, by my dear father's bedside; for he is again very ill. Last Tuesday was the Quarter Sessions, and he *would* go, and he seemed so well that Mr. May thought it best to indulge him. Accordingly he went at nine a.m. to open the Court, sat all day next the chairman in Court, and afterwards at dinner, returning at two o'clock a.m., in the highest spirits—not tired at all, and setting forth the next day for a similar eighteen hours of business and pleasure. Again he came home delighted and unwearied. He had seen many old and dear friends, and had received (to use his own words) the attentions which do an old man's heart good ; and *these*, joined to his original vigour of constitution and his high animal spirits, had enabled him to do that which to those who saw him at home infirm and feeble, requiring three persons to help him from his chair, and many minutes before he could even move—would seem as impossible as a fall of snow between the tropics, or the ripening of pineapples in Nova Zembla.

" All this he had done but not with impunity. He has caught a severe cold ; and having on Saturday taken nearly the same liberties at Reading, and not suffering me to send for Mr. May, until rendered bold by fear I did send last night—he is now seriously ill. I am watching by his bedside in deep anxiety. . . ." While we agree with the excellent maxim of the old music hall song that " a little bit of what we fancy does us good," we find difficulty in reconciling the infirm invalid of Three Mile Cross, who required three persons to move him, with the gay old man who stayed out dining and wining till two in the morning. Which was the genuine article ? And his infirmities in no way impaired his capacity for spending money. In 1840, the land comprising the cottage garden was put up for sale, occasioning Mary Mitford much uneasiness. She thought it would be bought by some speculator who would charge her an inordinate rent. Eventually it was acquired for her by a friend, who also added a small farmyard to their domain. Such an acquisition proved irresistible to Dr. Mitford. " My father is so anxious for a cow," she said, " that I cannot object, else the buying the cow, the fitting-up the dairy and cow-house, and the purchasing the different utensils will come, I suppose, to thirty pounds."

It is nothing short of a miracle that, with all her anxieties and responsibilities, her own health did not break down completely under the strain. She was, indeed, reaping what she had sown, with the added castigation that her affections were involved. Lady Ritchie,* in her charming but inaccurate introduction to *Our Village*, states that she was born to be tyrannised over, implying a lack of spirit and will-power. But it must have taken considerable will power to keep going at all during those anxious years. We think the true explanation is that being a lonely and affectionate woman, she clung tenaciously to her more obvious ties; and it was only when her emotions were involved that she showed a lack of will-power. But the strain took great toll of her strength, and she suffered from almost continuous attacks of nausea which prostrated her for weeks on end.† "After all, a wretched life is mine," she told Elizabeth Barrett. "Health is gone; but if I can but last while my dear father requires me; if the little money we have can but last; then it would matter little how soon I, too, were released." In the summer of 1841, to add to her troubles, she was involved in what might have been three serious accidents. While out driving, her horse bolted, and it was only due to the presence of mind of her servant that she escaped with nothing more than bad bruises. Then one night, while writing by candlelight in her bedroom, her clothes caught fire; and on another occasion, while inspecting a half built house with a friend, he fell through the floor, dragging her after him. Her spine was jarred to such an extent that for some considerable time she was unable to turn in bed.

All this time she was spending far more money than she was receiving, and on two occasions, in July 1841, and

* *Our Village*, with an introduction by Anne Thackeray Ritchie, 1910.

† From the details of this illness which she gave to a friend, it would seem that she was suffering from serious intestinal trouble.

February 1842, she had to implore Harness to release further monies from the trust funds. Her repugnance at making these appeals can well be imagined.

"Three Mile Cross,
Feb., 1842.

I sit down with inexpressible reluctance to write to you, my ever dear and kind friend, because I well know that you will blame me for the occasion; but it must be said, and I can only entreat your indulgence and your sympathy. My poor father has passed this winter in a miserable state of health and spirits. His eyesight fails him now so completely that he cannot even read the leading articles in the newspaper. Accordingly, I have not only every day gone through the daily paper . . . but, after that, I have read to him from dark till bedtime, and then have often (generally) sat at his bedside almost till morning . . . expecting the terrible attacks of cramp, three or four of a night, during which he gets out of bed to walk the room, unable to get in again without my assistance. I have been left no time for composition—neither time nor heart—so that we have spent money without earning any.

What I have to ask of you, then, is to authorize Mr. Blandy* to withdraw sufficient money to set us clear with the world, with a few pounds to start with, and then I *must* prefer the greater duty to the less—I must so far neglect my dear father as to gain time for writing what may support us. . . . I believe, when these debts are paid, his own spirits will lose that terrible depression, broken only by excessive irritability, which has rendered this winter a scene of misery to himself and such a trial to me.

Do not fancy, my dear friend, that I cast the slightest blame on my dear father. The dejection and the violence belong to disease fully as much as any other symptom. If anybody be to blame, *I* am the person, for not having

* Mr. J. J. Blandy, her man of business in Reading.

taken care that he should have no anxiety—nothing but age and infirmity—to bear. God forgive me for my want of energy! for suffering myself to be wholly engrossed by the easier duty of reading to him! I will not do so again.

. . . Do not refuse me this most urgent prayer, and do not think worse of me than you can help! If you knew all that I have gone through this winter—alone, day after day, week after week—you would wonder that I am still left to cumber the earth. Nothing could bear up under it but the love that is mercifully given to the object of anxiety—such love as the mother bears to her sickly babe. Once again may Heaven bless you, my ever kind friend! . . .

Ever gratefully yours,

M. R. Mitford."

There is something pathetic in her determination to shield her father from the censure that she knew his conduct would incur from Harness: but no amount of juggling with words, no smooth and polished phrases could hide the fact that he, and not she, was the cause of their acute financial embarrassments. That she was aware of this fact is evident from a passage in a letter to Elizabeth Barrett: "My father sees me greatly fatigued—much worn—losing my voice even in common conversation; and he lays it all to the last drive or walk—the only thing that keeps me alive—and tells everybody he sees that I am killing myself by walking or driving; and he hopes that I shall at last take some little care of myself and not stir beyond the garden. Is not this the perfection of self-deception?" It was indeed: but it was still self-deception. We do not believe that Dr. Mitford deliberately tyrannized over his daughter, for deliberation implies thought, a process which had never taken place in the Doctor's mind. But ignorance of the law does not lessen the crime, although equity demands that the fact should be taken into account

Her only consolation at this time was her friendship with Elizabeth Barrett, who had returned from Torquay and taken up residence in Wimpole Street in September, 1841. Their meetings, however, can only have been rare, for she was unable to leave her father. We know, however, that she was in London for three days at the end of 1841, and she spent a night with John Lucas and his wife at the beginning of 1842, when she met the artist, Hablot Browne. It may have been on this occasion that she brought up a young spaniel, Flush, as a present for her friend, for the first reference to this celebrated animal occurs in a letter of E. B. B.'s dated 2nd March.* But if they did not see one another frequently, letters passed between them twice a week, and there is no doubt that both derived pleasure from the correspondence. " You are far too good, my most dearest, in what you say of my poor letters," wrote MaryMitford. " They come from my heart, and therefore go to yours—but that is all their merit—merit to us only—to the lover and the loved." This was indeed the golden age of their friendship with warm-hearted sympathy and encouragement on one side, and a diffidence, tempered by a lively curiosity on the other. Elizabeth Barrett had still feelings of affection and admiration for her friend. And the harassed, careworn woman at Three Mile Cross, watching half the night at her father's bedside, poured out her heart to E. B. B. in the full flood of her generous nature : " My love and my ambition for you often seems to be more like that of a mother for a son, or a father for a daughter (the two fondest of natural emotions), than the common bonds of even a close friendship between two women of different ages and similar pursuits. I sit and think of you, and of the poems that you will write, and of that strange, brief rainbow crown called Fame, until the vision is before me as vividly as ever a mother's heart hailed

* Elizabeth Barrett frequently signed her letters by her initials which did not change after her marriage.

the eloquence of a patriot son. Do you understand this? and do you pardon it? You must, my precious, for there is no chance that I should unbuild *that* house of clouds; and the position that I long to see you fill is higher, firmer, prouder than ever has been filled by woman. It is a strange feeling, but one of indescribable pleasure. My pride and my hopes seem altogether merged in you. Well, I will not talk more of this; but at my time of life, and with so few to love, and with a tendency to body forth images of gladness and of glory, you cannot think what joy it is to anticipate the time. . . ."

It was as well that she had found someone else to love; someone upon whom to lavish her affections; for her father's long life was drawing to its close, and her martyrdom, of which she bore the scars for the remainder of her mortal life, was coming to an end.

XVIII

1842-1844

It was only during the last few months of his life that Dr. Mitford was wholly incapacitated. In March of 1842, he had an attack of English cholera, from which he seems to have made a good recovery, for in April we find Elizabeth Barrett telling Haydon " . . . I heard from our dear mutual friend Miss Mitford, my very precious friend Miss Mitford, a few days since;—and that she speaks with some thing more [of] hope of the infirm state of her father than her anxieties have suffered her to do for a long while past."* At all events, he had recovered sufficiently in June to entertain the members of the Reading Whist Club to dinner. However about July, he had what must have been a paralytic seizure, for he lost the use of his left hand and arm, and his left side was affected. From then until the end of his life, he was a helpless invalid, and could not move without the help of several persons. By early September, however, he had recovered sufficiently to attend the stone laying ceremony of the Reading Room in Reading, although it took four men to lift him from his carriage. His daughter, too, was present, and she was overwhelmed by the kindness shown to her. She told Elizabeth Barrett: " If ever I am ungrateful enough to bemoan my isolated position, I ought to think over the assemblage in the morning, [at the ceremony] and at the evening tea party and concert (where my father insisted on my appearing for an hour), in order to feel the thankfulness that thrilled through my very heart at the true and honest kindness with which I was received. It was an enthusiasm

* *Letters from Elizabeth Barrett to B. R. Haydon*, (ed. Martha Hale Shackford, 1939.) 1st April, 1842.

of man, woman and child—hundreds—thousands—such as I can hardly venture to describe, and it lasted all the time I stayed. Indeed, the pleasure amounted to pain, so confusing was it to hear the overpraise of which I felt myself unworthy." But her joy must have been short-lived, for soon after this her father was again seriously ill—probably with another stroke. His life hung in the balance, and her days and nights were spent at his bedside. There was no one but herself and the servants in the house—no relative or friend present to give her support. In her loneliness and anxiety she confided to Elizabeth Barrett all the hopes and fears which she was unable otherwise to express: "... dearest Miss Mitford's letters from the deathbed of her father make my heart ache as surely almost as the post comes," wrote E. B. B. to a friend. "There is nothing more various in character, nothing which distinguishes one human being from another more strikingly, than the expression of feeling, the manner in which it influences the outward man. If I were in her circumstances, I should sit paralysed—it would be impossible for me to write or cry. And she, who loves and feels with the intensity of a nature warm in everything, and seems to turn to sympathy by the very instinct of grief, and sits at the deathbed of her last relative, writing there, in letter after letter, every symptom, physical or moral—even to the very words of the raving of a delirium, and those, heart-breaking words! I could not write such letters; but I know she feels as deeply as any mourner in the world can."*

Elizabeth Barrett, with ten brothers and sisters wholly devoted to her, surrounded by loving care and every comfort, who had never known—and never was to know—the privations and humiliations resulting from lack of money, who never suffered from acute loneliness, could not understand the craving of the solitary soul for sympathy, nor the necessity for unburdening the over-anxious mind.

* *Letters of E. B. B.*, i, 111, 1897.

Her sheltered existence made her remote from the world; and in none of her letters does she display the slightest understanding of the influence of conditions on her friend's life and character. For the woes of suffering humanity in the abstract, she had a lively sympathy; but the woes and sorrows of this particular friend were beyond her comprehension. She told Haydon on November 6th "It [Dr. Mitford's state] is a strange prolongation of life in death—and her spirits [Mary Mitford's], so elastic ordinarily, seem to fail and falter."* This perhaps was not very surprising under the circumstances. Mary Mitford, in her simplicity was, probably unaware of this lack of comprehension; but it was obvious to the more subtle E. B. B. Many years later she wrote, ". . . I think I understand her better on the whole than she understands me (which is not saying much). . . ." But one can love without understanding, and generous gifts of expensive food came down from London to Three Mile Cross. There must, indeed, have been a constant supply, for Mary Mitford wrote: "No, my precious! do not send anything else *yet*: perhaps, by-and-by, a few oysters, but not this week, Mrs. Cockburn† having sent a brace of grouse." And she reported that her father had drunk five glasses of claret with a friend, which she took to be a sign of slight amendment.

But the sands were running out, and Dr. Mitford passed his time in praying and listening to the Gospels which his daughter read to him. For the remaining few weeks of his life, this extraordinary man was resigned and composed; no torments of uneasy conscience darkened his last hours, and he waited for death with calmness and resolution. On December 1st, he had an alarming relapse, and a few days later he became unconscious. At six o'clock on the morning of December 10th he, who had ruined his wife and crucified his daughter, sank peacefully into death.

* *Letters from E. B. B. to B. R. Haydon*, p. 9, 1939.

† Mrs. Robert Cockburn who, as Mary Duff, was beloved by Lord Byron as a child. He refers to her in *When I Roved a Young Highlander*.

He was buried in Shinfield church beside his wife on 15th December, and his daughter had a brass plate fixed on the grave with the inscription: "Here lye ye bodyes of George Mitford and Mary his wife ye said George died ye 10th day of December Anno Domini MDCCCXLII in ye full hope of a joyful resurrection."* His funeral caused something of a sensation in the neighbourhood. "The chief gentry of the country sent to request to follow his remains to the grave," his daughter wrote: "the six principal farmers of the parish begged to officiate as bearers; they came in new suits of mourning, and were so deeply affected that they could hardly lift the coffin. Every house in our village street was shut up; the highway was lined with farmers and tradesmen, in deep mourning, on horseback and in phaetons, who followed the procession; they again were followed by the poor people on foot. The church and churchyard were crowded, and the building resounded with tears and sobs when the coffin was lowered into the vault." No doubt, as Chorley states, the respect paid to Dr. Mitford was principally on her behalf, for she was much beloved: at the same time we think it probable that he was liked in the neighbourhood—at any rate among the village folk to whom his genial manners, his sporting propensities, his leniency as a magistrate and his acts of generosity (even though they were at his daughter's expense) would certainly prove popular.

Dr. Mitford's only legacy was one of debt which, despite the diminution of the trust funds in recent years, amounted to between eight and nine hundred pounds. His daughter stated "Everybody shall be paid, if I sell the gown off my back or pledge my little pension." Fortunately such drastic measures were not necessary, for it was suggested that a public subscription should be raised. Many of her

* Interesting details of the discovery of this plate, which had been concealed when the church was "restored" in the last century, are given in *Notes and Queries*, 8th Aug., 1936.

friends co-operated and Mr. Walter, the proprietor of *The Times*, undertook that the appeal should appear in that journal and the *Morning Chronicle*. A copy of this document, which was also circulated privately, came into our hands recently.

"To all who take an interest in their fate it has been well known that, for a very long time, the late Dr. Mitford owed his chief support to the literary exertions of his daughter. During the last four years those exertions were but too frequently interrupted by the demands which his failing eyesight and declining health made upon her services, as reader and nurse; and when he died at the advanced age of eighty-two, after a most protracted and expensive illness, it could hardly be deemed surprising that debts of between eight and nine hundred pounds should have accumulated; the rather that the failure of a publisher within that period had occasioned a loss to nearly half that amount;* so that, after the incessant labour of five-and-twenty years, after relinquishing her late mother's fortune, and three legacies left exclusively to herself, Miss Mitford is unhappily overwhelmed by embarrassments, which she has no power to prevent, which her father has left no means to defray, and to discharge which the small pension of a hundred-a-year that she owes to Her Majesty's Bounty, is manifestly inadequate.

She was however preparing to meet, as best she might, at whatever sacrifice and by whatever exertion, this heavy responsibility, when some friends to whom the circumstances became known proposed a Public Subscription, for the purpose of paying debts incurred, not through extravagance and wantonness, but to supply the wants of age and infirmity, and to surround with needful comforts the dying bed of a beloved parent.

* This may have been the failure of the publisher of *Finden's Tableaux*.

In furtherance of this design, the co-operation of those to whom the memory of the father is endeared by old and pleasant associations, as well as of those who may take an interest in the character of the writings of the daughter, is earnestly solicited. That which would fall with a crushing weight upon one solitary and almost destitute woman, will be but little felt when divided among the affluent and the many."

(Then follows a list of gentlemen in the county who were prepared to receive subscriptions.)

The response to this appeal was immediate. Within four days £450 had been donated and by the 26th March, the sum had risen to £1,300. All her friends gave generously, and in addition, collected subscriptions from others. Among those who contributed were the Queen Dowager,* the Archbishop of Dublin, the Bishop of Durham, the Dukes of Bedford and Norfolk, the Duchess of Norfolk, Lords Landsdowne, Northampton, Fitzwilliam, Spencer, Radnor, Lady Sidmouth, Lady Byron, Lady Dacre, Joanna Baillie, Maria Edgeworth, Fanny Trollope, Mrs. Opie, Tom Moore, Samuel Rogers, Horace Smith (*Rejected Addresses*), James Morier (*Haji Ba Ba*), Mrs. Cockburn, Charles Boner, Kenyon, Talfourd, Milman, Miss Fox, John Walter and many others. The young Queen Victoria also subscribed, but requested that her name should not be mentioned, as she gave from her private income " and fears being subjected to solicitations." Mary Mitford was intensely and humbly thankful for this kindness and generosity. On giving a friend news of the progress of the subscription, she wrote : " . . . . my health is so bad, and my poverty so great, that my friends hope there may be sufficient for the purchase of a small annuity—and this is what they are now trying for. I never before had an idea of my own popularity ; and I have on two or three

* Widow of William IV.

occasions shed tears of pure thankfulness at reading the letters which have been written to, or about, me. . . . I only pray to God that I may deserve half that has been said of me. So far as the truest and humblest thankfulness may merit such kindness, I am perhaps, not wholly undeserving, for praise always makes me humble. I always feel that I am over-valued ; and such is, I suppose, its effect on every mind not exceedingly vain-glorious." She who had given so much, who had sacrificed herself without stint was now, with that justice which occurs more frequently in this life than might be supposed, receiving ; and from henceforth, although she was never a rich woman, she had sufficient for her modest needs. The subscription exceeded £1,600, and the balance, after the debts had been settled, with her pension, the remainder of the trust funds and her royalties, made up her small income. At this time anat tempt was made to obtain an increase in the pension. One of the gentlemen who collected subscriptions for her was the Rev. Wildman Yates, of Ellesmere, Shropshire ; and he wrote to Sir Robert Peel on her behalf. But his efforts were unsuccessful, for the Minister replied : " The whole of the very small sum now at the disposal of the Crown for the grant of Civil List Pensions which is applicable for the current year has been appropriated."*

Although the debts were settled, her other legacy, that of shattered health, was not so easily disposed of, for she still suffered—and continued to suffer until the end of her life—from the terrible nausea, sickness and insomnia caused by her gastric attacks. Without doubt her sufferings can be attributed to the prolonged anxieties she had sustained, but her condition was not improved by the damp and dilapidated state of the cottage, which was again in need of repair. There seems to have been some question of her moving at this time, for she told Harness that she had been offered a cottage at Caversham ; and Elizabeth Barrett

* B.M. Peel Collection.

wrote to Haydon, "As to her coming to London, although you say 'no,' I say 'yea,'—because I am selfish and have flattered myself into fancying that she might live here almost as cheaply, and in certain respects, *social* respects, more pleasantly. But her wishes are against it—and I am not *so* selfish as to struggle against the natural flow of them."* However Mr. Blandy, her man of business, persuaded the Court of Chancery to put the cottage in order, and as her medical attendant, Mr. May, advised that the smell of paint would be fatal to her, she decided to take a holiday in Bath and Devonshire. "At present I am very poorly," she wrote, "and look upon moving with such dread that, but for being driven out by the paint, I don't think I could muster courage for to-morrow's journey." She has left an account of this visit to Bath in her *Recollections*. She lodged in Milsom Street, and was accompanied by a servant. The difference between her published comments and those in her letters provides an entertaining example of the artist's skill in creating pleasant fictions from unpalatable facts; for although she states that she owed Bath "all gratitude" because she went there "with health and spirits so shattered by a long illness and great sorrow" and returned "in the course of a few weeks . . . completely restored in mind and body," she did not, if her letters are to be believed, enjoy the visit. For one reason, the weather was bad and it rained nearly every day; and then she was ill for a great deal of the time with gastric trouble. No doubt there were some pleasant interludes, such as when she called on Landor at his lodgings and examined his miscellaneous collection of paintings, which, she comments, "it was dangerous to praise" for he was in the habit of bestowing any picture admired by his guest, and she was presented with a night view of Vesuvius, by Wright of Derby.† An entertaining sidelight on these visits is provided by one of Elizabeth

* *Letters from E. B. B. to Haydon*, p. 20.

† Joseph Wright, A.R.A., 1735-1797.

Barrett's letters: "Miss Mitford is in Bath, where she spent one week and is about to spend two, and then goes on her way into Devonshire. She amused me so the other day by desiring me to look at the date of Mr. Landor's poems in their first edition, because she was sure it must be fifty years since, and she finds him at this 1843, the very Lothario of Bath, enchanting the wives, making jealous the husbands, and 'enjoying' altogether the worst of reputations. I suggested that if she proved him to be seventy-five,* as long as he proved himself enchanting, it would do no manner of good in the way of practical ethics."†

Another visit she enjoyed was to Bishop Baines, principal of the Catholic College at Prior Park. All her life she had a sympathy with those professing the old faith, although she never felt inclined to change her own—"for my part I hate conversions." But the antiquity and historical tradition of the Catholic Church appealed to her, and she wrote of the Bishop, "I do not know when I have been so thoroughly interested as by Bishop Baines and his secretary, Mr. Bonomi, the old priest and the young. The Bishop is the very incarnation of taste, combined with an intelligence, a liberality, a gracious indulgence most rare among Protestant clergymen, who, frequently excellent, are seldom charming; while the younger one is full of sweetness and purity. My maid . . . is much afraid of my turning Catholic, and I have been really amused to-night at her fears. But one may love the good of every faith, and put the Catholic Bishop by the side of the Protestant Archbishop with no injury to any person, least of all to oneself." After a fortnight in Bath she went on to Bristol to meet Mrs. Trollope and she was "charmed with the old city." She visited places of historical interest and spent the afternoon with Joseph Cottle, friend and publisher of Southey, Coleridge and Wordsworth. But her health was so bad

* He was sixty-eight.
† *Letters of E. B. B.*, i, 137.

that when she arrived at the station to go to Devonshire, she changed her mind and caught the train home instead.

If she obtained little pleasure from this trip, she was dreading even more the return to the empty cottage; and it was something of a relief to find that the builder, in her absence, had been neglecting the work; that the place was not ready for habitation and that in consequence she was obliged to take a room in the cottage belonging to the mother of one of her servants. From there, she was able to supervise the workmen, and at the same time avoid the smell of paint. By the following month, June, she was sufficiently restored in health to pay a short visit to London, where she was overwhelmed with invitations and engagements—"the result of going to town so seldom, and staying so short a time." She met Mrs. Gore, the novelist "as worldly as her books," saw John Lucas's pictures and heard Adelaide Sartoris sing.* It may have been on this visit, too, that she made the acquaintance of Charles Reade, for a few months later she asked him to stay at the cottage on the occasion of the opening of the Reading Room† at Reading, to which ceremony both Carlyle and Dickens had been invited. Of course she also called on Elizabeth Barrett. "The dark room in Wimpole Street was a great contrast to these scenes [the parties she had attended]. Oh, how I more and more love to admire its sweet and precious inmate!" she exclaimed. "There is nothing like her in this world—that is certain." She tackled the formidable Mr. Barrett on the question of moving his invalid daughter from town, "and," she added, "having left Mr. Kenyon to follow up the blow, I have great hopes that a change may be effected." This remark is significant, for it was just this very point—the refusal of Mr. Barrett, against medical advice, to allow his daughter to go to Italy during the winter—that finally alienated Elizabeth from her father,

* Sister of Fanny Kemble.

† This was probably on the site of the present Athenæum Club.

and paved the way for Robert Browning to take his place in her affections.*

Mary Mitford returned to the cottage about the middle of the month, and at once began to set it in order. No doubt the new decorations made the furnishings appear shabby, for she and her personal maid, Kerenhappuck (to whom she always referred—perhaps not unnaturally—as "K") were busy with renovations and improvements. "My present occupation is looking over Reading for cheap, pretty crockeryware—a little dinner service, and breakfast and tea, and dessert to match. Whether I shall succeed in my search I can't tell. I begin to fear not; but *that* is the way I have been making my poor cabin neat and clean, and light and bright, picking up cheap materials in carpets, chintzes, etc., and then making them up myself. We . . . have carpeted every room in the house by the work of our own fingers, and have just completed our sofa and chair covers, our muslin curtains and blinds, and a new dimity bed, which was just completed in time for a certain Miss ——, a self-invited guest, who is the finest specimen of Hibernian brass that I have ever seen in my life." Many guests—invited and self-invited—were to stay at the cottage during the next few years, until, indeed, her health became so bad that she was unable to receive them. She had the Mitford love of hospitality, and now that the expenditure was under her control, she was able to indulge in this pleasure to the limit of her modest means. Indeed, as she was never strong enough to do much visiting on her own account, this remained one of her principal amusements. To the end of her life she retained the faculty of making new friends, for her sympathy, her charming manners, her great conversational powers and her willingness to admire, endeared her to all who came to the cottage.

One of the guests who came that summer was the poet

* Contrary to the suggestion in a recent play, E. B. B.'s correspondence makes it quite plain that she was more fond of her father than he of her.

Richard Hengist Horne. He was a man whose reputation, great in his day, has proved ephemeral, although at least one of his poems, the epic *Orion*, should rescue it from oblivion. He was the friend and intimate of most of the literary figures of his day, including Robert Browning; and he corresponded and collaborated with Elizabeth Barrett, although they never met. His was a strange character, with more than a little of charlatanism in it;* but he has left interesting details, if in some places inaccurate, of Mary Mitford in the two volumes of Elizabeth Barrett's letters which he edited. Horne's first visit (the first of many) took place, it would seem, in August, 1843, for Elizabeth Barrett, with whom he was then corresponding, wrote on the 7th "At four o'clock to-morrow you will be at Three Mile Cross. . . ." and later in the same letter, "Do tell me how you are pleased, and exactly how you are impressed by the visit to Three Mile Cross. I will be secret beyond womanity, if you are frank beyond discretion. Barter your impressions with me, my dear Mr. Horne."† We do not know what revelations his "frankness beyond discretion" led him into; but he has left a charming general impression of his visits to the cottage.

"There used to be, and there no doubt still is, if I had but the courage to go and look at it, a small, old-fashioned cottage at Three-mile Cross, near Reading, which stood in a garden close to the road. A strip of garden was on one side, a little pony-stable on the other, and the larger part of the garden at the back. It was a comfortable-looking, but still a real village cottage, with no town or suburb look whatever about it. Small lattice windows, below and above, with roses and jasmine creeping round them all, established its rural character; and there was a great buttress of a chimney rising from the ground at the garden

* Gosse (*Portraits and Sketches*, p. 99, 1913) refers to him as "gay, tactless and vain to a remarkable degree," and says that ". . . . he himself, with his incredible mixture of affectation and fierceness, humour and absurdity, enthusiasm and ignorance, at once so effeminate, and so muscular, was better than all his tales."

† *Letters of E. B. B. to R. H. Horne*, i, 80, 81.

strip-side, which was completely covered with a very ancient and very fine apricot tree. There the birds delighted to sit and sing among the leaves, and build too, in several snug nooks, and there in early autumn the wasps used to bite and bore into the rich ripe brown cracks of the largest apricots, and would issue forth in rage when any one of the sweetest of their property was brought down to the earth by the aid of a clothes prop, guided under the superintending instructions of a venerable little gentlewoman in a garden-bonnet and shawl, with silver hair, very bright hazel eyes, and a rose-red smiling countenance. Altogether, it was one of the brightest faces any one ever saw.

" 'Now my dear friend,' would she say, 'if you will only attend to my advice, you will get that apricot up there, which is quite in perfection. I have had my eye upon it these last three weeks, wondering nobody stole it. The boys often get over into the garden before any of us are up. There now, collect all those leaves, if you will be so good—and those too—and lay them all in a heap just underneath, so that the apricot may fall upon them. If you don't do that, it will burst open with a thump. There! now push the prop up slowly, so as to break the apricot from the stalk; and when it is down, do not be in too great a hurry to take it up, as it's sure to have a good large wasp or two inside. Wasps are capital judges of ripe wall-fruit, as my dear father used to say. A little lower with the prop!—more to the left—now just push the prop upwards, and gently lift—again—down it comes! Mind the wasps! three, four—mind!—perhaps that's not all—five!—I told you so!'

" 'How angry they are!'

" 'Not more, my dear friend, than you and I would have been under the circumstances.'

" . . . It would be impossible for any engraving or photograph, however excellent as to features, to convey a true likeness of Mary Russell Mitford. During one of these visits, Miss Charlotte Cushman* was also staying at the cottage, and exclaimed the first time Miss Mitford left the room, 'What a bright face it is!' This effect of summer brightness all over the countenance was quite remarkable. A floral flush overspread the whole face, which seemed to carry its own light with it, for it was the same indoors as out. The silver hair shone, the forehead shone, the cheeks shone, and, above all, the eyes shone. The expression was entirely genial, cognoscitive, beneficent. The outline of the face was an oblate round, of no very marked significance beyond that of an apple, or other rural 'character;' in fact, it was very like a rosy apple in the sun. Always excepting the forehead and chin. The forehead was not only massive, but built in a way that sculpture only could adequately delineate. Miss Barrett, in a note to a friend concerning Miss Mitford, described her forehead as of the ancient Greek type, and compared it to her idea of *Akinetos*, or the Great Unmoved,† although we may doubt whether the amiable authoress of *Our Village* would have felt very much pleased or complimented by the unexpected comparison. Howbeit, this brain-structure accounted to me for the fact that Miss Mitford's conversation was often very superior to anything in her books. Having on one occasion suggested this, she said, smiling 'Well, you see, my dear friend, we must take the world as we find it, and it doesn't do to say to everybody, all that you would say to one here and there.' And presently afterwards, when alluding to several persons, without mentioning any names, for she was a very politic lady of the old school, Miss Mitford added: 'One has to think twice before speaking once, in order to come down to them; like talking to children.'

"This build of head, and strong outline of head and face, will go far to explain the strength of character

* The American tragic actress.
† An allusion to *Orion*.

displayed by Miss Mitford during the early and most trying periods of her life, with her extravagant and selfish father. It may also equally account for her general composure and presence of mind, both on great occasions and others, trifling enough to talk and write about, but of a kind to test the nerves of most ladies. For instance, in driving Miss Mitford one day in her little pony-chaise on a morning visit, she so riveted my attention on the special point of a story, that I allowed one wheel to run into a dry ditch at the roadside, and the pony-chaise must of course have turned over, but that we were ' brought up ' by the hedge. ' Hillo ! my dear friend ! ' said Miss Mitford ; ' we must get out.' We did so ; the little trap was at once put on its proper course, and, without one word of comment, the bright-faced old lady took up the thread of her story."

These anecdotes paint a pleasant picture of her life at this period, of calm repose, of well merited rest, of dignity and composure acquired through privation and suffering ; and it was meet and right that it should be so. Her life was passed in the quiet enjoyment of the more simple pleasures, in reading, in entertaining her friends and in gardening, interspersed by occasional short visits to London to see Elizabeth Barrett. What did these two clever women discuss during their long tête-à-têtes? Possibly French literature, to which they frequently referred in their correspondence, and in which they were both passionately interested. ". . . She [Miss Mitford] . . . praises the French writers—a sympathy between us, that last, which we wear hidden in our sleeves for the sake of propriety," wrote E. B. B. And then there would be the new books to criticize and the current literary gossip to talk over, for both of them, it must be admitted, took a keen interest in these mundane matters. Mary Mitford, though she lived in seclusion in the country was, through her many contacts, always well-informed, and many witnesses have testified to the excellence of her conversation.

"... She was stronger and wider in her conversation and letters than in her books," wrote E. B. B. many years later to Ruskin, "... The heat of human sympathy seemed to bring out her powerful vitality, rustling all over with laces and flowers. She seemed to think and speak stronger holding a hand—not that she required help, or borrowed a word, but that the human magnetism acted on her nature, as it does upon men born to speak. ..."*

At the end of 1843, she was elected an honorary member of the new Literary Institute,† founded by J. S. Buckingham, the author and traveller. Associated with her in this honour was Agnes Strickland, the historian. Elizabeth Barrett, commenting on this fact to Horne, wrote: "I confess that I wondered a good deal at Mr. Buckingham's, or the Literary Institute's, selection of Miss Strickland as the second female Honorary Member. Nobody else to be found fit for the honour,‡ except Miss Strickland! And Miss Martineau, Mrs. Jameson, Maria Edgeworth, Mary Howitt, and Lady Morgan all alive—with long-established European reputations! ... for my own part, although it gave me cordial pleasure to hear of the honour won by, and honourably paid to, Miss Mitford, I should have been more pleased, even for her sake, and valued the appreciation more fully, if it had united her name to the names of these distinguished contemporaries, rather than severed it from them."§ E. B. B.'s judgment in literary matters was usually so excellent that it is a little astonishing to find her writing in this fashion. In our opinion, so far as Mary Mitford's reputation was concerned, it would have made very little difference whether her name were coupled with Agnes Strickland's or with any of the others' for, in creative ability and artistic skill, she was far superior to all of them. Harriet Martineau, although a public figure, was a

* *Letters of* E. B. B., ii, 216.
† This was a literary and social club in Hanover Square.
‡ This was in 1843, before her own reputation was established.
§ *Letters of* E. B. B. *to* R. H. *Horne*, i, 211.

didactic reformer who used her journalistic skill to propagate her views; Mrs. Jameson was a conscientious but not very enlightened art critic; Mary Howitt's writings, though painstaking are uninspired, and Lady Morgan was a boisterous and lively vulgarian. Of them all, Maria Edgeworth, with her large output of novels, had perhaps the most creative ability, although some of her characterisations are incredibly dull.

Little is known of Mary Mitford's movements during 1844, although in June she went to London for a week. She seems, however, to have been affected by the current craze for mesmerism started by Harriet Martineau's miraculous cure,* for her maid Jane, who was deaf, was mesmerized several times, " . . . but not, I believe," wrote Elizabeth Barrett, whose interest in the marvellous was always acute, " with much success curatively. As a remedy, the success has been far greater in the Martineau case than in others. With Miss Mitford's maid, the sleep is, however, produced; and the girl professed, at the third *séance*, to be able to *see behind her*—— "† a useful qualification in a maid. At the end of the year, the Queen visited the neighbourhood, paying a visit to the Duke of Wellington at Strathfieldsaye. This proved a gala occasion for the village children, for Mary Mitford took two hundred and ninety of them, in waggons lent by the local farmers, to the corner of Swallowfield Lane to watch the royal visitor. They called at her home at nine o'clock in the morning, were each presented with a flag, and then, accompanied by their teachers, went in procession to the appointed place. " We had chosen our place well," she told E. B. B., " for the Queen was escorted to that point by her noble host, who took leave of her just in front of our waggons, which looked between the laurels and the pink and white flags like so many masses

* Harriet Martineau was so convinced of her imminent demise at this time that she wrote her own obituary notice; but her prophetic powers were not highly developed and she lived for many years after its composition.

† *Letters of E. B. B.*, i, 220.

of painted-lady sweet peas. . . . After this we all returned . . . to my house, where the gentlefolks had sandwiches and cake and wine; and where the children had each a bun as large as a soup-plate, made doubly nice as well as doubly large, a glass of wine, and a mug of ale. All this seems little enough; but the ecstasy of the children made it much. They had been active from four o'clock in the morning. They had been shouting and singing all day. They did sing and shout all the afternoon, for I had made it my particular request to the schoolmistresses and masters that there might be no scolding or keeping in order—flinging ourselves upon the children's own sense of right. And well did they justify the trust! Never was such harmless jollity! Not an accident! Not a squabble! Not a misword. It did one's very heart good."

No wonder that she was beloved in the village; no wonder that the children, as they passed her window, dropped curtsies or bowed, for actions such as these must have endeared her to all.

XIX

1845-1848

In January, 1845, Robert Browning, on the advice of Kenyon, wrote to Elizabeth Barrett about her volume of poems published in 1844.* Thus began that remarkable correspondence between the two poets which ended only on their marriage on 12th September, 1846. From this, it is possible to follow Mary Mitford's visits to London with far more accuracy than in previous years and to elucidate the real sentiments of E. B. B. towards her. The first time she is mentioned is in a letter dated 5th February, before the two correspondents had met. "You do not know her, I think, personally," wrote E. B. B., "although she was the first to tell me . . . of the grand scene in *Pippa Passes*. *She* has filled a large drawer in this room with delightful letters, heart-warm and soul-warm . . . driftings of nature (if sunshine could drift like snow), and which, if they should ever fall the way of all writing, into print, would assume the folioshape as a matter of course, and take rank on the lowest shelf of libraries. . . ."† Unfortunately—for letters from such a writer to such a recipient would have had great interest—very few of the sheets in that drawer "fell into print." After Mary Mitford's death, Harness applied for them for publication, but E. B. B. told Ruskin: "Her letters were always admirable, but I do most deeply regret that what made one of their greatest charms unfits them for the public—I mean their personal details. . . . When I . . . with the greatest pain force myself to examine them (all those

* *Poems*, 1844.

† *Letters of Robert Browning and Elizabeth Barrett Browning*, i, 12, 1899.

letters she wrote to me in her warm goodness and affectionateness), I find with wonder and sorrow how only half a page here and there *could* be submitted to general readers—*could*, with any decency, much less delicacy."* And so, presumably, they were destroyed, since they have not, so far as we are aware, come to light. But if they were not suitable for publication at that time, they ought to have been kept for posterity; for it is on those "personal details" that historians and biographers depend for their material.

It is unlikely that Mary Mitford was aware of the developments in Wimpole Street for Elizabeth Barrett was reticent by nature and the circumstances of her life forced her to be discreet. It was not until June, six months after the correspondence had begun and a month after her first meeting with Browning, that she mentioned the "bare fact" of his having called upon her, "and reluctantly I did it, though placing some hope on her promise of discretion." Nothing emphasizes more clearly than the remarks in these letters the total lack of understanding between these two women: and if Mary Mitford, in the greater simplicity of her nature, never perhaps probed the depths and subtleties of her friend's character, E. B. B. in her turn, erred in her interpretation of the older woman's qualities. The letters are illuminating on this point, and they also show that E. B. B. felt something approaching to dislike of her friend at this period. "All to-day, Friday, Miss Mitford has been here!" she wrote on 1st November, 1845. "She came at two and went away at seven—and I feel as if I had been making a five-hour speech on the corn laws in Harriet Martineau's parliament . . . so tired am I. Not that dear Miss Mitford did not talk both for me and herself . . . for that, of course, she did. But I was forced to answer once every ten minutes at least . . . and so I am tired and come to rest myself upon the paper. Your name was not once

* *Letters of E. B. B.*, ii, 217.

spoken to-day. . . ."* Then again "Dear Miss Mitford comes to-morrow, and I am not glad enough. Shall I have a letter [from Browning] to make me glad? She will talk, talk, talk . . . and I shall be hoping all day that not a word may be talked of . . . *you*:—a forlorn hope indeed!"† And in 1846 she wrote, "To-day I had a letter from Miss Mitford who says that, inasmuch as she does not go to Paris,‡ she shall come for a fortnight to London, and 'see me every day'!! No time is fixed—but I look a little aghast. *Am I not grateful and affectionate?* Is it right of you, not to let me love anyone as I used to do?"§ How different this is from the early days of their friendship when Mary Mitford, through the exactions of her father, was kept in the country and E. B. B. was enquiring when she would be coming to town. Then her visits evoked very different feelings, or could this have been written: "Miss Mitford came to spend a day with me some ten days ago; sprinkled, as to the soul, with meadow dews. . . ."

It was only natural that with this new, and overwhelming, interest in her life, Elizabeth Barrett should feel impatient when anything occurred to postpone her meetings with Browning. Moreover, although he and Mary Mitford had never met she had expressed the view, despite her initial recommendation of *Pippa Passes*, that his writings were obscure,¶ and consequently E. B. B. felt jealous for his reputation. But these two facts scarcely justified the tone of the letters. Furthermore other people besides Mary Mitford—whose visits to London were infrequent—prevented Browning from coming to Wimpole Street, and they were not thus belittled. And just how much Elizabeth Barrett misjudged her friend's character is also

* *Letters of* R. B. *and* E. B. B., i, 263.

† Idem, i, 455.

‡ She was unable to go through lack of money, a servant having robbed her of a considerable sum.

§ *Letters of* R. B. *and* E. B. B., ii, 23 *et seq.*

¶ She was not by any means the only person who held this view. Wordsworth was another who professed the same opinion.

startlingly revealed: "... she sees the whole world in stripes of black and white, it is her way.* I feel very affectionately towards her, love her sincerely. She is affectionate to me beyond measure. Still, I always feel that if I were to vex her, the lower deep below the lowest deep would not be low enough for *me*. I always feel *that*. She would advertise me directly for a wretch proper,"† she confided to Browning. And on another occasion, "She hates ... and loves in extreme degrees." This perhaps was the most unjust of all the strictures. That Mary Mitford loved to excess, until it became a form of weakness, we know from her devotion to her unworthy father; but that she ever hated has yet to be proved. Scorn of conduct she considered unworthy she may have expressed—indeed undoubtedly did; but of hatred, with its sinister implications, no single instance can be evinced. In this same letter, E. B. B. added "She is too fervent a friend—she can be. Generous too, she can be without an effort; and I have had much affection from her—and accuse myself for seeming to have less—but——"‡

But what? we must ask. Perhaps she supplies the answer herself: "... to-morrow morning Miss Mitford comes to spend the day like the dear kind friend she is; and I, not the least in the world glad to see her! Why have you turned my heart into such hard porphyry? *Once, when it was plain clay, every finger (of these womanly fingers) left a mark on it—and now ... you see!*"§ Was it that she, knowing the love Mary Mitford bore her and which, until recently, was returned, had a sense of guilt, of betrayal, "I have had much affection for her—and accuse myself for seeming to have less—" towards her friend? And this feeling of guilt led her to denigrate and to disparage one who had recently been the object of her

* She was, on the contrary, far too tolerant, and to continue the metaphor, her view of the world was uniformly of one colour, and that a bright one.

† *Letters of* R. B. *and* E. B. B., i, 500.

‡ *Letters of* R. B. *and* E. B. B., i, 473.

§ The italics are ours. *Letters of* R. B. *and* E. B. B., ii, 289.

affections? The subtleties and convolutions of the human heart are the least capable of explanation, since logic plays no part in them; but we can find no other reason to account for the sudden change of attitude. Yet how unnecessary it was, and how unjust was E. B. B.'s estimate of her friend's reaction to the news of her love for Browning. "No single person will be more utterly confounded than she," she wrote, "when she comes to be aware of what you are to me now—and *that* I was thinking to-day, while she talked to never a listener. She will be confounded and angry perhaps—it will be beyond her sympathies—or if they reach so far, the effort to make them do so will prove a more lively affection for me, than, with all my trust in her goodness, I dare count on."* Confounded Mary Mitford may have been, and in that she was not alone, for the secret had been well kept; but it postulates a lack of understanding of her character to suppose that she could be angry over what was a cause for happiness to her friend. She may have experienced a sense of personal loss (although she did not betray it) for all the love of her warm nature was centred on E. B. B., but this in no way influenced her affections, and her devotion ended only with her life.

It is only fair, however, to point out that while E. B. B. was not the soft, gentle creature she has been depicted—she was too clever not to be caustic on occasions—she was not a malicious woman nor was she disloyal to her friends. It was only in her relations with Mary Mitford that her behaviour was open to criticism, and that "for reasons, for reasons," as she herself would have said. Whether we have interpreted these "reasons" correctly can never be definitely ascertained; but that they existed is beyond dispute.†

Throughout these two years, 1845 and 1846, Mary

* *Letters of* R. *B. and* E. *B. B.*, ii, 291.

† In addition to the passages quoted, there are many others scattered throughout E. B. B.'s correspondence, which support our view.

Mitford, apart from her occasional visits to Wimpole Street, followed her normal routine in the country, for her health, although not good, had not yet deteriorated sufficiently to keep her confined to the house. In the winter of 1845, she was still an active woman, taking long walks which were " not only the necessity of existence to me, so far as health is concerned, but also the chief means of my social pleasures ; for since I have made the grand discovery that a lantern is as good as a moon, I trot about at night with a maid, not merely to country neighbours, but to lectures and concerts in Reading, where I have a whole Mechanics' Institute as an object of interest and pleasure." At fifty-eight a walk of six miles at night was something of an achievement, following as it must have done, an active day. Despite all she had suffered and endured, she never lost—even when a helpless cripple—her zest for life nor her interest in affairs, both literary and social. Nor had her delight in entertaining diminished, for that summer many of her friends, among them Chorley, Lucas and Horne, visited Three Mile Cross. In addition, she made a new one, Charles Boner, the translator of Hans Andersen, with whom she remained on intimate terms for many years. Her powers of friendship were indeed astonishing : not only did she rarely lose an old friend, except in the natural course of events, but she retained the faculty of making new ones to the end of her life. It says much for her conversational powers, her charm of manner, that when she was over sixty, she became friendly, among a host of others, with Ruskin, Kingsley and James Payn, all of them considerably younger than herself. In an intellectual sense she never became old, for while her bodily powers became weaker and frailer, her zest for life and her interest in current affairs kept her mind youthful and vigorous. And the very fact that she accepted traditional standards and conventions, and had always done so, freed her intellect for the contemplation of other matters.

It was in August, 1845, when he was thirty years of age, that Boner first came to the cottage. He was on a visit to England from Germany, where he held the position of tutor to the children of the Prince of Thurm and Taxis at Ratisbon; and after staying a week with Wordsworth at Rydal Mount, he came, at the poet's instigation, to Three Mile Cross. This was the first of many visits—for he saw her whenever he was in England—and it resulted in a correspondence throughout which she acted as his adviser on literary matters. As he was then at the beginning of his career, her advice must have been most valuable. "*The Fir Tree* and *Red Shoes* [his translations from Andersen] seem to me exceedingly good," she wrote, "but unless these works be very profitable (which is an answer to everything,) I had rather see you writing prose of your own, and laying the foundation of a solid reputation." And in another letter, acknowledging some of his verses, she requested him to find someone else to act as his literary agent. "I live in the country, going rarely, if ever, to London, and then to one house only. I have as few literary friends and acquaintances as is well possible, and of the race of Editors and Journalists I know absolutely nothing. Then if I write to proprietors of magazines, or newspapers, or periodicals of any sort, requesting them to insert a friend's poem, the reply is sure to be that they overflow with poetry, but that they want a prose story from me, and most likely they trump up a story of some previous application, and *dun* with as much authority as if I really owed them the article, and they had paid for it. Now all this is not only supremely disagreeable to me, but makes me a most ineffective and useless mediator for you. You should have a man upon the spot, and not an old woman at a distance, hating the trade of authorship, and keeping as much aloof as possible from all its *tracasseries*...."

As has been stated before, she always maintained that she would never have written a line, had she not been obliged to do so; and now that her income was secure, her literary output, although not entirely ceasing, was certainly much reduced. Nevertheless it is not true that she had "as few literary acquaintances as is well possible," since she was friendly—and enjoyed being so—with most of the literary figures of her day; nor is it strictly true that she "hated the trade of authorship." What she disliked was being dependent on her literary output for money; and now that this necessity no longer arose, there is evidence that she was well content with her literary fame, and that when she came to take up her pen again, she derived considerable enjoyment from it. This question of authorship was always a source of disagreement between her and Elizabeth Barrett, for as Elizabeth Lee has pointed out, "she underrated the literary vocation, while Mrs. Browning was inclined to overrate it." Indeed E. B. B. wrote to Chorley, "It does appear to me wonderfully and mournfully wrong, when men of letters . . . take to dishonoring their profession by fruitless bewailings and gnashings of teeth; when, all the time, it must be their own fault if it is not the noblest in the world. Miss Mitford treats me as a blind witness in this case; because I have seen nothing of the literary world, or any other sort of world, and yet cry against her 'pen and ink' cry. It is the cry I least like to hear from her lips, of all others; and it is unworthy of them altogether. On the lips of a woman of letters, it sounds like jealousy (which it cannot be with *her*), as on the lips of a woman of the world, like ingratitude."* These remarks provide more evidence that E. B. B. never appreciated her friend's bitter struggle, nor could she, with her lack of worldly experience, understand the searing scars it had left on Mary Mitford's mind.

Another source of pleasure, besides her visitors, was the garden. That autumn she had a magnificent display of dahlias, and one of her seedlings was sold for £20, "the

* *Letters of E. B. B.*, i, 259.

highest price given for a dahlia this year," she told Emily Jephson, with whom she often exchanged horticultural details. " . . . I don't know what the nursery man (Mr. Bragge of Slough) means to call it. It is white, of the most exquisite shape and cleanness, tipped with puce colour. We have some very fine seedlings *this* year, and our great bed is also full of fine old dahlias—I mean those raised by other growers ; for I don't believe that we have one more than three years old, except the old Springfield, which I insist upon keeping for ' auld lang syne.' . . . What should I, who have only Flush to love me, and poor Ben and K. and K's little boy, do without flowers ? " The garden which was always kept in perfect order, must have necessitated a full time gardener. Even at this stage, when her income was greatly reduced, her domestic staff seems to have consisted of four persons ;* and her servants usually remained with her for long periods, probably because they " become, as they are in France, and ought, I think, always to be, really and truly part of the family."† At this period she had K., her personal maid " a most sensible young woman, who waits upon me, and walks out with me " ; another woman to do the household work ; Ben Kirby, who during Dr. Mitford's lifetime was house boy, and about whom she wrote the entertaining tale *The Tambourine*, and probably a man for the garden. Another occupant of the house was K.'s child " a little fatherless boy, who is the pet of the household." The first mention of this devoted servant occurs during Dr. Mitford's lifetime, but she seems to have left and returned later, owing to some gossip, probably in connection with her child. She eventually married Sam Sweetman, a groom, who joined the household about 1847 when her mistress was obliged to keep a pony chaise, owing to her crippling rheumatism.

* In the American edition of *Letters from Abroad to Kindred at Home*, Miss Sedgwick says that the Mitfords kept " two men servants, two or three maid servants and two horses."

† *Yesterdays with Authors*, by James T. Fields, (letter dated February, 1850) 1872.

It was in the winter of 1845-1846 that Mary Mitford first suffered from those attacks of rheumatism which, with increasing severity, lasted until the end of her life. On March 23rd, 1846, she told Boner: "You will be sorry to hear that I, generally so active, am quite crippled by rheumatism, and hobble about like a woman of ninety. I have some hope that it is the result of this most unusual season, and that when the real spring comes (for as yet we have only the name) and brings with it the primroses and the violets, I may be able to get out and look for them." That year, too, there was a slight resumption of her literary activities, for she edited a volume for children in French of selections from the works of Alexandre Dumas.* She was a little apprehensive about the reactions of her two English publishers, Messrs. Grant & Griffiths and Henry Colburn, to whom she was under contract; but as the French work was published by Rolandi and printed in Brussels, they were not in a position to protest. And in August, there was a new edition of *Belford Regis*, a copy of which she sent to Boner.

In the midst of these activities, she received a great shock in the death by suicide of her old friend, Benjamin Haydon. "He was my old and intimate friend and correspondent for above thirty-five years," she told Boner. "At one time he used to write to me three or four times a week, and although my occupations, and my business, and my dislike of letter writing had much diminished that closeness of intercourse, yet the friendship continued unbroken. This event quite upset me, and I have hardly recovered from it yet." Poor Haydon was the victim of his own unstable character, and the principal cause of his suicide was unsatisfied vanity. The bright hopes of his early days had not been fulfilled, and although other painters with less talent than himself achieved success, he, through

* *Fragments des Œuvres d'Alexandre Dumas choisis à l'usage de la jeunesse*, ed. par M. R. Mitford, 1846.

inordinate vanity which made him unable to cherish his worldly interests, had received affronts and humiliations. A short time before his death, he had sent boxes and pictures to Elizabeth Barrett at Wimpole Street* (which he had done on several previous occasions to prevent their seizure by creditors) among which was his portrait of Mary Mitford. He asked E. B. B. to keep it for his sake, but later wrote that he could not bear to part with it. Mary Mitford was much touched when she learned of this incident.†

But the principal event of 1846, was Elizabeth Barrett's marriage to Browning which took place secretly at Marylebone Church on September 12th. The news was communicated to Mary Mitford by a letter, presumably from E. B. B., and it must have given her a shock, for she can have had no indication of the affair. But her behaviour provided a quick refutation of the suggestion that she would be "angry" and that the marriage would be "beyond her sympathies," for E. B. B., replying to her friend's first letter after the marriage, says, "You are good, you are kind. I thank you from the bottom of my heart for saying to me that you would have gone to the church with me. *Yes, I know you would.*" She did not, of course, know anything of the sort, and for the last few months had harboured thoughts which were contrary to the spirit of this kindly suggestion. But whatever Mary Mitford may have felt—and it is impossible that she should not have experienced a sense of loss—her comments were commendably restrained. She had a dignity and self-control which, when she suffered through her affections, enabled her to conceal it. This was proved again and again by her loyalty to her father, and the same quality was manifest in this instance. "Did you hear that my beloved friend Elizabeth Barrett is married?" she asked Emily Jephson. "Love really is the wizard the poets have called him; a fact I

* They had corresponded but never met.

† The portrait remained for some years in the possession of Mr. Barrett. It is now in the Reading Museum.

always doubted till now.* But never was such a miraculous proof of his power as her travelling across France by diligence, by railway, by Rhône boat—anyhow, in fact; and having arrived in Pisa so much improved in health that Mrs. Jameson, who travelled with them, says she is 'not merely improved but transformed.' I do not know Mr. Browning; but this fact is enough to make me his friend." And to Boner she wrote "The great news of the season is the marriage of my beloved friend, Elizabeth Barrett, to Robert Browning. Do you know him? I have seen him once only, many years ago. He is, I hear, from all quarters, a man of immense attainment and great conversational power. As a poet, I think him overrated." Although she may have felt hurt, she never wavered in her affection. E. B. B., on the other hand, seems never to have regained her original feeling for her friend: but it is never easy to forgive those whom we feel we have wronged.

Continued ill health was her lot during the next two years, and as her sufferings increased her physical powers declined. In the winter of 1847, she was again crippled by rheumatism; and even when her condition ameliorated in the warmer weather, she remained exceedingly lame. It took her three hours, she complained, to walk a distance usually accomplished in one. By the autumn of that year, she had been obliged to buy a pony and was looking about for a suitable carriage. It may have been this animal which was so vicious that he kicked two carriages to pieces in one afternoon and had to be replaced by one whose habits were more suited to an elderly invalid. Rheumatism, unfortunately, was not the only cause of her sufferings, for she still had bouts of the gastric trouble

* This was a matter on which she had always been sceptical, frequently expressing the opinion that a marriage of convenience was more likely to prove successful than a love match. It is, therefore, all the more remarkable that T. J. Wise, in accounting for his forged first edition of the *Sonnets from the Portuguese*, should have evolved the fiction of Mary Mitford's being entrusted with their private printing. It was a bad psychological blunder to have imagined that Mrs. Browning would ever have entrusted love sonnets to her sceptical friend.

and in addition, in the spring of 1848 she had a bad attack of influenza which left her much weakened. Mrs. Browning writing from Florence, advised a visit to the sea; but her medical attendant would not allow her to take so long a journey, so she went, at the end of July, to Taplow. At first she seems to have benefited from the change; but in her desire to visit the interesting places in the vicinity, she overtaxed her small residue of strength, and by August 6th she was again "miserably ill" and was obliged to return home to rest.

Notwithstanding this background of ill health and weakness, visitors continued to come to Three Mile Cross, and among them, in January, 1847, on the introduction of Mrs. Cockburn, was John Ruskin. "Have you ever read an Oxford Graduate's *Letters on Art*?" she asked a friend. "The author, Mr. Ruskin, was here last week, and is certainly the most charming person that I have ever known. The books are very beautiful, although I do not agree in all the opinions; but the young man himself is just what if one had a son one should have dreamt of his turning out, in mind, manner, conversation, everything." And she told Boner in 1848, "John Ruskin . . . is a very elegant and distinguished-looking young man, tall, fair and slender—too slender, for there is a consumptive look, and I fear a consumptive tendency—the only cause of grief that he has ever given to his parents. He must be, I suppose, twenty-six or twenty-seven,* but he looks much younger, and has a gentle playfulness—a sort of pretty waywardness, that is quite charming." We wonder what she would have said had she known the true character of her visitor, the abnormalities and cold cruelty of his dual personality. But perhaps, with her recognition that mental states had often physical causes, she would only have exclaimed "Poor fellow!" This was the first visit of many, and in the summer of 1848, Ruskin took his young and beautiful wife,

* He was born in 1819.

she who caused him such a physical revulsion, down to Three Mile Cross. Effie Ruskin told her parents—" . . . we came down here to Reading [they stayed at the Bear Inn] and last night we took tea at Miss Mitford's who is a dear old lady and lives three miles from here. She has a beautiful garden from which she gave me a bouquet, she is very fond of John and being very poor her house is a little cottage with wee rooms. . . . She is now 60 and is energetic and, I think, very romantic. . . ."*

Mary Mitford's name was not associated with the great reforms and movements which convulsed the country during her lifetime—the circumstances of her life prevented that—but she nevertheless took a lively interest in current affairs. Had she been free, however, it is doubtful whether she would have played any active part in them: hers was not a thrusting, forceful personality, and she had too much worldly wisdom to believe that any particular individual or system would bring about the millennium. She believed in doing her duty in that station of life into which she had been born; and although herself perpetually in need of money, she always gave to deserving cases. After her father's death, when she had more leisure, she interested herself in the affairs of the neighbourhood; and one of the schemes she laboured for was the establishment of lending libraries for the poor. Her collaborator in this plan was Lovejoy, the Reading bookseller, whose shop was in London Street. He was a man of exceptional ability, whose library was so well stocked that it was considered to be a rival to Mudie's. We have been privileged to examine some of the papers left by his successor, Miss Langley, and we found that among those who patronised the shop were Walt Whitman, Swinburne, Richard le Gallienne, the Duke of Wellington, Charles Reade, Dickens and many others. In this plan for village libraries, she also had the assistance of William Chambers, the Edinburgh publisher

* *The Order of Release*, ed. Sir. W. James, pp. 114 *et seq*, 1947.

and proprietor of *Chambers's Journal*, who made her acquaintance about this time. He has left some interesting impressions of her. After saying that he went to see her on every possible occasion, he continues: "In her character she was a matchless specimen of a well educated Englishwoman, correct in taste and feeling, clever and self reliant. . . . Although considerably advanced in life, she had the liveliness and winning manners of a child. Some women never seem to grow old, and she was one of them. Her tongue ran on so incessantly concerning the details of village life, that each of my visits might have afforded the materials of a popular article. Short in stature, and with a tall gold-headed cane in hand, she invited me to walk with her through the adjoining green lanes in the neighbourhood; at every step the trees, wild flowers, and birds offering objects of garrulous remark."*

This year, too, Boner, who was visiting England, was frequently at Three Mile Cross, and in the summer the genial Boston publisher, J. T. Fields, armed with an introduction from Kenyon, came to the cottage. Like many other people, he was attracted by the unusual beauty of her voice which, he said, was the most magnetic he had ever heard, and which had "a peculiar ringing sweetness in it, rippling out sometimes like a beautiful chime of silver bells." Fields has left a vivid account of this first visit to the author of *Our Village*: "The cottage where I found her was situated in the high road between Basingstoke and Reading; and the village street on which she was then living contained the public house and several small shops near by. There was also close at hand the village pond full of ducks and geese. . . . The windows of the cottage were filled with flowers, and cowslips and violets were plentifully scattered about the little garden. I remember the room into which I was shown was sanded, and a quaint old clock behind the door was marking off the hour in small

* *Chambers's Journal*, Jan. 28th, 1882.

but very loud pieces. The cheerful old lady called to me from the head of the stairs to come up to her sitting room to converse with her. . . ."* This was the first of many visits, and they corresponded till the end of her life. Fields was a generous friend, and her letters contain many references to his thoughtful kindness. Nevertheless it says much for her own charm that nearly all those who came to make her acquaintance purely as a literary celebrity, remained to serve her.

* *Yesterdays with Authors*, J. T. Fields, p. 264, 1872.

XX

1849-1852

During 1849 she seems to have had some respite from her perpetual ill health, and in January she felt so much better that she was planning a visit to Paris. This was a long cherished scheme which, for one reason or another, had never materialized, but for which now the auspices seemed propitious. Henry Chorley, and her companion at Taplow the previous summer, a Mr. Hinton, were to accompany her; and she was pleased at the prospect of being in the French capital when Prince Louis Napoleon, whom she admired, was President of the Republic.* When it became known that she was to make this trip, she received many letters of introduction; and in this connection she told Boner: " Everybody says that my name will be sufficient introduction, and so forth. Now that is a very pretty speech; but even if it were true, which I do not believe, it would not follow that one could go about proclaiming one's name or pinning one's card upon one's shawl." Nevertheless, she was destined not to cross the channel, for ill health once again intervened and prevented her from travelling. Mrs. Browning wrote: " . . . what are your plans for the summer. Do you think of Paris seriously? Am I not sceptic about your voyages round the world? It's about the only thing that I don't thoroughly believe you *can* do."* The truth was, indeed, that she had become so frail that in spite of slight ameliorations from time to time, it was not safe for her to be away from home, where she could obtain rest and medical attendance, for more than short periods.

* He was elected president in 1848.

† *Letters of E. B. B.*, i, 400.

Since E. B. B.'s marriage in 1846, there had been a steady exchange of letters between them. It can well be imagined that to the woman in Italy, unable to obtain new publications and remote from literary news, Mary Mitford's letters, containing all those "personal details" must have been most acceptable. The two friends exchanged views about French literature and politics (they both admired Napoleon III, but for different reasons) and discussed with avidity the authorship—then unknown—of *Jane Eyre*. When the older woman settled the problem, "It [*Jane Eyre*] was really written by a Miss Brontë, [sic] a clergyman's daughter, diminutive almost to dwarfishness—a woman of thirty, who had hardly ever left her father's parish in Yorkshire," Mrs. Browning commented ironically: "I certainly don't think the qualities, half savage, and half freethinking, expressed in *Jane Eyre* are likely to suit a model governess or schoolmistress; and it amuses me to consider them in that particular relation." When a letter eventually arrived at Three Mile Cross from the Yorkshire parsonage, no doubt it was forwarded to Italy. And it was in the spring of 1849, too, that Mary Mitford received the news for which she had been impatiently waiting—that her beloved friend had given birth to a son.* The joyful tidings were conveyed to her by Robert Browning in a letter which, she told Boner, was the first she had ever received from him.

For the greater part of that year her health seems to have been sufficiently good to permit a certain amount of activity. In September, she spent a day at Whiteknights, near Reading, then the property of Baron Goldsmid whose daughter became her friend, to meet Cobden and his wife. "He impressed me exceedingly," she told Boner. "I expected to find a very clever, powerful man, but coarse and elderly—a man out of the counting-house. On the contrary, he is young-looking, full of taste, grace, elegance

* Robert Wiedeman Barrett Browning, b. 9th March, 1849.

and refinement, playful and gentle in the highest degree. His wife is a true English beauty. . . ." Unfortunately this day in the open air brought on an attack of neuralgia, which lasted for some time and caused her acute pain. Then in December, her servant who drove the pony chaise and looked after the garden caught smallpox, which was rife in the neighbourhood; and although she was advised to send him away, she thought it her duty to have him nursed in the house. The infection spread to K.'s little boy, causing great anxiety to both his mother and her mistress. Fortunately the child recovered, but even in February of the following year, "people still pass on the other side of the way," she told Boner, "and a carriage stops and leaves a card and makes a hurried inquiry." It is indeed remarkable that in her poor state of health, she was not attacked by the malady. But such are the vagaries and inconsistencies of nature that she escaped unscathed and in March she reported that "ever since violeting began I have walked eight or nine miles every day," a feat she had been unable to perform for several years.

There is no doubt that her rheumatic condition was greatly accentuated by the bad state of the cottage. The walls were mouldering with damp, the rain came through the roof and the windows, and in every high wind the small panes rattled and fell in. She determined that if the Master in Chancery would not permit the necessary repairs, she would find another cottage, and in May she had actually taken the long threatened step of giving notice to quit. The difficulty was to find another suitable habitation, but she already had in view the cottage at Swallowfield, a village three miles further along the Basingstoke road, to which she removed the following year.

It is indicative of her increased strength that she allowed herself to be persuaded, by Henry Chorley, into literary composition again that summer. He had taken over the editorship of the *Ladies Companion*, a journal belonging to

Bradbury and Evans, which was then in a precarious state; and no doubt he felt that contributions from her would help to increase the journal's circulation. These were to be a series of papers entitled *Readings of Poetry, Old and New*, and were to consist of extracts from her favourite authors.* The papers, augmented in number, were eventually published as a book under the title of *Recollections of a Literary Life* and were remarkable for two things: they contained much interesting autobiographical matter, written in her own discursive style, and they verified Mrs. Browning's assertion that "when she [Mary Mitford] read a book, provided it wasn't written by a friend, edited by a friend, lent by a friend, or associated with a friend, her judgment could be fine and discriminating on most subjects."† Thus among the gods of our literature, we find W. C. Bennett‡—"the ubiquitous Bennett," as Mrs. Browning called him—and several other manufacturers of verse, personal friends of hers, whose productions are now mercifully forgotten. But with these exceptions, the book is a testimony to her taste and learning. For instance, when writing of Walter Savage Landor in the chapter *Poetry that Poets Love*, she says: "To no one can the words that I have placed at the head of this paper apply more perfectly than to Mr. Landor. No poetry was ever dearer to poets than his. Nearly fifty years ago, we find Southey writing of and to the author of *Gebir*, with a respectful admiration seldom felt by one young man for another; and, from that hour to the present, all whom he would himself most wish to please have showered upon him praises that cannot die. The difficulty in selecting from his works is the abundance; but I prefer the *Hellenics*,

* They were published in the *Ladies Companion* from July, 1850 onwards. The last one appeared on 31st May, 1851.

† *Letters of E. B. B.*, ii, 217.

‡ W. C. Bennett, who was a friend of hers and with whom she corresponded, was a watchmaker by trade. His poems, which had a certain vogue, are certainly some of the worst in the English language. Sixty-two of her letters to him, mostly concerned with business, are in the Henry E. Huntington Library, California.

that charming volume, because few, very few, have given such present life to classical subjects." These views are identical with those expressed by Sidney Colvin in his admirable study of Landor,* written thirty years later. Landor's poems are esoteric and have only ever appealed to the few ; and who will deny his astonishing feeling for, and intimacy with, past ages ? The *Recollections* might, in fact, be termed the first of the popular anthologies, for although the extracts she chose are now well known, they were not so then, except in literary circles.

The uncertainty over her place of residence persisted throughout 1850 and the following year. Her notice to quit had galvanised the myrmidons in Chancery to action, and an estimate was obtained for putting her house into order. But it was apparently too costly for by April she had taken the Swallowfield cottage, " a good, comfortable, soundly built cabin, standing high and dry at the end of a lane, a little way out of the road from Reading to Basingstoke." In the meantime, she was offered a cottage in Wales which, however, she declined. She did not want to leave the neighbourhood she knew and loved so well, and she feared, in a remote district, being unable to obtain the books she required. " I have the habit of running over almost every book of any note that is published," she commented ; and the facilities for doing so were provided by Lovejoy, the Reading bookseller. In July, she was waiting to hear whether Mrs. Browning, who was in Paris, would come to London, and she told Boner that her lameness was so bad that she would not visit the metropolis, unless for this reason, despite the attractions of the Great Exhibition. But the Brownings arrived, and she departed hastily to the capital for a week to be with her friend. " A strange thing it seemed to see her walking about like other people," she commented to Boner, after the visit. " She and her husband are now gone to winter in Paris. . . .

* *Landor* (*English Men of Letters Series*), Colvin, 1884.

They have a pretty little boy, but it was odd to hear the English parents and the English nurse talking to him in Italian. I suppose next year they will all talk to him in French, and when English will take its turn, God knows." Her time, when not spent with her beloved friend, seems to have been fully occupied. Her lameness did not prevent her from visiting the Exhibition in the company of Lucas, and inspecting the pictures at the British Gallery. She saw Ruskin, who told her that he contemplated abandoning art for natural science, and she spent a great deal of time with her new friend, Miss Goldsmid.

On her return, she must have been fully occupied with the preparations for the removal to Swallowfield which took place at the end of September, 1851. The cottage she had chosen still stands to-day. It is brick, of Flemish bond with dark headers. There have, however, been alterations, for a left wing has been added and two bay windows, and the pond shown in the engraving is no longer there. The cottage stands in the fork of two lanes and the immediate vicinity is open and unwooded, whereas when she was in residence it was surrounded by shrubs and trees. Indeed if she were to revisit not only this locality but the whole neighbourhood which she knew so intimately, we feel that she would have some difficulty in recognizing it, and this despite the fact that many of the buildings she described are still standing. The major difference between now and a hundred years ago lies in the disappearance of natural objects, the ponds and particularly the trees, for the country must have been much more wooded then than now. Her own transition from one home to another was simple. "I walked from the one cottage to the other on an autumn evening, when the vagrant birds, whose habit of assembling here for their annual departure gives, I suppose, its name of Swallowfield to the village, were circling and twittering over my head." But the transportation of her possessions was a more complicated affair. She possessed about six thousand books which, according to the man who carried out the removal, weighed four tons, and their arranging on new shelves occupied some time: the task was not finished two months later. Anyone who has moved quantities of books will appreciate the utter confusion which must have reigned until they were all safely stowed away on shelves. Then new carpets had to be bought and fitted, and the garden made. No plants had been brought from Three Mile Cross and she appealed to her friends for roots and seedlings. But despite the dislocation, she was charmed with her new residence. " . . . I like the place," she told Boner. " It is exceedingly convenient, the neighbours, high and low, are delighted to get us, and the drives and walks are charming. Indeed, in quiet pastoral beauty it is impossible to exceed this lovely valley of the Loddon, with its green water-meadows and its magnificent trees. . . ." And of course as soon as she was settled, down came the visitors, Dean Milman and his wife, J. T. Fields and possibly Charles Kingsley, whom she met at the end of that year, and whose personality made a strong impression on her. " Mr. Kingsley took me quite by surprise in his extraordinary fascination," she wrote. " I have never seen a man of letters the least like him. . . . Mr. Kingsley is not only a high-bred gentleman, but has the most charming admixture of softness and gentleness, with spirit, manliness and frankness—a frankness quite transparent—and a cordiality that would win any heart."

In the midst of the removal, she was called upon to supply material for another volume of her *Recollections*. The papers which had been appearing in the *Ladies Companion* were now being published by Bentley as a book. She had intended that the work should consist of two volumes, but the publisher desired a third. The success of this work, which appeared early in 1852, was immediate and gratifying, and she told Miss Goldsmid, " Ever since it has been published I have had, day by day, letters upon letters, packets upon packets, books upon books, from all parts of the country . . . not merely from enthusiastic girls and young poets from Oxford and Cambridge, but from people the most unexpected—grave old merchants . . . and professional men . . . who find relief from their mind-weariness in the soothing delights of poetry. I should be afraid to tell you how many strangers have written to me during the last three months; and I hail it, not merely as a mark of personal kindness to myself, but as a pregnant proof of the interest taken in the main subject of the work." Nevertheless this book, which brought her so much commendation, was the cause of a coolness in E. B. B.'s feelings towards her, for in Chapter 14, Vol. 1, in which she gave extracts from the works of Elizabeth and Robert Browning, she also revealed details of her friend's private life.* These concerned the death by drowning of Edward Barrett, Mrs. Browning's favourite brother, who had accompanied her to Torquay in 1838: and the incident was referred to because, the author explained, she had so often been asked what was the shadow that had passed over E. B. B.'s young heart which "saddened her bloom of youth, and gave a deeper hue of thought and feeling, especially of devotional feeling, to her poetry." Here is the description of the tragedy. "One fine summer morning her favourite brother, together with two other fine young men, his friends, embarked on board a small sailing-vessel for a trip of a few hours. Excellent sailors all, and familiar with the coast, they sent back the boatmen, and undertook themselves the management of the little craft. Danger was not dreamt of by any one; after the catastrophe no one could divine the cause, but in a few minutes after their embarkation and in sight of their very windows, just as they were crossing the bar, the boat went down, and all who were in her perished. Even the bodies were never found. I was told by a party who were travelling that year

* This paper had not appeared in the *Ladies Companion.*

in Devonshire and Cornwall, that it was most affecting to see on the corner houses of every village street, on every church-door and almost on every cliff, for miles and miles along the coast handbills, offering large rewards for linen cast ashore marked with the initials of the beloved dead; for it so chanced that all the three were of the dearest and the best; one, I believe, an only son, the other the son of a widow."

The Brownings were in Paris when their attention was drawn, by a French journalist, to this passage. Mrs. Browning was very distressed, so much so that she was unable to read it herself and asked her husband to do so, with certain omissions. She was morbidly sensitive, and could not bear any reference, even from her husband, to her brother's death, even though it had taken place fourteen years before. At that time she was, in addition to her natural grief, overcome by remorse, for it was on her behalf that Edward had remained in Cornwall, somewhat against his father's wishes. Furthermore she dreaded the publicity these revelations would entail, and feared to read references to the event whenever her name was mentioned in the press. She at once wrote to her friend: "My very dear friend, let me begin what I have to say by recognizing you as the most generous and affectionate of friends. I never could mistake the least of your intentions; you were always, from first to last, kind and tenderly indulgent to me—always exaggerating what was good in me, always forgetting what was faulty and weak—keeping me by force of affection in a higher place than I could aspire to by force of vanity; loving me always, in fact. Now let me tell you the truth. It will prove how hard it is for the tenderest friends to help paining one another, since *you* have pained *me*. See what a deep wound I must have in me, to be pained by the touch of such a hand. Oh, I am morbid, I very well know. But the truth is that I have been miserably upset by your book, and that if I had had the least imagination of your intending to touch upon certain biographical details in relation to me, I would have conjured you by your love to me and by my love to you, to forbear it altogether. . . . He [Browning] tells me (and *that* I perfectly believe) that, for the facts to be given at all, they could not possibly be given with greater delicacy ; oh, and I will add for myself, that for them to be related by anyone during my life, I would rather have *you* relate them than another. But why should they be related during my life ? There was no need, no need."* Now this letter was most magnanimous, considering the offence, for we cannot but believe that before such facts were published, her consent should have been obtained. There was nothing harmful or injurious in their relation, but Mary Mitford ought to have known that E. B. B. would dislike their publication. But she belonged to a more robust generation, one accustomed to cut and thrust, and, on occasions, to savage attacks such as abounded in the *Quarterly* and *Blackwood's*. She was more frank and outspoken than her friend, and with her flair for those "personal details," it probably never occurred to her that what she had written would wound and hurt. Indeed in any one else, she would have deemed such hypersensitivity as mere ill-bred affectation, and in most cases, she would have been right. But in this instance, she was undoubtedly at fault ; and it is a pity that the incident could not have closed with E. B. B.'s magnanimous letter and her own assertion that she would rather her whole book had perished than that it should have given her friend a moment's pain. Unfortunately Mrs. Browning thought fit to comment on the indiscretion at some length, and in a contemptuous fashion, to her friends. How much kinder it would have been if she had restrained her remarks to those which she made to Kenyon : " She [Miss Mitford] upset me by her book, but had the most affectionate intentions, and I am obliged to her for what she meant."

* *Letters of E. B. B.*, ii, 45.

The success of the *Recollections* was far greater than the author had anticipated, and Bentley asked for a portrait—which was painted by Lucas—to adorn future editions and to appear in his *Miscellany* for 1852. Indeed the book was so popular that months after publication she was still receiving ten to twenty letters a day, and it had been reprinted in Paris and the U.S.A. One enthusiastic American, the wife of a college professor, invited her to stay for two or three years, and bring her entire household. But she had difficulty, poor woman, in moving from room to room, let alone undertaking a voyage across the Atlantic, for her rheumatism had returned in full force. And that summer, she was prostrated for over a month with a high fever, which greatly debilitated her. Indeed she had become so much of an invalid that she was unable to go to London in the summer of 1852 to see the Brownings: and E. B. B., although she was in England for several months and paid other country visits, did not find time to go to Swallowfield. It is possible that the incident of the *Recollections* was still rankling, but it was her last chance to see her old friend, although, of course, she did not know it. Had she come, she would probably have been shocked at the change which had taken place. From an active woman, Mary Mitford had become a complete invalid, not able to see visitors till two in the afternoon, and then only for a short period, lest the excitement should bring on an attack of nervous prostration. "I can hardly crawl from room to room," she wrote, "and never expect to walk the length of my little garden again—am lifted in and out of a very low pony-carriage, and from step to step upstairs to bed. Then, in bed, I cannot stir, and have all the length of the spinal column, all round the loins, and across the shoulders, a soreness which renders every position painful. It is just as if I had been soundly beaten, so that, after a little interrupted sleep, I am more fatigued in the morning than when I went to bed at night." William Harness, hearing that she was ill, came down for the day and was so upset by her appearance—he " thinks me breaking fast "—that he stayed three weeks, in order to be able to look after her. When he left, he retained his lodgings in the village so that he could return later in the year. But such was her indomitable spirit that she continued, in spite of her manifold physical disabilities, to receive visitors; and Lady Russell, her friend of thirty-four years, surrounded her with every care and attention, calling constantly at the cottage. Her friends still came down from London—among them a new one, Bayard Taylor, the American traveller—to spend an hour or two in her company: so that in this period of intense physical suffering she, who had never spared herself, was rewarded by the care and devotion of her friends.

But the culminating blow to her already shattered health was a serious accident when out driving in the grounds of Swallowfield Park, the home of Lady Russell. She was being driven through a gate when, presumably, the carriage overturned, and she was flung, with great violence, on to the hard road, sustaining severe injuries. No bones were broken but, although she did not know it, her spine was injured and she lost all power in her lower limbs and her left arm.

XXI

1853-1855

This accident was the beginning of the end, although such was her vitality that she lingered on for another two years, a helpless cripple, suffering great pain. And when we read of the agony she endured, and of the fortitude and dignity with which she bore it, we can only pay her this tribute—that she knew how to die.

It is characteristic of her that, when describing the accident, she refrained from mentioning the name of the driver of the pony chaise whom, we suppose, must have been her servant Sam. He had, a year previously, married the faithful K., who, shortly after the accident, gave birth to a child, and was thus unable, at the time of crisis, to attend to her mistress. Sam, however, stepped into the breach, and lifted the invalid about " with a tenderness, a handiness, and a power that no woman could have," and superintended " a giddy young maid and a stupid old nurse after a fashion that nobody would believe without seeing." But her condition was serious. She was lifted into, and out of, bed, and could not change her position without external aid. Her left arm was bound tightly to her body, and she had lost all power in her legs. Mr. May, however, was hopeful that when the finer weather came, and she could sit out in the garden, her condition would improve.

Her mental faculties, however, were unimpaired; and within a few weeks of her accident, she was contemplating a second series of *Recollections*. This time she intended to devote some chapters to French literature, and asked Boner to obtain for her certain poems by Casimir Delavigne.

She also told him, characteristically, that if her plan matured, she would review his book *Chamois Hunting in Bavaria*, which had been recently published. However, by February of 1853 such progress as she had made—being able to stand for half a minute and drag one foot after another—was terminated by a spell of cold weather; and she relapsed once more into helplessness, with a recrudescence of pain. The plan of a second series had therefore to be abandoned; but this by no means terminated her literary labours. In March, she corrected the proofs of a second edition of the *Recollections* and, later in the year, she was preparing an edition of her *Dramatic Works*,* and finishing her novel *Atherton* on which she had been working for a number of years. The preface to her plays contains much autobiographical information, as well as facts of great interest to all students of the drama. The activity of her mind in this short period before her death was truly astonishing. There is something pathetic, yet admirable, that almost to the end of her life she should, with a will-power which overcame her physical sufferings, practise her art; and that what had proved such a hard taskmaster for so many years should, in the end, prove a consolation and distraction.

Her mental activity was greatly in excess of her physical powers, and this probably hastened her end. For she could not rest; and within a few weeks of her accident, she was again receiving visitors. Besides Lady Russell and her daughters, whom she described as wading through mud to see her that winter, she saw a great deal of Charles Kingsley who, living at Eversley, was only six miles away. He has left a colourful description of her at this time. "I can never forget the little figure rolled up in two chairs in the little Swallowfield room, packed round with books up to the ceiling, on to the floor—the little figure with clothes on, of course, but of no recognized or recognizable pattern; and somewhere out of the upper end of the heap,

* Published in 1854.

gleaming under a great deep globular brow, two such eyes as I never, perhaps, saw in any other Englishwoman—though I believe she must have had French blood in her veins, to breed such eyes, and such a tongue, for the beautiful speech which came out of that ugly (it was that) face: and the glitter and depth, too, of the eyes, like live coals. . . ."* The first mention of James Payn, the novelist and editor of the *Cornhill*, occurs in her correspondence of that year, although they had met earlier, probably in 1852. Payn, whose father had been her girlhood's friend, was a young man of twenty-three at the time, and he has written of her: "I well remember our first interview. I expected to find the authoress of *Our Village* in a most picturesque cottage, overgrown with honeysuckle and roses, and set in an old fashioned garden. Her little cottage at Swallowfield, near Reading, did not answer this picture at all. It was a cottage, but not a pretty one, placed where three roads met, with only a piece of green before it. But if the dwelling disappointed me, the owner did not. I was ushered upstairs (for at that time, crippled by rheumatism, she was unable to leave her room) into a small apartment, lined with books from floor to ceiling, and fragrant with flowers; its tenant rose from her armchair with difficulty, but with a sunny smile and a charming manner bade me welcome. My father had been an old friend of hers, and she spoke of my home and my belongings as only a woman can speak of these things. Then we plunged *in medias res*—into men and books."†

She was of considerable assistance to him in his literary career, giving him introductions to anyone he wanted to know, for, he says, "She seemed to me to have known everybody worth knowing, from the Duke of Wellington (her near neighbour) to the last new verse maker whom I [he wrote poems in his youth] had superseded."‡ And

* Quoted by James Payn (*Some Literary Recollections*, 79, 1884).
† *Some Literary Recollections*, James Payn, p. 78, 1884.
‡ Idem, p. 79.

again " . . . she had very considerable influence in the world of letters, which was always at the service of her friends. She was never tired of furthering my own ends, even when she did not quite approve of them. . . . I had been brought up in the country, without the least link to literature in any direction, and she gave me introductions to everybody I wanted to know."* It was armed with two of her introductions, to Harriet Martineau at Ambleside and de Quincey at Lasswade, that he went north that year, and caused her to comment sympathetically to Boner, " Young James Payn . . . is gone to the Lakes to finish a volume of poems . . . and to try to regain his health, for he has been during the winter at death's door, and is exactly the charming lad that so often goes off in consumption—full of beauty, mental and physical, and with a sensibility and grace of mind such as I have rarely known." Harriet Martineau she had known for many years, but the previous year had seen a renewal of her epistolary intercourse with the de Quincey family. We have not been able to ascertain whether she ever met de Quincey—for she corresponded on terms of intimacy with many persons whom she had never seen—but we think it likely that they became acquainted about 1821—possibly through Charles Lamb—when they were both contributors to the *London Magazine*. At all events, she seems to have been in correspondence with him intermittently for a number of years and, after her death, he wrote to his daughter Florence, " You would, of course, see [in the newspapers] the death of Miss Mitford. I was sincerely grieved. . . ."†

After her accident, she was confined to her room for twenty-two weeks, being wheeled from the bed to the fireside and back again. When the finer weather came, she was lifted downstairs, sometimes into her pony chaise which could, however, only proceed at walking pace for

* *Some Literary Recollections*, p. 79.
† *De Quincey : Life and Writings*, H. A. Page, ii, 98.

fear of causing her pain; and sometimes into the garden on a seat under an acacia tree. How she loved that tree "waving its delicate foliage, and bending to every breeze like drooping feathers." Indeed her interest in nature never waned, and her letters at this period abound in descriptions of her garden and flowers. It almost seemed as though her confinement had made her powers of observation on the scenes of her limited vision all the keener. "My love of fragrant flowers brought me last night a singular visitor," she told Boner. "When putting me to bed K. broke into a variety of exclamations, pointing all the while to the candlestick. Looking as she directed, I saw there a dark looking caterpillar. It moved, and there was the reflection of a tiny green light. It was a glowworm. On the table were jars of pinks and roses, and there had been a jar of wild honeysuckle. Doubtless the insect had dropped from the flowers. After some consultation we extinguished the candle, and Sam deposited the candlestick in front of the house. Ten minutes after, the glowworm had crawled to the grass, I hope to live its little life out in peace and comfort. Was it not strange? K., who knows my old love for those stars of the earth, says that now I cannot go to them they come to me."

Unfortunately Mr. May's prognostication of a return of strength in the finer weather was not fulfilled, and she became more and more feeble. But her courageous spirit triumphed over her physical weaknesses and enabled her to continue with her work. She told Boner that except to distant friends, she was reducing her correspondence to the merest notes, in order to be able to finish *Atherton*. She worked on this through the autumn of 1853 and the first three months of the following year. There is reason to believe, indeed, that she was forced to do so, for her long illness had proved a considerable drain on her slender resources. But here again help was vouchsafed from an unexpected quarter, for the Dean of Windsor put her case before the Queen, and the result was a special grant. She told her friend Hugh Pearson, the Rector of Sonning, who no doubt had drawn the Dean's attention to her plight: "I did write as respectfully as possible to Colonel Phipps begging him to offer my humble and dutiful thanks—such being, I believe, the proper form—to Her Majesty; merely adding that nothing but the urgent claims of a most severe illness, which had now lasted nearly two years, could alone have induced me to avail myself of the Dean of Windsor's kind intervention by appealing to Her Majesty's bounty." Then she added with pathetic pride, "My only objection . . . would be to have the grant put into the papers as the consequences of 'reduced circumstances,' because without the terrible pull of illness there would have been nothing of the sort—nor ought there to have been—on my part."

Atherton is, perhaps, the least successful of all her original work, and except for the beautiful style in which it is written, has little to commend it. The plot is forced and unnatural, and although some of the characterisations are good, the book lacks the spontaneity of her earlier work. Her talents were not suited to novel writing, and she could not sustain the interest of a full length plot. Ruskin, however, liked it and wrote "I have just finished *Atherton*, to my great regret, thinking it one of the sweetest things you have ever written, and receiving from it the same kind of refreshment which I do from lying on the grass in spring. My father and mother, and an old friend and I, were talking it over to-day at dinner, and we were agreed that there was an indescribable character about it, in common with all your works—and indescribable perfume and sweetness, as of lily of the valley and honey, utterly unattained by any other writer, be it who he or she may." The book had a phenomenal success which gladdened the heart of its suffering author; and she told a friend that the demand was so great that Mudie's library was obliged to keep four hundred copies in circulation. It is nothing short of a miracle that it was produced at all, for she was prostrate for the entire winter. In February, 1854, she wrote: "For four months I have been in a terrible state—just got from my bed to the fireside, I hardly know how, for every time I expect to be the last. Unable to rise from my seat, to stand for a moment, to lift either foot from the ground, and when lifted into bed again, unable to turn or to move the least in the world, lying on my back like a log. The influenza came on, and my life was saved by two table-spoonfuls of champagne in water twice a day, which I am still compelled to take. Indeed it is nourishment that keeps me alive. The moment that power goes I shall sink. In this state was nearly all *Atherton* written—in the midst of the tremendous pain of rheumatism in every limb, in the loins, and, above all, in the chest, and with such loss of power that I am obliged to have my pen dipped in the ink for me, not being able to raise my hand."

To that most beloved of all her friends, Elizabeth Barrett Browning, she wrote:

"Swallowfield, March 29th, 1854.

Weaker and weaker, dearest friend, and worse and worse; and writing brings on such agony that you would not ask for it if you knew the consequences. It seems that in that overturn the spine was seriously injured. There was hope that it might have got better; but last summer destroyed all chance. This accounts for the loss of power in the limbs, and the anguish in the nerves of the back, and more especially in those over the chest and under the arms. Visitors bring on such exhaustion, and such increase of pain that Mr. May forbids all but Lady Russell. Perhaps by the time you arrive in England I may be a little better. If so, it would be a great happiness to see you, if only for half an hour.

May God bless you, my beloved friend, and all whom you love!

M. R. Mitford."

Mrs. Browning was most distressed by this letter. She implored her old friend not to attempt to write again, but asked that K. should send the news. "In any case," she added, "I shall see you this summer, if it shall please God; and stay with you the half hour you allow, and kiss your dear hands and feel again, I hope, the brightness of your smile."* This hope was not to be realized, for she did not come to England again until after Mary Mitford's death. But Boner, who was not due till 1855, advanced his visit by a year and came over in June so that he might see her once more. His visit, as it turned out, was attended by almost fatal results, for the excitement and exertion of talking brought on an attack of breathlessness which left her prostrate. Both her servants thought she was dying, but thanks to their excellent care, and her own indomitable will, she rallied once more. She had reluctantly to ask Boner not to come again, because it would be a grief to him "to shake the last sands in the hour glass." Another visitor that year had been Talfourd, who had spent two hours by her bedside. The meeting between these two old friends had been warm and cordial, and all past misunderstandings were forgotten. He was much affected by her enfeebled condition, and yet within a fortnight he himself was dead.† She commented sadly "We both, I believe, felt it to be a last parting, though neither dreamed which thread of the cord would soon be parted."

She was fully aware that she was dying ("I am in my death sickness") and regarded the prospect with equanimity. Even in this state of debility, she derived a calm enjoyment from life. "I am sitting now at my open window, not high enough to see out, but inhaling the soft summer breezes, with an exquisite jar of roses on the window-sill, and a huge sheaf of fresh-gathered meadow-sweet giving its almondy fragrance from outside; looking on blue sky

* *Letters of E. B. B.*, ii, 164.

† He died suddenly of apoplexy on 13th May, while delivering a charge to the grand jury at Stafford. His last word was "sympathy."

and green waving trees, with a bit of road and some cottages in the distance, and K.'s little girl's merry voice calling Fanchon* in the court." And she told Harness, "I am still as cheerful as ever, which surprises people much. Is it uncommon?" Nevertheless her mind was disturbed by religious doubts. It was not that she was a woman without faith, although she rarely referred to the subject, but that her reason rebelled against some of the ritual of the Church of England. But after meditating upon the matter, she came to the conclusion that "the mystery being above our finite faculties, the only way is to take it exactly as it is written, and throw ourselves on the mercy of God through the great Mediator." She believed that the long visitation of her illness had been sent to draw her closer to God, and after some delay, due to physical weakness, she received the Sacrament from Hugh Pearson. "I think you will approve of my having done so," she told Harness, "not merely as a Christian, however unworthy, but as adhering to the Church of England, which, with all its faults, is the most large and liberal of the many English sects. . . . I have twice gone through the Gospels, and once through the whole of the New Testament, since we met; and I *believe* with my whole mind and heart that divine history. Still, dearest friend, I find it difficult to realize; and I am troubled in prayer with wandering thoughts. Pray that He may quicken my faith and deepen my repentance. I feel fully my own unworthiness, and that my hope must be in His mercy. Pray for me, dear friend." Thus she, at the end of her anxious and careworn existence, found peace and consolation. And it was fitting that it should be so, for her life had been a long self-sacrifice, and if she had sinned, it was through excess of love. Yet when she had thus composed her mind, and accepted the faith into which she had been born, she wrote characteristically to another friend: "I tell you this [about her religious

* Her dog.

sentiments] . . . because it is a faith to avow and not to conceal; but you may well imagine that I neither preach myself nor deal in holy gossip of any sort." Even on her deathbed she was free from all cant, and that dignity which had sustained her through all her sufferings, did not fail her at the supreme moment.

All through the summer of 1855 her frail pulse beat its uncertain measure, but in the autumn there came a slight amendment. ". . . I am certainly better than a month ago," she told Boner, "though still confined to my chair night and day, sitting on a water cushion, with no other change than from being propped by air-cushions, to having my feet lifted on another chair. It has not been thought safe to risk the exertion of my being lifted into bed. . . . Still the first breeze will probably—certainly (humanly-speaking), carry the withered leaf from the tree, though at present the symptoms are improved." As the result of this slight improvement, she was again allowed visitors, but only one a day for an hour or two; and in October, when writing to thank Ruskin for gifts of wine, she invited him to Swallowfield—"But only if you are at home and can do it without the slightest inconvenience." And when he accepted and arranged to see her two days running (possibly by staying in the locality) she said "I do not write to provoke a reply, but only to tell you that I am all the better for the great happiness of anticipating your visit. . . . Another reason why I write is to entreat you to dine at my poor cottage. You must, dear friend—everybody does. You cannot imagine that I should have the folly or the bad taste to offer you anything that would give you the lesser vexation of putting my little household out of the way. You shall have nothing but a cutlet and a brace of birds, and some of your excellent father's wine. But you must dine here at six o'clock on Wednesday or Thursday, and by so doing and not coming till four you will give me exactly the sort of rest which will enable us to go on talking again for an hour or perhaps two hours afterwards, without fatigue. The first day we will be quite alone—so we will on the second if you prefer it. . . ."

The kindness and attention of her friends gladdened her heart and certainly lightened the burden of her sufferings. The Ruskins, father and son, sent her wine ; other friends supplied game which was, with stimulants, almost her only sustenance and she received books and gifts from many people, particularly from America where she was much beloved. But of all the attentions she received, one which gave her the most pleasure was a poem addressed to her by Walter Savage Landor who, with that courtesy for which he was distinguished, wrote :

"Bath, July 24, 1854.

Dear Miss Mitford,

It would be ingratitude in me who have received so much enjoyment and instruction from your writings were I never to make an acknowledgment of it. My only hesitation in sending these verses was occasioned by the fear that, in an excess of politeness, you might fancy it necessary to write a line in reply. Pray do not think of it. Your friend Miss Day will inform me of your health, which I most anxiously hope is improving.

Believe me, dear Miss Mitford,
Yours sincerely,
W. S. Landor."

"*To Mary Russell Mitford*

The hay is carried, and the hours,
Snatch, as they pass, the linden flowers ;
And children leap to pluck a spray
Bent earthward, and then run away.
Park-keeper ! catch me those grave thieves
About whose frocks the fragrant leaves,
Sticking and fluttering here and there,
No false nor flattering witness bear.

I never view such scenes as these,
In grassy meadows girt with trees,
But comes a thought of her who now
Sits with serenely patient brow
Amid deep sufferings ; none hath told
More pleasant tales to young and old.
Fondest was she of Father Thames,
But rambled to Hellenic streams ;
Nor even there could any tell
The country's purer charms so well
As Mary Mitford. . . .
Verse ! go forth
And breathe o'er gentle breasts her worth,
Needless the task ; should she see
One hearty wish from you and me,
A moment's pain it may assuage,
A rose-leaf on the couch of age."

Her letters of this period are so animated and vital that it is almost impossible to believe she was dying. Even in December, when her small access of strength was fast ebbing, and when her "feeble fluttering pulse, which can often hardly be found," was only kept beating by stimulants, she still managed to write ; and on Christmas Day, 1854, she sent a long letter to Boner containing comments on current affairs. Yet she had little more than a fortnight to live. A week later she was so ill that her life was once again despaired of, but she rallied and was able to write : "It has pleased Providence to preserve to me my calmness of mind, clearness of intellect, and also my power of reading by day and by night ; and, which is still more, my love of poetry and literature, my cheerfulness and my enjoyment of little things. This very day, not only my common pensioners, the dear robins, but a saucy troop of sparrows, and a little shining bird of passage, whose name I forget, have all been pecking at once at their tray of breadcrumbs outside the window. Poor pretty things! how much delight there is in common objects, if people would but learn to enjoy them." On January 8th she wrote her last letter; it was to Hugh Pearson. "This day week I had a terrible shake, being New Year's Day. I had many letters to answer, which brought on exhaustion of the brain, and such an attack of retching, that both Sam and K. thought me dying; so did Lady Russell and Mrs. Hunter, who called and would come up. I got over it through ten glasses of brandy, a wineglass each, not more watered than it would be for sale, but it has left me much weaker; and yesterday I had a return of those terrible neuralgic jars running through every limb, from which I have latterly been free. To-day I am better; but if you wish for another cheerful evening with your old friend, there is no time to be lost."

Two days later, her sufferings were at an end. She died on 10th January, at five o'clock in the afternoon. Her passing was so peaceful that Lady Russell, who had been with her all day, did not know which moment was her last: and as she lay dead, her face bore an expression of intense tranquillity and repose.

Her funeral took place on 18th January and was conducted by Hugh Pearson; and she was accompanied to her last resting place by William Harness and George May, her executors, and her servants, Sam and K. She lies in a corner of the beautiful churchyard at Swallowfield, in the shade of the trees in Swallowfield Park, and within sight and sound of a tributary of the Loddon she loved so well.

Thus she only survived the father to whom she had sacrificed health and worldly prospects by thirteen years and one month.

We shall have failed in our task if we have not made it clear that hers was an essentially noble nature, strong enough to endure vicissitudes and responsibilities such as do not usually fall to the lot of woman. For over twenty years she supported her parents, and although the selfishness and extravagance of her father placed upon her an almost intolerable burden, she was rarely heard to complain. Her salient qualities were graciousness, dignity and loyalty, combined with the imperturbability and polished manners of a woman of the world; and it was this strain of worldliness in her character which prevented her from ever descending to mawkishness and sentimentality.

Of her work it is only necessary to quote Mrs. Browning who, writing to R. H. Horne on the subject of *Our Village*, says: "The *Village* . . . is my favourite. If read by snatches, it comes on the mind as the summer air and the sweet hum of rural sounds would float upon the senses through an open window in the country, and leaves with you for the whole day a tradition of fragrance and dew. . . . She is in fact a sort of prose Crabbe in the sun, but with more grace and less strength; and also with a more steadfast look upon scenic nature—never going higher than the earth to look for the beautiful, but always finding it as surely as if we went higher. She is 'matter of fact,' she says, which may be so, but then she idealizes matter of fact before she touches it, and thus her matter of fact is as beautiful as the matter of phantasy of other people. . . . In my own mind . . . she herself is better and stronger than any of her books; and her letters and conversation show more grasp of intellect and general power than would be inferable from her finished compositions. . . . In her works, however, through all the beauty there is a clear vein of sense, and a quickness of observation which takes the character of a refined shrewdness. . . . And is she not besides most intensely a woman, and an Englishwoman?"*

* *Letters of E. B. B. to R. H. Horne*, i, 150 ff.

APPENDIX I

Genealogy of Mary Russell Mitford

I Roger Mitford, Lessee of Heddon tithes, temp. Elizabeth.

= Anne dau. of —— who apparently survived him as she is stated to have succeeded to the lease of the Heddon tithes.

II Oswald Mitford, son of the above, who succeeded to the above tithes.

= Ellen, dau. of ——. She was party to a suit in 1602.

III, IV, V } Several generations here missing.

VI John Mitford of the Dam Mills near Ovingham and afterwards of the Tyne Mills near Hexham. Will proved at York 13.6.1727.

= *circa* 1678 Catherine, dau. of George Bates. She was buried 2.6.1730 having had issue:

1. Robert, bap. 20 Feb., 1679.
2. George, bap. 5 June, 1682.
3. John of the Tyne Mills, bap. 25.12.1686.
4. Thomas, bap. 31.8.1691.
5. George of Hexham, *vide infra.*
6. Three daughters.

VII George Mitford of Hexham (5th son), bap. 9.4.1694, surgeon and apothecary. Buried 25.3.1750.

= Elizabeth, dau. of —. Porter.

They had issue:

1. Francis Mitford of Hexham, *vide infra.*
2. George Mitford of Morpeth, bap. 16.6.1726.
3. John, bap. 4.7.1727.
4. Seven daughters.

VIII FRANCIS MITFORD of Hexham, surgeon, bap. 17.5.1722, buried 10.5.1768.

= Jane, dau. of William Graham, curate of Hexham. She was buried 25.11.1765, having had issue:

1. William, bap. 8.3.1759 in Holy Orders, lived at Douglas, Isle of Man, died *circa* 1834.
2. George Mitford of Alresford, *vide infra*.
3. Two daughters, Elizabeth *ob. inf.*, and Dorothy Mary, bap. 12.5.1763.

IX GEORGE MITFORD of Alresford (2nd son), b. 15.11.1760, d. 10.12.1842.

= Mary, dau. of Rev. Richard Russell, Rector of Ash and Vicar of Overton, Hants. She died 2.1.1830 having had issue:

1. Francis, bap. 12.11.1786, d. 23.11.1786.
2. Mary Russell, b. 16.12.1787, d. 10.1.1855.
3. ? a son.

The above information kindly supplied by Captain the Hon. Bertram Mitford.

APPENDIX II

Medical Record of Dr. Mitford

One of the problems which has proved most difficult to solve has been the question of Dr. Mitford's medical degree. As a result of our investigations, we have come to the conclusion that the published statements on the subject, by his daughter and others, are not true. In her *Recollections* Mary Russell Mitford says that her father was "a graduate of Edinburgh, a house pupil of John Hunter;" and in the Doctor's Obituary Notice in the *Annual Biography*, some of the details of which she supplied, under the heading *George Mitford, M.D.*, it is stated: "Being a younger son, he was brought up to the profession of medicine, studied at the University of Edinburgh, and was for three years a house-pupil of the celebrated John Hunter in London." But as we have remarked elsewhere, his name does not appear on the roll of students of the medical faculty, nor is it among those who obtained their M.D.'s at the university. In those days, the doctorate was the only university degree in medicine, but it was by no means necessary to possess it to qualify as a member of the profession. Those in practice, and in the hospitals, had often only slight qualifications. They might be apothecaries, or have passed the examination of the Company of Surgeons, but frequently medical qualifications were only obtained after several years' experience in practice or in the hospitals.

If we examine the relevant dates in Dr. Mitford's career, we shall see that it would have been almost impossible for him to have passed any time at a university. He was born in November, 1760, and in 1780, in his twentieth year, was on the staff at Haslar Hospital. If we deduct the three years he was supposed to have spent as Hunter's pupil, he would have been seventeen on *leaving* the university.

According to the *Annual Biography*, however, " . . . Dr. Mitford resided at Alresford, in Hants, and then having taken his degree in medicine, he practised for a few years as a physician in Reading." This would place the conferring of the degree about the years 1789-91; but as we knew he did not obtain it at Edinburgh, we consulted the published records of other universities, as well as those of the Royal College of Surgeons, the Royal College of Physicians and the Royal College of Surgeons of Edinburgh. His name, however, was not on any list of graduates. We also applied to the Society of Apothecaries, but they were unable to help us. Harness, however, states that the degree was obtained before Dr. Mitford set up in practice at Alresford, that is to say before his marriage. As he left Haslar in September, 1782, and did not marry until October, 1785, it is just possible, although improbable, that some of this interval was spent in study; or alternatively he might have then been with Hunter, and have studied at a university until he went to Haslar when he was twenty. But at which university?

In none of Mary Mitford's letters have we discovered any references to her father's degree. On the contrary, when writing to him, the letters were always addressed to George Mitford, Esq., and never to "Dr. Mitford." The award was entirely posthumous, in the *Annual Biography*, *The Times*, other obituary notices and in the *Recollections*. As Mary Mitford was a truthful woman, it is certain that Dr. Mitford was either a "graduate of Edinburgh" or she sincerely believed him to have been one. We can only conclude that, with his childish love of official positions, and his adolescent vanity, he must have attached sufficient importance to a university education to have claimed the privilege for himself.

APPENDIX III

Works of Mary Russell Mitford

Miscellaneous Poems	1810
Miscellaneous Poems, 2nd edition, with 23 additional poems	1811
Christina, the Maid of the South Seas	1811
Watlington Hill	1812
Ode to Genius	1812
Weston Grove	1812
Narrative Poems on the Female Character (Blanch and The Rival Sisters)	1813
Julian, a tragedy	1823
Our Village, Vol. I	1824
Our Village, Vol. II	1826
Foscari, a tragedy	1826
Our Village, Vol. III	1828
Rienzi, a tragedy	1828
Dramatic Scenes	1828
Our Village, Vol. IV	1830
Stories of American Life by American Authors, ed. M. R. Mitford	1830
Our Village, Vol. V	1832
Lights and Shadows of American Life, ed. M. R. Mitford	1832
Charles the First, a tragedy	1834
Belford Regis, 3 vols.	1835
Tales for Young People, 6 vols.	1837
Country Stories	1837
English Bijou Almanack for 1843	1843
Fragments des Oeuvres d'Alexandre Dumas choisis à l'usage de la Jeunesse par Miss M. R. Mitford	1846
Recollections of a Literary Life, 3 vols.	1852

Atherton and Other Tales, 3 vols.	1854
Dramatic Works, 2 vols.	1854

This list does not include her contributions to the magazines and annuals.

APPENDIX IV

It has not been possible to ascertain when the portrait of Mary Russell Mitford by John Lucas, in the National Portrait Gallery's Collection, was painted.

This portrait was acquired by the Trustees in 1875, after Lucas's death, and it came from his studio. It had been supposed for many years that it was an original painting by John Lucas. It is, however, obviously the painting, or an exact copy of the painting, engraved as a frontispiece to Mary Russell Mitford's *Dramatic Works*, published in 1854, and there described as by Haydon.

Comparison with a photograph of the portrait (head only) believed to be the original by B. R. Haydon now in the Reading Museum and Art Gallery reveals certain similarities : for instance the pose, shadows and head dress are the same, but the features have been fined down. Unfortunately the provenance of the Reading portrait is unknown. It must however be reasonably certain that Lucas painted the National Portrait Gallery's portrait basing it on Haydon's and reducing the scale, and that the Lucas version was engraved for the *Dramatic Works* 1854. When this work was carried out, is a matter of conjecture ; but it is reasonable to suppose that at some time Haydon's portrait was either in Lucas's possession, or he had easy access to it. He was well qualified to improve on the original, which was considered by her friends to be a caricature. He met Mary Russell Mitford in 1828, a little more than three and a half years after Haydon's portrait had been executed, and he was therefore familiar with her appearance at that period.

INDEX

A

Abbey School, Reading, 12, 15, 31, 34
Abbott, Mr., 207
Agate, James, 50*n*
Alexander, Emperor of Russia, 116
Alhambra, the, 96
Alnwick Castle, 60
Alresford, 1 *et seq.*, 111, 120, 137, 311
Alton, 47
Anderson, Elizabeth, 5
Angiolini, Mdme., 74
Annual Biography, 15, 310
Ash, 1
Athenæum, The, 211, 213*n*, 221
Atholl, Duke of, 16
Austen, Jane, 11, 12*n*, 26, 119, 137, 138
Austen, James, 120*n*
Aynsley, Lady Charles, 16, 18, 57, 60-64, 67, 78, 112
Aynsley, Lord Charles, 16, 17, 18, 56, 59, 62, 64*n*
Aynsley, Gawen, 16

B

Babington, William, M.D., 28
Baillie, Joanna, 83, 137, 253
Baines, Bishop, 256
Banister, Charles, 37*n*
Banister, J., 37*n*
Barrett, Edward, 289, 290
Barrett, Edward Moulton, 225, 257, 276*n*
Bates, William, 141, 142
Bath, 19, 255
Bath Hotel, 55
Baxter, George, 212
Beaumont, Colonel, 57
Beaumont, Mrs., 57 *et seq.*
Bedford, Duke of, 253
Benhall, 82
Bennett, W. C., 285
Bentley, Richard, 209, 288, 292
Bertram House, 41, 45, 46, 48, 52, 55, 68, 71, 78, 98; advertised for sale, 101; mortgage on, 103; sale, 106; title deeds of, 107, 112; Chancery suit over, 125, 128
Bertram, Sir Robert de, 45
Biographia Literaria, 123
Biographical Sketches (Martineau), 111, 193*n*
Blackwood's Magazine, 116*n*, 168, 170, 171, 174
Blamire, Dr. 72*n*
Blamire, Mrs., 72
Blandy, J., 107, 244, 255
Bocking, 64, 112
Bodleian Library, 142*n*
Body, Mr. 128, 129
Bolton, Lord, 103
Boner, Charles, 253, 271, 275, 280, 286, 294, 301, 305
Book of Memories (Hall), 27, 181, 182
Borderers, The, 216
Botley, 71, 73
Bounty, Mutiny on, 88
Bowles, W. L., 23
Bradbury & Evans, 285
Brentford, 20
Bristol, 19, 256
British & Foreign School Society, 116
British Museum, 110, 127, 142*n*
Brompton, 75
Brontë, Charlotte, 283

Brontë, Emily, 138
Brougham & Vaux, Lord, 48, 84
Browne, Hablot, 246
Browning, Elizabeth Barrett, 78, 95*n*, 114, 134, 138, 202, 209, 218; description of, 218, 223; opinion of M.R.M's. work, 228, 230; poem to M.R.M., 235, 246, 348, 250, 254, 257, 259, 262, 263, 266 *et seq.*, 273, 276; marriage, 276, 282, 285, 289-291, 300, 307.
Browning, Robert, 122, 216, 266 *et seq.*, 277, 283, 289
Browning, Robert Wiedeman, 283, 287
Buckingham, J. S., 263
Buller, Dr. W., 4, 5
Buonaparte, Lucien, 97
Burdett, Sir Francis, 48
Burney, Captain, 92
Burney, Fanny, 92, 111
Burns, Robert, 110
Butler, Rev. S., 97
Butts, The, Reading, 18, 210
Byron, Lady, 253
Byron, Lord, 83*n*, 110*n*, 147, 148, 250*n*

C

Calonne, C. A. de, 35
Campbell, Thomas, 96, 97, 118, 142
Capheaton, 59
Carlton House, 102
Carlyle, Thomas, 257
Castle Hill, Reading, 13, 14
Cathcart, Mr., 186, 207
Catherine, Grand-duchess of Russia, 116
Chabannes, Marquis de, 99, 135
Chamberlayne, William, 109
Chambers, William, 115*n* 279
Chamber's Edinburgh Journal, 215, 280
Chamois Hunting in Bavaria, 295
Chancery Court, 49, 108, 109
Charizi, Jehuda, 81
Charlemagne, 97*n*
Charmouth, 26
Chatham, Earl of, 25
Chelsea, 21, 31
Chillingham Castle, 63
Chiswick House, 218
Chorley, Henry, 212, 217, 221-223, 240, 271, 277, 282, 284
Christ's Entry into Jerusalem, 121 128
Chronicle of the Cid, 96
Clark, Mary Anne, 78*n*
Clarrisa Harlowe, 110
Cob, The, Lyme Regis, 26
Cobbett, William, 47, 71, 73, 79, 84
Cobden, Richard, 283
Cochrane, Lord, 48, 118
Cockburn, Mrs. Robert, 250, 253, 278
Colburn, Henry, 277
Coleridge, E. H., 22
Coleridge, S. T., army experiences, 22, 51*n*, 91; opinion of M.R.M's. verses, 93, 95, 111, 122
Coley Avenue, Reading, 13, 14, 18, 21
Coley Park, Reading, 38*n*, 103*n*
Colman, George, 172
Colvin, Sir Sydney, 286
Commitment Books (King's Bench Prison), 29
Cook, Captain, 92*n*
Cornhill, The, 296
Cottle, Joseph, 256
Cotton, William, 8
Covent Garden Theatre, 74, 122, 137, 145, 147-153, 159, 161, 175
Cox's Museum, 21
Critic, The, 74
Cromwell, Oliver, 1
Cromwell Road, 21
Cumberland's British Theatre, 183, 184
Cure for Heartache, A, 74
Cushman, Charlotte, 261

D

Dacre, Lady, 217, 220, 253
Daniel, George, 183
Darley, George, 227
Davenport, R. A., 93, 100, 109*n*, 196
Dawson & Wratislaw, 107
Deane, Mathias, 19
Delavigne, Casimir, 294
Devonshire, Duke of, 195, 217, 227
Diaries of Macready, 122, 171, 207, 216, 221
Dickens, Charles, 122, 257, 279
Dickers, Mary, 2
Dickinson, Catherine, 119, 128*n*, 134, 152
Dickinson, Charles, 117, 128*n*
Dorchester, 27
Doria, Andrea, 138
Drury Lane Theatre, 110, 122, 159, 161, 165, 180

E

Eaton Square, 21
Eclectic Review, 80
Edgeworth, Maria, 110, 137, 253, 263
Edinburgh Review, 79, 155*n*, 157*n*
Edinburgh University, 3, 15, 16*n*
Egham, 136
Egyptian Hall, Piccadilly, 121
Elford, Lady, 124
Elford, Sir William, 88, 94, 96, 100, 101, 109*n*, 110, 113, 114, 119, 121, 123, 124, 129, 133, 134, 136, 140, 141, 143, 150, 151, 159, 161, 164, 179, 180, 209, 240
Elliot, Charles, 106, 109, 125, 128
Elliston, R. W., 159, 166, 167
Emma, 111
Encyclopædia Britannica, 82*n*
Enfield, 56
English Bards and Scotch Reviewers, 110
English Opera House (The Lyceum), 156, 212
English Wits (Russell), 50
Eversley, 295
Examiner, The, 153

F

Fairchild Family, The, 13*n*
Falloden, 63
Farley Hill Court, 119, 128
Fields, J. T., 280, 288
Fiesco, Giovanni, 138
Finden's Tableaux, 226*n*, 230, 235, 252*n*
Flush, 114
Folkestone, Lord, 48, 74, 81
Forrest, Mr. (American Actor), 228
Forster, John, 122, 216
Forty Thieves, The, 51
Fox, the Hon. Caroline, 220, 253
Fox, Charles James, 48, 61*n*, 68, 78
Framlington, 62
Frazer's Magazine, 196-199
Freemason's Tavern, 117
Fulham, 112

G

Gallery of Illustrious Literary Characters, 141, 142
Gallienne, Richard le, 271
Gebir, 285
Gentleman's Magazine, 142, 222*n*
George III, 41, 124
Gifford, William, 82, 83
Giles, Jacob, 7, 8
Goldsmid, Miss, 283, 287
Good Words, 3*n*
Gore, Mrs. Charles, 257
Gore, Capt. the Hon. Edward, 213
Graham, Dr., 28*n*
Graham, Jane, 2
Graham's Club, 69

Grammar School, Reading, 12, 121
Grazeley, village of, 47, 48, 70, 128
Grazeley Court, 40, 45
Great Exhibition, 1851, 286
Grenville, Lord, 68
Grey, Earl, 63, 64
Guy's Hospital, 28

H

Hall, S. C., 27*n*, 181, 230*n*
Hall, Mrs. S. C., 181, 188
Hampton Court, 136
Hans Place, (No. 22), 31, 32, 36, 41, 43, 51, 73, 81, 116
Hans Place, (No. 33), 116
Harness, Dr., 4, 5, 9, 29, 37*n*, 103
Harness, the Rev. William, 9, 11, 28, 37, 43, 46, 70, 85, 99*n*, 117, 142, 155*n*, 169-171, 174, 186, 189, 191, 205, 217, 228, 229, 233, 244, 292, 306, 311
Harrow School, 70
Haslar Hospital, 4, 28*n*, 72*n*, 311
Hatchett's Hotel, 20, 55*n*
Havell, Edmund, 131
Haydon, B. R., 7*n*, 121, 128, 136, 138, 147, 149, 153*n*, 167, 169, 178, 188, 248, 250, 255, 275, 314
Haymarket Theatre, 21, 74
Hazlitt, William, 51*n*, 112*n*, 123, 141*n*, 155
Heckfield Grange, 38
Heckfield, Vicar of, 38
Hemans, Felicia, 137, 229
Henry the Eighth, 51
Hexham 2; parish register 4*n*, 54, 67
Hexham Abbey, 57
Hill, Constance, 13, 131
Hill, Lucy, 136, 143
History of Alresford (Robertson), 1*n*
History & Antiquities of the Borough of Reading (Man), 41
History of Medicine (Garrison) 28*n*
History of Selbourne (White) 110
Hodgson, Rev. Francis, 97
Hofland, Barbara, 121, 125, 126, 152, 181, 188, 234
Hofland, T. C., 121
Holland, Lord, 48, 86, 97, 110*n*
Hompesch, Baron von, 49, 69*n*
Horne, Richard Hengist, 259, 271, 307
Howitt, Mary, 3*n*, 263
Howitt, William, 213
Hunt, Leigh, 121, 127
Hunter, John, 3, 311
Hyde Park Corner, 20

I

Isley, 84
Ion, 216, 220*n*, 221
Irish Lottery, 30
Irving, Washington, 161*n*
Isle of Man, 88

J

James, Miss, 119, 136
Jameson, Anna, 263, 277
Jane Austen: Facts and Problems, 120*n*
Jane Eyre, 283
Jeffrey, Francis, 148, 149*n*, 155*n*, 216
Jephson, Emily, 212, 274, 276
Jerrold, Douglas, 220, 236
Jew, The, 37
John Bull, 153
Julie, (Rousseau) 110

K

Kean, Edmund, 123, 175
Keats, John, 121
Kelly, Fanny, 136

Kemble, Charles, 145, 148-151, 159, 161, 167, 173, 175, 177, 180
Kemble, Fanny, 195
Kensington Gardens, 74
Kent, Duke of, 117
Kenyon, John, 202, 218, 238, 240, 253, 266, 280, 291
Kerenhappuck, 258, 278, 294, 298, 301, 306
Kew Palace, 136
King's Arms, Reading, 12
King's Bench, Court of, 107
King's Bench Prison, 29
King's Regiment of Light Dragoons, 21
Kingsley, Charles, 271, 288, 295
Kirby, Ben, 274
Kirkley Hall, 56, 59, 62, 63
Knowles, Sheridan, 161*n*

L

Ladies Companion, 284, 288
Ladies Magazine, 142, 156, 160
Lady Geraldine's Courtship, 95*n*
Lalla Roohk, 112
Lamb, Lady Caroline, 117
Lamb, Charles, 82*n*, 121, 122, 136*n*, 141*n*, 162, 166, 180, 297
Landor, W. S., 216, 217, 255, 285, 304
Landseer, Edwin, 217
Langley, Miss E., 279
Lansdowne, 2nd Marquis of, 117
Lansdowne, 3rd Marquis of, 219, 253
Latournelle, Mrs., 12
Lawrence, Sir Thomas, 123, 186
Lefevre, Shaw, 38, 42, 63, 64, 124
L'Estrange, the Rev. A. G., 9
Letters (Seward), 110
Letters from Elizabeth Barrett to B. R. Haydon, 248, 250, 255,
Letters of Elizabeth Barrett Browning, 218, 228, 231, 236, 249, 256, 263, 264, 267, 273, 282, 285, 290-291, 301
Letters of Elizabeth Barrett Browning to R. H. Horne, 209, 259, 263, 307
Letters of Robert Browning to Elizabeth Barrett Browning, 266-270
Letters of Samuel Taylor Coleridge, 22*n*
Letters on Art (Ruskin), 278
Leverian Museum, 21
Life and Friendships of Mary Russell Mitford (Roberts) 10*n*, 23*n*, 28*n*
Life and Times of Mrs. Sherwood, 12
Life of Byron (Moore), 83*n*
Life of Coleridge (Gillman), 22
Life of Mary Russell Mitford (L'Estrange) 2*n*
Life of Nelson (Southey), 111
Linwood, Miss, 73
Lisle, Abbe de, 35
List of Graduates in Medicine in the University of Edinburgh, 16*n*
Literary Gazette, 238
Literary Institute, 263
Literary Life of the Rev. William Harness, 9*n*, 70
Literary Pocket Books, 127
Little Harle Tower, 56, 59, 62, 64
London, 19, 27; the Mitfords' residence in, 28, 68, 73, 79, 112, 116, 119, 136, 208, 286
London Magazine, 141, 142, 143*n*, 153, 154*n*, 162, 297
London Road, Reading (No. 39), 31, 41
London Street, Reading, 277
Longman, Hurst, Rees and Orne, 75, 91, 97
Lorraine, Lady, 57 *et seq.*
Lorraine, Sir William, 57
Louis XVI, 12, 35*n*
Lovejoy, G., 131, 132, 279, 286
Lucas, John, 36*n*, 188, 216, 227, 246, 257, 271, 287, 292, 314
Lyme Regis, 24, 25
Lyme Regis (Wanklyn), 25

M

Maclise, Daniel, 142*n*, 196, 197
Macready, W. C., 122, 137, 139, 145, 147, 149-151, 154, 158, 161; quarrel with M.R.M., 166-171, 175, 207, 216, 221
Maginn, William, 142*n*, 196-199
Marlborough, 5th Duke of, 121
Marmion, 80
Martineau, Harriet, 111, 193*n*, 208, 222*n*, 263, 297
Mary Russell Mitford and her Surroundings (Hill), 13, 131
Marylebone Church, 276
May, George, 240, 255, 294, 298, 300, 306
Mechanics' Institute, Reading, 271
Medical Register, 16
Melbourne, Viscount, 229
Melville, Viscount, 51
Memoires (Marmontel), 110
Merchant Taylor's Hall, 116
Merry, Mr., 203
Mill Hill School, 121
Milman, Dean, 175, 201, 216, 253, 288
Milton, Fanny—see Trollope, Fanny
Mirror, The, 132, 133*n*
Miscellany, The, 292
Mitford, village of, 2, 56
Mitford, Bertram, 55, 56, 59, 61, 75, 78, 106, 188
Mitford, Dorothy Mary, 54, 309
Mitford, Elizabeth, 54, 309
Mitford, Francis, 2, 3, 4, 54, 308, 309
Mitford, Francis (brother of M.R. M.), 6, 309
Mitford, George, 2; education, 3; marriage, 4; appearance, 5, 9; political opinions, 10; practice in Reading, 13, 31; character, 14, 85, 99, 102, 104, 187; medical degree, 15, 309; gambling, 15, 199; financial difficulties, 24, 27, 68, 98, 101, 135, 251; imprisonment, 29, 99, 30, 36; ambitions, 40, 46, 50, 53, 55, 63, 65; as a literary agent, 15, 75, 81; 84, 149, decision to leave Bertram House, 100, 129, 133, 157, 160; illness, 165, 231, 241, 248; 176, 200, 205, 207, 209, 240, 245; death, 250, 309
Mitford, George of Morpeth, 3, 16, 56, 62, 64, 308
Mitford, the Rev. J. R., 82
Mitford, Sit John de, 45
Mitford, Mary (sister of Lady Charles Aynsley) 62, 75, 78
Mitford, Mary (mother of M.R. M.), 2; marriage 4; character, 16, 98; 27, 36, 37, 41, 48, 50, 55, 63, 65, 71, 86, 98, 105, 134; illness, 100, 161, 173; on Jane Austen, 120, 164, 178; death, 191, 309
Mitford, Mary Russell, birth, 1, 6; childhood, 7; first visit to London, 19; residence in Lyme Regis, 25-27; residence in London, 28-31; wins lottery, 30; education 32-39; appearance, 36, 181; habits of reading, 44, 110; her letters, 49; visit to Northumberland, 54-67; attitude to her father, 65, 69, 85; visit to Cobbett, 71; *Miscellaneous Poems*, 71, 76, 77, 80-82, 2nd ed., 94; *Dramatic Works*, 82, 152, 295; *Christina*, 88, 93; *Blanch*, 93, 95; *Watlington Hill*, *Weston Grove*, 109; *Narrative Poems*, 109, 116; first attempt at drama, 110; love of Nature, 113; decision to remain single, 114; meets Talfourd, 121; *Our Village*, 125, 130, 136, 143, 156; *1st vol.* 161-165, 3rd ed., 172; *2nd vol.* 174, 177; *3rd vol.* 179; *4th vol.* 193; *5th vol.*, 200, 201;

diary, 127; move to Three Mile Cross, 128; *Fiesco*, 137, 139; *Foscari*, 140, 144-146, 147-151, 159, 175; magazine work, 141, 148, 161; *Rienzi*, 137, 144, 159, 161, 165-170, 184; *Julian*, 148, 151, 153, 157; income 1823, 156, 157; money difficulties, 158, 177, 205, 233, 244, *et seq.*; bad health, 160, 165, 193, 201, 231, 275, 277, 292, 303; *Charles I*, 161, 172, 195, 207; quarrel with Macready, 167-170; *Gaston de Blondeville*, 175; *Dramatic Scenes*, 175, 176; garden, 178, 212, 273; *Inez de Castro*, 179, 195; *Otto*, 185, 189, 228, 240; father's jealousy, 186, 187; religious opinions, 190-192, 206, 302; *Stories of American Life*, 193; *Sadak and Kalasrade*, 196, 212; *Lights and Shadows of American Life*, 201; *Atherton*, 202, 295, 298, 299; *Belford Regis*, 209-211, 275; *Tales for Young People*, 209; visit to London for *Ion*, 216-222; meets E.B.B., 218; affection for E.B.B., 224, 225, 246; pension, 229; edits *Finden's Tableaux*, 230; father's exactions, 236, 245; *Bijou Almanack*, 240; visit to Bath, 255; E.B.B's. marriage, 276; moves to Swallowfield, 281; *Recollections of a Literary Life*, 285, 288, 292, 294; accident, 293; death, 306, 309, 314
Mitford, Admiral Osbaldistone, 55
Mitford, Roger, 3, 308
Mitford, Sibella de, 45
Mitford, William, 4, 54, 88, 309
Mitford, Colonel William, 189
Monck, Bligh, 38, 103
Monck, Sir Charles, 61
Monthly Magazine, 51*n*, 79
Montrose, Duke of, 172
Moore, Thomas, 112, 253
More, Hannah, 33
Morgan, Lady, 263
Morier, James, 253
Morning Chronicle, 84*n*, 111, 112*n*, 116, 123, 252
Morpeth, 2, 56, 59, 62, 64
Mosse, Mrs., 27
Mount Coffee House, 100
Moustiers, Count de, 12
Moxon, Edward, 238*n*
Murray, Lord Charles—see Aynsley, Lord Charles.
Murray, John, 91

N

Napoleon, Emperor, 97*n*, 116
Napoleon II, 282
National Book League's Poetry Exhibition, 75*n*
National Portrait Gallery, 36*n*, 314
Newcastle School, 3
New Monthly Magazine, 138, 142, 143, 162, 177
New Times, 128
Northumberland, Duchess of, 60 *et seq.*
Notes and Queries, 116*n*, 164, 251

O

Odiham, 37
Ogle, Captain, 21
Ogle, Nathaniel, 56, 59, 62, 63, 64, 67, 100
Ogle, Dr. Newton, Dean of Winchester, 4, 21, 48, 56
Ollier, C. & J., 127
Opie, Mrs. Amelia, 80, 112, 137, 253
Opie, John, R.A., 46
Orion, 259
Osbourne, Dorothy, 50
Overton, 2, 103, 119, 120*n*
Oxford, 73
Oxford Street, 52

P

Paddington, 21
Palmer, Fyshe, 119, 124
Palmer, Lady Madelina, 119
Paradise Lost, 33
Parker, Charles, 196
Payn, James, 44*n*, 271, 296
Pearson, the Rev. Hugh, 299, 302, 306
Peel, Sir Robert, 229, 254
Percy, Lady Emily, 61
Percy, Lady Julia, 61
Perry, James, 84, 111, 112*n*, 116, 118, 123, 136
Perry, Mrs., 136
Phillips, Sir Richard, 51
Piccadilly, 74
Pickwick Papers, 122
Pippa Passes, 268
Pitt, William, 25
Pleasures of Friendship, 97*n*
Poetical Register, 51, 89*n*, 93, 100, 109*n*
Portraits and Sketches (Gosse), 259
Pratt, S. J., 78, 91
Pride and Prejudice, 111, 120
Prior Park, 256
Proctor, Bryan Waller, 171, 216
Provoked Husband, The, 51
Prussia, King of, 116
Public Record Office, 29*n*, 45, 49*n*, 106*n*

Q

Quarterly Review, 80 *et seq.*, 84, 162, *et seq.*
Quincey, Thomas de, 141*n*, 297

R

Radcliffe, Mrs., 175*n*
Raggett, Mr. and Mrs., 37*n*
Reade, Charles, 257, 279
Reading, M.R.M's. first residence in, 11; 2nd residence in, 31, 40; social customs in early 19th century, 41; races, 42, 70; 48, 55; elections, 63, 124; 105, 125, 128, 130; Greek plays in, 146; Reading Room, 248, 257, 258
Rejected Addresses, 110
Regent, the (afterward George IV), 102, 116, 172
Reminiscences (Macready), 155
Rhymed Plea for Tolerance (Kenyon), 202
Richard III, 137
Richmond, 48, 118, 136
Ritchie, Lady, 243
Rivers, Lord, 38
Rivington, F. C. & J., 91
Roberts, W. J., 23
Robins, George, 176, 201
Robins, Messrs., 99, 101, 106, 107, 176
Robinson, Henry Crabb, 166, 203
Robinson, Mathew, 38
Roddam, 62
Rogers, Samuel, 216, 253
Rowden, Frances, 33, 52, 73, 74, 81, 87, 97, 116, 195*n*
Royal Academy, 73
Royal Institution, 118
Royal Society, 89
Royston, 56
Ruskin, Effie, 279
Ruskin, John, 44, 266, 271, 278, 287, 299, 303
Russell, Sir Henry, 134*n*
Russell, Lady, 134, 293, 295, 300, 306
Russell, Dr. Richard, 1, 10, 27, 51, 93
Rydal Mount, 272

S

St. Giles's Church, Reading, 13
St. Laurence's Church, Reading, 13
St. Mary's Church, Reading, 13, 18
St. Paul's Cathedral, 21
St. Quintin, Count de, 12, 15, 31, 34, 49, 55, 99, 135

St. Quintin, Mrs. de, 12, 15, 33
St. Quintin, Victoire, 55
Sartoris, Adelaide, 257
Saunders & Otley, 215
Saxmundham, 82
Scotch Corporation Hall (Fetter Lane), 111
Scott, John, 143
Scott, Sir Walter, 82*n*, 83*n*, 92, 111, 149*n*, 186
Search After Happiness, 33
Sedgewick, Catherine, 194, 237
Sedgewick, Kate, 194
Selby, Mr., 61
Sense and Sensibility, 111
Seraphim and Other Poems, 235
Sheridan, R. B., 48, 51*n*, 78, 84
Sherwood, Mrs., 13, 15, 31
Shinfield, 45
Shinfield Church, 45, 136, 143, 165*n*, 192, 251
Shrewsbury, Lord, 103, 107, 108
Sidmouth, Viscount, 41
Sidmouth, Lady, 253
Simonds, Messrs., 106
Sketch Book (Irving), 161
Smith, Horace, 110, 253
Some Literary Recollections, (Payn), 44*n*, 220*n*, 296, 297
Somerville, Mary, 229
Sonnets from the Portuguese, 277*n*
Southampton, 111
Southampton St., Reading, 13, 14
Southey, Robert, 81, 96, 111, 285
Spain, 96
Spring Gardens, 21, 73
Squire, Sir John, 138*n*
Staël, Madame de, 112
Stanfield, Clarkson, 180, 216
Steventon (Hants.), 119, 120
Strathfieldsaye, 38
Strawberry Hill, 136
Strickland, Agnes, 263
Suffolk, Lord, 75
Surrey Institution, 109
Sussex, Duke of, 117, 124
Swallowfield, 284; removal to, 287, 292, 295, 296, 303
Swallowfield Park, 135, 293, 306
Swan Inn, Three Mile Cross, 130
Sweetman, Samuel, 274, 294, 306
Swinburne, A. C., 59*n*
Swinburne, Sir John, 59

T

Tales of Fashionable Life (Edgeworth), 110
Talfourd, Mrs. T. N., 218, 221
Talfourd, Thomas Noon, 121, 133*n*, 138, 139, 141, 143, 144, 145, 147, 151, 152, 156*n*, 166, 169, 180, 193, 203, 209, 216: quarrel with M.R.M., 219, 253, 301
Tankerville, Lord, 63
Taplow, 278
Tavistock House, 11, 123, 124
Taylor, Henry, 132, 274, 284
Temple Bar Magazine, 202*n*
Terry, Mrs., 38
Thalaba, 81
Thompson Martin, Mr., 98
Three Mile Cross, 110, 112; Mitfords' removal to, 128, 129 *et seq.*; cottage at, 130-134, 223; garden at, 178, 179; sightseers to, 201; visitors to, 226, 237-239; structural alterations to, 232, 259-262, 278, 280, 279
Thurm and Taxis, Prince of, 272
Ticknor, George, 226
Times, The, 23*n*, 252
Took's Court, 75
Tower, The, 21
Town Hall, Reading, 42
Traditions, The, 31
Traits of Nature (Burney), 111
Tree, Ellen, 216
Trevelyan, Sir John, 59
Trollope, Anthony, 38*n*
Trollope, Fanny, 38, 175, 176, 184*n*, 253, 256

U

United States, 93, 97, 116, 138, 184; M.R.M's. views on, 194, 208; M.R.M's. invitation to, 292

V

Valpy, A. J., 9, 75
Valpy, Dr., 12, 15, 55, 75, 81, 121, 122, 146
Vestris, 74
Victoria, Queen, 253, 264, 299
Victoria Theatre, 207
Virginius (Knowles), 161*n*
Vittoria, battle of, 112

W

Wade's Mill, 56
Wallington, 59
Walpole, Horace, 136
Walter, John, 203, 252, 253
Waltham Cross, 56
War Office, 23
Wardle, G. L., 78, 81
Warrior's Return (Opie), 80
Water Colours, Exhibition of, 73
Waverley, 111
Webster, Daniel, 237
Wellington, Duchess of, 117
Wellington, Duke of, 38*n*, 118, 264, 279, 296.
Westminster Abbey, 21
Westminster Hall, 51
Whitbread, Samuel, 51; M.R.M's. Lines to, 52, 78, 117
Whiteknights, Reading, 121, 283
Whitman, Walt, 279
Whittaker, George, 161, 173, 174, 193
Wickham, 9, 10
Willis, Nathaniel Parker, 208
Wilson, Professor, 6, 149
Wilson, Mrs., 112
Wimpole Street, (No. 50), 246, 268, 271, 276
Winchester, 6, 48
Windsor, 136
Windsor, Dean of, 298
Wise, T. J., 277*n*
Wokingham, 119, 136
Wolcot, 56*n*
Wordsworth, William, 91, 121, 122, 202, 216, 217, 218, 268*n*, 272
Wortley, Montagu, Lady Mary, 50

X

Ximenes, the Misses, 74
Ximenes, Sir Morris, 74*n*

Y

Yates, Rev. Wildman, 254
York, Duke of, 78*n*, 112, 175
Young, Mr., 145, 167, 180